Binary Options Unmasked

Simple instruments with devastating power

Arm yourself with knowledge, *before* you trade

By Anna Coulling

www.annacoulling.com

Binary Options Unmasked

© 2014 Anna Coulling - All rights reserved

All rights reserved. No part of this book may be reproduced or transmitted in any form, or by any means, electronic or mechanical, including photocopying, recording, or any information storage and retrieval system, without prior permission of the Author. Your support of Author's rights is appreciated.

Disclaimer

Futures, options, binary options, stocks, bonds, commodities and spot currency trading have large potential rewards, but also large potential risk. You must be aware of the risks and be willing to accept them in order to trade in the futures, options, binary options, stocks, bonds, commodities and foreign exchange markets. Never trade with money you can't afford to lose. This publication is neither a solicitation nor an offer to Buy/Sell futures, options, binary options, stocks, bonds, commodities or currencies. The information is for educational purposes only. No representation is being made that any account will or is likely to achieve profits or losses similar to those discussed in this publication. Past performance of indicators or methodology are not necessarily indicative of future results. The advice and strategies contained in this publication may not be suitable for your situation. You should consult with a professional, where appropriate. The author shall not be liable for any loss of profit, or any other commercial damages including, but not limited to special, incidental, consequential, or other damages.

Who This Book Is For?

If you are even thinking of dipping a toe into the world of binary options, this book is for you. Even more so, if you are a novice or inexperienced trader.

Binary options are some of the most powerful, yet potentially destructive financial instruments to hit the trading world in the last few years. Appearing simple and uncomplicated, they offer the short term speculative trader the opportunity to make money fast, based on simple yes/no propositions. However, beneath this simplicity lies a web of complexity, rarely revealed or explained in detail. For the unwary, there are many hidden dangers, and used in the wrong way they are likely to destroy your capital fast.

If you want to learn how to avoid the pitfalls and traps lurking in this market, this book is for you. Binary options are perfectly valid trading instruments, but you have to understand the risks, and manage those risks accordingly.

What This Book Covers?

Binary Options Unmasked has been written to provide an objective and balanced view on this relatively new trading instrument.

All market instruments carry risk, some more than others, and this is no different with binary options. No speculator or investor should ever invest or speculate in an instrument about which he or she has little or no knowledge. There is no right or wrong way to approach the markets, only the right way for you, and I hope this book will explain all you need to know about binary options. The pros and cons, the risks, and yes, the scams you need to watch out for. Like any new market, it has attracted more than its fair share of the 'get rich quick' merchants, keen to make a fast buck before moving on.

Starting with the probabilities and risks involved in binary options, the book moves on to consider trading techniques to harness their power. These include using volume price analysis, and trading on multiple charts, incorporating both tick charts and more conventional time based charts. From binary options, the book moves forward to binary spreads, which are now becoming increasingly available and explains how to use these in hedging strategies to manage risk.

Each topic and instrument is explained with both charts and schematic illustrations to help you learn more quickly.

If you want to discover more about binary options before entering this market, this is the book for you.

Table of Contents

Foreword   9

An introduction to this book which explains who I am, why I wrote this book, and what I hope you will gain from reading it. Binary Options Unmasked is just that. The world of binary options is not all it seems, but if you are prepared to take the time and understand these instruments, it will be time well spent.

Chapter One : The Binary Battlefield   13

It's a complicated world where even the word binary has lost its meaning in the context of these instruments. Here I explain the various profiles of fixed odds, binary probabilities and everything in between as well as the crossover and linkages from sports betting to financial trading.

Chapter Two : Odds & Probabilities   21

In this chapter I explain the core differences between a fixed odds proposition, and one based on probabilities. In addition, I also introduce the concept of time which is one of the pivotal principles of trading both binary and vanilla options.

Chapter Three : Off Exchange Binary Brokers   37

Binary products can be broadly classified as either 'off exchange' or 'on exchange'. In this chapter the world of off exchange brokers is explained, as they are often the starting point for many traders. It is these brokers who are increasingly under the spotlight from the regulatory authorities, alarmed at their proliferation.

Chapter Four : On Exchange Binary Brokers   47

On exchange binary options offer a more flexible alternative to the on exchange products. These instruments resemble, and are more akin, to vanilla options both in their construction and also the trading environment.

Chapter Five : Risk & Reward Ratios Explained   75

In this chapter I explore risk and reward ratios, to help explain why most binary option traders struggle to make money. It also explains why an 'on exchange' binary option is such a powerful proposition.

Chapter Six : Shifting The Probabilities Using Volume Price Analysis   87

A short introduction to volume price analysis, a trading method I have used for almost twenty years. It is powerful and simple, and once learnt can be applied to any chart in any market, and is the perfect method to analyze intraday charts trading binary options. Using this approach will help you to trade with confidence on any chart from minutes to hours, and from days to weeks.

Chapter Seven : Volatility Explained — 105

Volatility lies at the heart of options trading. In this chapter you will discover where and how to interpret volatility quickly and easily, using a variety of tools, indicators and indices.

Chapter Eight : Binary Option Products — 141

Here I introduce the most popular binary option products available today. I explain what they are, how they work and how to approach them as traders.

Chapter Nine : Vanilla vs Binary Options — 151

A vanilla option is very different to a binary option. In this chapter I explain the main differences between these two instruments. In particular, I explain the risk and reward profiles of both in more detail, and how these compare when considering the binary option from 'on exchange' brokers.

Chapter Ten : Preparing To Trade Binary Options — 161

Regardless of whether you are trading 'off exchange' or 'on exchange' binary options, the starting point is always the same. It starts with the chart, and here I explain the steps to take as you prepare to trade binary options.

Chapter Eleven : Binary Options Strategies — 191

In this chapter I walk you through several trading strategies starting with the simple, before moving on to the more complex as I show you how to use a binary option to manage risk in an underlying market. I also explain the mapping of strategies, which is a vital ingredient of trading success in the binary world.

Chapter Twelve : Are Binary Options For Me? — 207

The debate continues as to whether these new instruments are betting or trading. Here I give you my own thoughts, and in reading the book I hope you will be able to form your own opinions, based on a sound knowledge and understanding of these unique and powerful instruments.

Acknowledgements & Trading Resources — 211

I owe a huge debt of gratitude to many people and organizations. In this section you will find a range of free trading resources which I have used throughout the book. These resources include where you can find free live prices and charts for yourself.

Testimonials

Here are just a few of the many email testimonials. If you would like to read more simply visit my Amazon author page which you can find here:

http://www.amazon.com/Anna-Coulling/e/B00CYN13VQ/ref

Last week I bought your book A Complete Guide to Volume Price Analysis through Amazon. For all the books and investment courses I bought your book is the easiest to understand. I read your book once and already understand the market better.

First off, I loved your books - they've helped me piece together the last bits of the trading puzzle I've been working on for years. You articulate the actions of the professionals better than anyone I've come across.

Forex for beginners, was a great read. Your description of the trade was first rate, and the use of multiple time frames a revelation.

I am only half way finished with your VPA purchased from Amazon & I'm so appreciative of the excellent information in your book. What I appreciate most is your teaching style... You have this engaging narrative authority coupled with wonderful/insightful analogies that makes your book so entertaining as well. I must say after reading more than a dozen books "4-5 rating via Amazon", yours & perhaps another book are the only two that I have found to be OUTSTANDING!

I'm have almost finished my first read of your VPA book. It is what I've been looking for and the book is transforming my trading philosophy. Thank you for writing such a great and informative book. Anna, I'm both hungry and excited about developing a mastery in VPA.

I have put together a system for timing the SP500, and it has been constructed without volume, as volume did not give me reliable results with my buy/sell signals. However, after just reading your book "A Complete Guide to Volume Price Analysis", I will be giving volume a second look, and likely a place in my system. I would like to say thanks for putting this bundle of knowledge together

---

I just wanted to let you know that I purchased your book on kindle, and I am reading it for the second time. I think this book is very well written and has helped me read the charts better. I think your book is under priced!!

Just a quick message to say that I love your book. Your explanations of the psychology of market dynamics really got me thinking, and I very much like your warehouse/retail metaphor.

Hi Anna! - Thank you so much for writing such a valuable knowledge regarding financial trading. I'm a beginner, but from all the books, articles and studies I've made regarding forex, your books (I bought the two of them in Amazon) have definitively been the most valuable to me.

Foreword

The goal of a successful trader is to make the best trades - money is secondary

Alexander Elder (1950 -)

We all dream of financial freedom. Of finally giving up the day job, and never having to worry about money again. No more worrying about paying the bills, or working in a job we hate. No more commuting, no more boss, and no one to tell us what to do or when. Imagine working from home with just a computer and a broadband connection. A better quality of life for our family. More time with our partner. More time with our children. More time to actually enjoy life, and with enough money to buy those luxury items we have always dreamed about. The fast car, the holiday home, the boat perhaps. All of these things and more, are now within our grasp. All we have to do is forecast whether a market is rising or falling in the next few minutes, and by how much. It sounds so simple.

What could be easier?

This is the dream of many traders, but is one few ever achieve, and sadly it remains just that, a dream. It is also the message many binary brokers promulgate with slick marketing campaigns and some clever tricks, guaranteed to lure you in with promises of get rich quick returns, using a small amount of trading capital. Every emotional lever is used, with binary options promoted as the quick and easy way to fulfill your dreams. This is further endorsed by the less scrupulous internet marketers, who see this as the next get rich quick opportunity for themselves.

The binary brokers share some blame. However, as you will discover there are some excellent ones, but these are few and far between. The regulatory authorities in many countries have become so alarmed by the explosion of this market, many have banned this form of trading completely. Some consider binary options as speculative trading instruments with regulation then falling within the financial services sector, whilst others consider them betting and gaming and regulated accordingly. The latter are generally countries who see this market as one for potential economic growth, and therefore take a more relaxed approach to the risks.

It is a market which is growing exponentially, and gaining in popularity as more and more traders are drawn to it like moths to a flame. And traders are drawn for one reason, and one reason only. Simplicity. I could explain binary options in one short paragraph. In fact in chapter one I do just that.

So, why have I written a book on the subject?

Let me draw a parallel here with the forex market which has many similarities. Ten years ago you would have been hard pressed to find a forex broker, let alone be able to place a trade easily. The internet changed all that, and the forex market was promoted as a 'get rich quick' scheme - no knowledge required. Gradually over the years, the retail trader and investor has become wise to the scams, sharp practice and over hyped marketing messages. The market has matured, aided by the regulatory authorities with traders of all levels becoming increasingly knowledgable. Long term success requires effort, good money management and a deep understanding of price action and market behavior.

With the forex market maturing, and brokers finding it increasingly difficult and expensive to attract new business, binary options have stepped in as the next 'hot instrument'. Sitting somewhere between fixed odds and vanilla options, binary options have it all, offering a broad range of markets, and not just forex. Their hook is 'simplicity'. Like a simple pack of cards, all you are being asked to do is to guess whether the next card is higher or lower than the last.

A simple decision, with a simple outcome. Simplicity in spades.

But sadly, this is where the good news ends and the bad news starts because the majority of binary options traders lose, and lose quickly. And the reason is because in most cases you are trading 'against the house', and just as in Las Vegas the house always wins, given the odds are always stacked in their favor. If all this sounds rather depressing, help is at hand because this book covers all you need to know, and more about binary options. Nothing is held back.

However, binary options elicit strong opinions. Some people consider them gambling - pure and simple, whilst others consider them just another trading instrument. It is certainly true for some types of binary option, these are no more than a bet. However, if you are prepared to avoid these and delve deeper into the world of binary trading and binary spreads, these are perfectly valid instruments, provided you are prepared to use them in the same way as any other instrument. In other words, a derivative of the spot or cash market, and as such, any analysis always starts with the chart.

Binary options are just another instrument to consider. They have many advantages and some disadvantages. They may be appropriate for you or they may not. Much will depend on your trading strategy and style. But in reading this book, you will at least be able to make a considered and balanced decision for yourself, and you will also be able to select a reputable and reliable broker.

Used wisely, binary options have plenty to offer. Use them foolishly and you will lose your money - fast.

Who Am I?

If you have discovered any of my other books, you will already know volume price analysis lies at the core of my trading methodology. To me this approach just makes sense. It is what I fervently believe will help you to succeed as a trader, so you can fulfill your own dreams. It is the trading method I have used for over seventeen years in all markets. And the reason is because it works, and to me just makes sense. It is an approach based on common sense and logic. The logic of volume and price action is these are the only two leading indicators we have. And for trading using binary options I believe this approach is critical to your success. As is trading in multiple timeframes, another core trading principle. Trading on tick charts also has a place here, particularly for intra day trading.

At this point, you may be wondering who I am, and why you should believe anything in this book. Here is a little about me, and details of the places where you can check out my credentials. And before you read on, rest assured I have **no financial relationship whatsoever** with any of the companies mentioned in the remainder of this book.

I began my own trading career back in the 1990s, before the days of the internet, and started trading index futures using price and volume. In those days there were no online brokers, and all the data came in via a satellite feed. Orders were placed by phone with the broker, and executed and filled on the floor of the exchange. It was very stressful, not least because of the time delay in getting filled or when the data feed broke down, which happened regularly.

Since those heady days, I have traded virtually every market and every instrument. As an options trader, my approach was based on one of the most conservative yet popular strategies, namely covered call writing. Options are a particular favorite of mine, and whilst binary options are a very different instrument, nevertheless they do share many important underlying characteristics.

My trading experience has given me the grounding I needed to succeed, which is what I want to share with you in this book.

My trading philosophy is, in essence, very simple and akin to the ubiquitous KISS, except my version is Keeping It Super Simple.

I have found over the years the best results come from having an approach that is uncomplicated, not least because the markets are complex enough. Trading may not be easy, but it is straightforward.

My trading techniques are based on chart analysis, backed by my view of the broader fundamentals and related market sentiment, which provide me with the framework against which the markets move each and every day. However, it is I who make the decision to trade - no one else.

As I say in my webinars, live trading rooms and seminars, there are only two risks in trading. The first is the financial risk, and the second is the risk on the trade itself. Nothing else.

The first is easy to quantify and manage. This is pure and simple money management. The second, the risk of the trade itself, is much more difficult to assess. This is what we need to quantify every time we open a new position or consider taking a position in the market. The questions we always have to answer are: What is the risk on the trade? What is the probability of success? Am I taking on too much risk, and how do I measure that risk?

In a nutshell, this is what I want to share with you in this book. I want to arm you with the knowledge, skills and tools so you too can become a confident, consistent and profitable binary options trader. Like me, you will be able to make your own discretionary trading decisions based on your analysis of the price and market activity, coupled with the underlying fundamental and relational picture.

This is the approach I also use in my market analysis which is taken by a number of leading financial portals such as www.investing.com where you will find over 400 articles and analysis covering a variety of markets.

I write daily market analysis and commentary on my personal site, www.annacoulling.com which currently has over 700 articles. Here you will also see, over the years I have been invited to speak by the Chicago Mercantile Exchange www.cmegroup.com and I am also a regular presenter and contributor for The Money Show www.moneyshow.com. You will also find me at www.seekingalpha.com and www.traderkingdom.com.

I have published over 50 web sites, all of which have free content covering a variety of trading and investing topics, along with several dedicated Facebook pages. This is one www.facebook.com/learnforextrading and you can also follow me on Twitter at www.twitter.com/annacoull or tune in to one of my many recorded trading webinars at www.youtube.com/acoull.

Alternatively, you can simply Google my name.

So let's get started as we unmask the world of binary options together.

Anna

Chapter One

The Binary Battlefield

To turn $100 into $110 is work. To turn 100 million into $110 million is inevitable

Edgar Bronfman (1929 - 2013)

In many ways, this is perhaps the most difficult chapter to write, as the world of betting and trading move ever closer with a consequent blurring of the boundaries. And indeed may be one of the reasons you have purchased this book, as you would like to understand and clarify the differences between these two worlds. However, understanding the differences and where these boundaries are drawn, is paramount in having a clear view of where one stops, and the other starts. Binary options now seems to be the battlefield on which these two opposing forces face one another.

My purpose in writing this book is *not* to come down on one side or the other. My aim is to try to highlight what I believe are the pros and cons of these instruments. To consider both sides, and from there to draw conclusions on the best trading strategies to adopt. By the end of the book, I hope you will have a balanced view with which to make your own decision.

We are all different, with varying risk tolerances. What is high risk for one person, may be low risk for another. All I can do here is to present the case, both for and against binary options, and to consider the alternative ways to use them, of which as you will see there are many. But as with any new approach to financial trading, if we can understand the instrument's strength and weakness, then we can make balanced decisions on the best way to use them.

Understanding the odds and probabilities will also help you to assess and quantify the risk in using binary options, as well as other instruments.

Speculating and investing, by their very nature carry risk. It is for us as traders, to quantify these risks and to make our own decisions, according to our own risk appetite. The issue with the world of binary options, and here let me refer to them in the broader context of 'binary trading', is the boundaries between sports betting and financial trading are now very blurred indeed. To the extent that even those involved in the financial world, including the media, seem to be confused.

The forums too reflect this confusion with strongly held views, similar to those between technical and fundamental traders, with neither able to see the other's point of view. The same is true here. Mention the word 'binary' in a trading forum, and instantly a heated debate will ensue. One side will label it betting, short and simple. The other will argue it is trading, and never the twain shall meet.

So, in order to bring some clarity to this debate let me start with the word binary itself, which seems to be the catalyst for so much argument and confusion.

In the nineteenth century the word 'gay' simply meant happy, joyful, carefree, and was an adjective. During the course of the twentieth century the meaning of the word changed completely, not only in the context of everyday language, but also in its use as a noun. And this example, in many ways highlights the issues surrounding the term 'binary option'. It is, after all just a term with which to describe a trading instrument, and in many respects we are simply arguing about semantics.

Therefore, let me draw a line in the sand.

Whether the instruments are referred to as binary options, binary bets, fixed odds bets, fixed odds, binary betting, binary trading, fixed odds trading, or digital options, all of these 'definitions' have two things in common:

- Your risk is always limited and can never be exceeded
- Your profit is always limited and can never be exceeded

The above statements are not to be confused with percentage returns. These are the numbers you will often find quoted as part of the marketing message. Whilst the percentage returns can vary, and do, the underlying risk/reward profile remains constant.

Could the definition above be considered radical or innovative? Any trader or investor worth their salt will limit their risk. Only a fool or gambler will trade with unlimited risk. But risk can be limited in many ways.

In the financial world, a stop loss is perhaps the most obvious, taking us out of the market if a position moves against us, thereby protecting our greatest asset, namely our trading capital. We can limit loss by hedging in other markets. We can also limit loss with conservative trading strategies using options, and finally one could even consider limiting loss as the maximum invested in a share or stock.

In the sports betting world, limited loss is as old as the hills. Bet on a race or a sports event of any kind, and your loss is limited. It is limited to the amount of your bet. Go to the casino and bet on the roulette wheel, your risk is limited again and is simply the amount you bet. Once your wager or bet is placed that's it. You cannot lose any more than the amount bet. In other words, your downside risk is limited.

It is this aspect of the 'limited risk' of these instruments which is marketed most vigorously by the binary brokers. Which is rather odd given most traders always limit risk anyway.

The other side of the equation is limited risk is counterbalanced by limited profits. This is a far more serious issue, and one with dramatic and potentially damaging implications. As it undermines one of the core principles of financial trading success. In many ways this takes us immediately to the core issue of the binary trading debate. And the issue is this.

Longer term trading success is not based on the simple maths of positive and negative outcomes. It is not a question of simply shifting from a 50/50 ratio to 60/40, or 70/30. A trader can be consistently successful with fewer positive outcomes than negative, **provided** the losers are small and the winners are large.

And herein lies one of the fundamental issues with these instruments. There is no facility to 'uncap' the profit side of the equation. This is not to say an instrument with a limited profit profile is a necessarily a bad thing.

In fact, this approach is common in the world of vanilla options, where strategies are adopted to limit both risk and reward.

However, these strategies and others, are used only under certain market conditions and not all the time. In other words, on a discretionary basis.

At this point let me explain this in more detail. Vanilla options simply refer to those options available through a central exchange, such as the CME, whilst so called 'exotic options' refers to binary options. These terms are just a simple 'hook' with which to differentiate between the two. This book is about binary options, or as they are sometimes called 'exotic options'. However, we will be touching on vanilla options to draw parallels and to explain various points throughout the book. Vanilla options are very different instruments and I will be writing several books in the future to explain them in more detail. For the purpose of this book I will explain everything you need to know about vanilla options as they relate to binary trading.

But to return to the maths of trading success. We can be successful as speculative traders with more losing trades than winning trades, even as 'low' as achieving three positive trades for every seven negative trades. This is premised on the fact that these three positive trades will outweigh our seven negative trades, provided the losses are small and the profits are relatively large. However, holding a positive position to maximize the profit available is one of the most difficult aspects of trading, but it does underpin the essential maths of long term consistent success. Therefore, if you are trading an instrument which restricts both your profit and loss, you will be facing a constantly uphill struggle.

One could also argue that perhaps this is one of the reasons success in betting is such an elusive goal.

At this point you may be thinking I am favoring the betting fraternity, but this is not the case at all and quite the reverse. My purpose in writing this book is to try to help you understand all aspects of the binary option instrument and to use it appropriately. As you will discover, it is not one to be used unthinkingly or in an overly simplistic way. And it is one of the many ironies of the binary world that it is marketed as both simple and for the novice trader. Whilst the first of these statements is undoubtedly true at a superficial level, the second is most certainly not.

The power of a binary is only revealed when used in more sophisticated ways, which I explain as we move through the book. This is not to say they are not suitable for novice traders, because in many ways they are. However, only used in the correct manner. I hope, even if you have never been involved in trading or investing, by the end of this book you will be able to make an informed decision about binary options for yourself. That's my goal.

How Has Betting Changed?

At this point, let me explain how betting in the sports world has changed in the last decade, which will help you to understand how and why these approaches are increasingly being adopted in the financial world.

If we start with traditional sports betting, before the advent of the internet, the opportunities available for betting and gambling were limited, to say the least. In the UK, horse racing, football, rugby and cricket were the most popular, with betting offered via a network of high street bookmakers. The bets offered were simple limited risk and limited reward. Your bet was your maximum loss, and if your selection won, then you would receive your stake and any profit based on the odds quoted. And one important point here is this type of bet was also characterized in another way. In horse racing, any bet was always on selecting a horse to win, not one to lose.

All of this changed with the advent of two catalysts. First came the internet, and second came the betting exchanges. These factors combined to change the face of traditional betting in three distinct ways:

- Betting 'in running' was introduced
- Betting on losers became available
- Betting exchanges created 'peer to peer' betting

Let's examine these one by one, and believe me they are all directly relevant to binary options.

Betting In Running

Betting in running has been one of the most radical changes to traditional betting. Prior to its introduction a bet was placed at the start of an event, and then settled at the end of the event, either as a winning bet or a losing one. In other words a fixed risk and reward profile, with a fixed duration for the event.

The advent of in running, allows bettors to place a bet during an event, live betting if you like. Your bet can be placed at any time during the event, with the odds being offered constantly changing to reflect the probabilities of the event occurring. In a football match for example, after a goal is scored, it is possible to bet on the latest odds, which reflect the probability of one team winning and the other losing. If the other team equalizes, the odds change as the prospect of a draw becomes more likely.

In the racing world it has suddenly become possible to bet on a horse based on the odds being offered live. The same applies to tennis, cricket and a host of other sports. Suddenly, with in running betting it is now possible to bet live on a player, event, outcome, number of goals scored, corners, runs scored, wickets to fall, in fact anything you can think of.

Unlike the old type of odds, which were fixed at the start of the race, with betting in running, odds have become dynamic, constantly changing to reflect the ebb and flow of probabilities.

Time now becomes important. No longer does it simply reflect the 'duration' of the event, but now time itself governs the probabilities, with the time left to the end of the event impacting probabilities 'in running'. After all, the closer to the end of an event, the less likely an event may or may not happen. If a team is losing heavily with only minutes left to play, this would be reflected in the odds, and the probabilities of the event happening or not.

What has also become standard practice in the last few years is to allow in running bets to be closed out early, either to take a profit or to stop a loss developing further.

Betting On Losers

Betting on winners is intuitive. A horse wins a race. A match is won. A player wins an event. Betting on losers is counter intuitive, and yet is now standard within the betting industry. In betting on a winner, we are betting the 'event' will happen. In betting on a loser we are betting the 'event' will **not** happen. A very different proposition. Instead of the horse winning the race, we are now betting the horse will **not** win the race. The player will **not** win the match, or the team will lose the game and **not** win.

This revolution in the betting world has come about largely through the advent of the betting exchanges. These have brought private individuals together, allowing one person to act as the bookmaker, to lay the bet. Peer to peer betting. Laying a bet is betting the event will not happen. Betting on losers has now become standard in all sporting events.

Betting Exchanges

Betting exchanges have revolutionized the world of betting. Until their arrival, the traditional bookmaker was king. Suddenly with the arrival of the betting exchange, peer to peer betting has become possible, and the traditional in built profit of the bookmaker hidden in the odds, is no longer relevant. The betting exchange now stands at the centre, matching the two parties together, in much the same way as a futures exchange does in the financial markets. Betting has finally arrived in the 21st century.

And what happens in the world of betting flows into the world of the financial markets fairly soon after. This is where we are now with binary options encompassing all these aspects in one simple instrument.

I mentioned in the foreword to this book I would explain binary options in one paragraph, and if we take each word in turn, then this will help to explain what the instrument is, and how it works.

A binary is simply a different way to count, using just two numbers. Zero and one. All computer logic is built on the foundation of binary numbers, the simple 'yes/no' switch of a zero or a one, from which complex operating systems are constructed. The term binary has been adopted in the trading world in this context, to describe a trading instrument which only has two possible outcomes. A 'yes or no' answer if you like. In other words, 'the event', will either occur or not. There is no other possible outcome.

For example, I might ask you if you think it will rain tomorrow? If you think it is going to rain, you answer yes, but if not the answer is no. There is no other possible outcome. Either it rains or it doesn't. In probability theory (of which much more later), these are referred to as 'mutually exclusive' events, because it is impossible for them to happen together. Another example would be a head or a tail when tossing a coin. Only one outcome is possible, either a head or tail. And now the word binary itself is increasingly being replaced with the word digital, just to add to the confusion.

At this point you could conclude a bet is a type of binary, and I would have to agree. That's exactly what it is, and herein lies all the confusion. In many ways the word binary is irrelevant because you could use words such as 'button', 'switch', 'polar', almost anything which has a yes/no, or an 'on or off' connotation. The industry just happens to have chosen the word binary, but the meaning of the word from a trading perspective is meaningless.

The second word is option which is where the whole field of binary trading becomes very grey. Vanilla options have been available as trading and investing instruments for many years, but are a very different instrument. And whilst there are common principles which apply to both, which I will explain in detail later, the risk profiles of these instruments are very different. Just to recap on the terms exotic and vanilla options. This is all this means. An exotic option loosely refers to a binary option, whilst a vanilla option refers to those quoted on a central exchange such as the CME (Chicago Mercantile Exchange).

For our purposes here, and for the time being, just think of the word option in the context of the binary option, as whether you are agreeing or disagreeing with the proposition of an event happening or not.

In summary. A binary option (or a digital option if you prefer), is an option to purchase to agree, or purchase to disagree, with an event which can only have two outcomes. It either happens, or it doesn't. But, here is the key point. The event has to happen or not happen within a predetermined period of time. Time is one of the principle governing factors and an immensely powerful force, not just in the world of binary options, but in all options markets. But again I am going to cover this in detail shortly, but first things first.

Let's take a simple example of a binary option, which could be as follows:

Will the price of gold be above $1,225.30 per ounce in the next 15 minutes, or below?

You will be presented with two possibilities, something along these lines:

- *Will the price of gold be above $1,225.30 per ounce in the next 15 minutes?*
- *Will the price of gold be below $1,225.30 per ounce in the next 15 minutes?*

Alongside will be quoted some odds for the event, and an explanation that success or failure will be measured against the underlying spot gold price.

If you think the answer is yes, the price of gold will be above $1,225.30 per ounce in the next fifteen minutes you purchase the first proposition, but if you think the answer is no, you purchase the second proposition. All you do is then wait 15 minutes. If you are correct you win, but if not you lose. Does this sound simple? Yes, because in principle it is. This is the simplest type of binary option, and often referred to as the 'up/down' bet. There are many other types, which again I will explain as we move forward, but the underlying principle is the same. You are essentially being asked to decide whether an event, in this case the price of gold, is likely to happen or not, and all that is required is a simple yes or no answer. This is what I referred to as the simplicity of the instrument in my introduction.

The questions that follow are whether this is betting, trading, or investing? After all I could argue all we are ever attempting to do, whether as speculators or investors, is to answer this very question. Is the market going up or down? Or perhaps more accurately, up, down or sideways, a choice which is also catered for in the binary options world. However, what we are also attempting to forecast here is not simply whether the event will happen or not, but also whether it will happen **within** a predetermined period of time.

This is literally the '*game changer*' and is the aspect least understood by speculators in the world of exotic options, but most understood by those in the world of vanilla options. And to complicate it further, there is another factor namely volatility. Volatility is where the world of probabilities, odds, risk and return collide.

To return to our original example and to use a simple analogy. Trying to forecast the price of gold in fifteen minutes time, is the equivalent of trying to forecast the position of the favorite in a horse race, seconds or minutes from the start. Most people have enough trouble trying to forecast which horse will win, let alone where a particular horse might be at some point during the race.

And whilst time does define the end of the race, at least this is known in advance, and the horse is trained and run accordingly. During the race many other factors come into play, with the horse perhaps held back by the jockey, maybe boxed in on the rails, perhaps not fully fit, or simply having an off day. There are all sorts of factors and many more, which would dictate the position of our horse during the race.

Trying to weigh all of these up to arrive at a decision is almost impossible. If this is the case, and I fully accept the above analogy is far from perfect, why are binary options considered such a simple instrument? Let's take a look and start to unmask what a binary option really is, once the flesh has been removed from its bones.

In the next chapter we are going to take a look at the odds and probabilities which go hand in hand with binary options, and the binary market in general. This will help to frame the risk profile of these instruments, and from there we can then move on to consider how to shift the probabilities of success in our favor.

Chapter Two

Odds & Probabilities

The price pattern reminds you that every movement of importance is but a repetition of similar price movements, that just as soon as you can familiarize yourself with the actions of the past, you will be able to anticipate and act correctly and profitably upon forthcoming movements

Jesse Livermore (1877 - 1940)

In the first chapter we explored the sports betting world, and the reason for this is simple. Many of the recent innovations in sports betting are now being adopted in the financial trading world, under the umbrella term of binary, and in understanding the sports betting approach, I believe will help you to understand the world of binaries. This catch all term is now being applied to all and every instrument, as traders and speculators rush to embrace this new approach to trading.

At this point I think it would be useful if I lay out what I believe are the core differences between a binary option and a fixed odds bet. You may disagree with what I believe these differences to be, and you may even think this is merely semantic, which could also be true. However, the fact remains this is a very grey area, and all I am trying to do here, before we delve into the platforms, quotes, odds and probabilities, is to lay down some definitions of what I believe are the differentials.

Binary Options vs Fixed Odds

Let me first start by trying to compare these two terms, which I hope will help to clarify the remainder of this chapter. In chapter one we have already seen the following statements are always true, for each instrument:

- Your risk is always limited and can never be exceeded
- Your profit is always limited and can never be exceeded

Now let's look at those areas which are not common to each:

- A binary option is quoted in probabilities whilst a fixed odds trade is generally quoted in cash or a percentage cash return

A binary option can be closed at any time during the event a fixed odds trade generally cannot

And this, in simple terms is what I believe distinguishes a binary option from a fixed odds trade. This is important as you will see in the following and subsequent chapters.

But before we start to consider some actual examples, let me highlight the one principle which differentiates binaries and fixed odds from every other form of trading or investing. And that single principle is time. I touched on this concept in chapter one, but now I want to explain it in more detail here.

The Significance Of Time

In the world of options, whether binary or otherwise, and even in the context of betting, time plays a pivotal role. Time can be either your friend or your enemy, and whether it is working for you or against you will ultimately depend on how you have positioned yourself in the market.

As the event nears its natural conclusion time slips away ever faster. And this is what I meant by the game changer I referred to in chapter one. It is a game changer for three reasons.

First, what we are trying to forecast is not *if* an event will happen, but also to forecast **within what timeframe** this event will occur. This is very different to all other forms of trading and investing, and which is why options, in the purest sense, are wasting assets. Options can and do expire worthless, a concept many traders struggle to grasp. After all, why would we want to buy anything which can and does go to zero? And it is time which creates this wasting effect.

Second, in introducing the time element into the probability of an event occurring or not, the wasting aspect of time is reflected in the probabilities. This is perhaps self evident once we start to think of this in terms of a horse race again.

Third and finally, as the event nears its conclusion, time has a dramatic effect on the probabilities quoted. Again, this is perhaps self evident. After all, if the event is almost at an end and our selection can either win or lose, the yes/no probability will swing wildly. The same principle applies whether this is a horse race or a binary option in the financial world.

If we take a horse race as our simple example. Suppose our horse is last in a big field of runners, with only a furlong left to run, and we have bet on our horse to win. The probabilities of our horse suddenly surging from last to first and winning the race would be very low indeed.

However, consider another race with perhaps 100 yards to run. And here our horse is second or third, with all three horses now neck and neck in the race to the line. The probability of a win would now be very high, but one which would also be swinging wildly as there are only two possible outcomes. Either the horse wins or it does not win. With every stride nearer the finish line, the probabilities would be changing, and changing very quickly. Until perhaps the final few strides where you might see the probabilities swing dramatically from a very high probability, to a very low probability in a matter of seconds.

Now, along with the above characteristics of time, there is a further perhaps more subtle aspect which applies.

In a sports betting event the time of the event is fixed to a precise day and time. The 139th running of the Kentucky Derby starts at 6.24 pm at Churchill Downs. There is no choice for you to make, other than to decide whether to place a bet. The race ends at different times, depending on the speed of the runners.

In fixed odds in the financial world, it is very different. Here, you may have the opportunity to decide when the event starts depending on whether the broker offers this choice. If they do, you can decide to run your Kentucky Derby race at 6.24 pm, or 6.25 pm or whenever you choose. The choice is yours. The length of the event will then be precisely defined by the duration you select. But the key point is you choose when it starts.

In binary options it is different again. Here the start and finish time of the event are defined. The event starts at 6.24 pm and for a 15 minute event, finishes at 6.39 pm.

But what does this mean from a betting or trading perspective?

In the sports betting example, you have no choices to make other than selecting a runner. Imagine for a moment you believe your horse has a better chance of winning if the ground is wet. Can you change the date and time of the race to suit your horse? The answer is no. You have to make a selection on the day of the race, and weigh up the odds.

Moving to fixed odds trading. Does the choice of ground become an option? And the answer is yes. Why? Because now it is you who decides when the race starts. The broker is waiting for you to place a bet, but *you* decide when the race starts. This is an important aspect which we will cover in more detail as we move deeper into the subject, but it is a significant point, and one which is often lost in the betting/binary argument. After all, if you are choosing when your event is run, is it possible to weight the probabilities in your favor? And the answer is yes, ***most definitely.*** And when we are dealing with a financial instrument which has technical, fundamental and relational aspects, our understanding of how to forecast future price action using volume price analysis, will shift the probabilities in your favor. I explain volume price analysis later, and have written a separate book on the subject.

Binary options differ again. Here we are presented with a menu card of events. Each event on the menu has a ***specific*** start and end time. We cannot choose the start, but what we ***can*** choose is where we wish to join the race. This is equivalent to betting in running. Once in, we can also choose to leave the race if we wish.

Whilst the event has a fixed end point, nevertheless we have the option to join at any time. This is an entirely different dynamic in terms of time. Remember that probability and time are inextricably linked. In our horse racing event with our selection trailing along in last (and which we have backed to lose), we can then take advantage of the erosion of time and make it work in our favor, as there is little time left before the event finishes. The odds, or the probability of the horse winning would be low, allowing us to take a very low risk/low return bet. The binary option allows us to have time working for us, rather than against us. An issue we will explore further in more detail later.

It is important to appreciate at this stage, the erosion of time is not linear. This is a further aspect of binary options we will look at when considering price, and the underlying derivative. But for now let's concentrate on time.

As the event starts we have plenty of time left for our event to happen (or not). However, as the clock begins to tick down, the less time there is available for our event to occur. And the closer we get towards the end of our event, then the wasting aspect of time increases exponentially. This is all shown in the simple schematic in Fig 2.10.

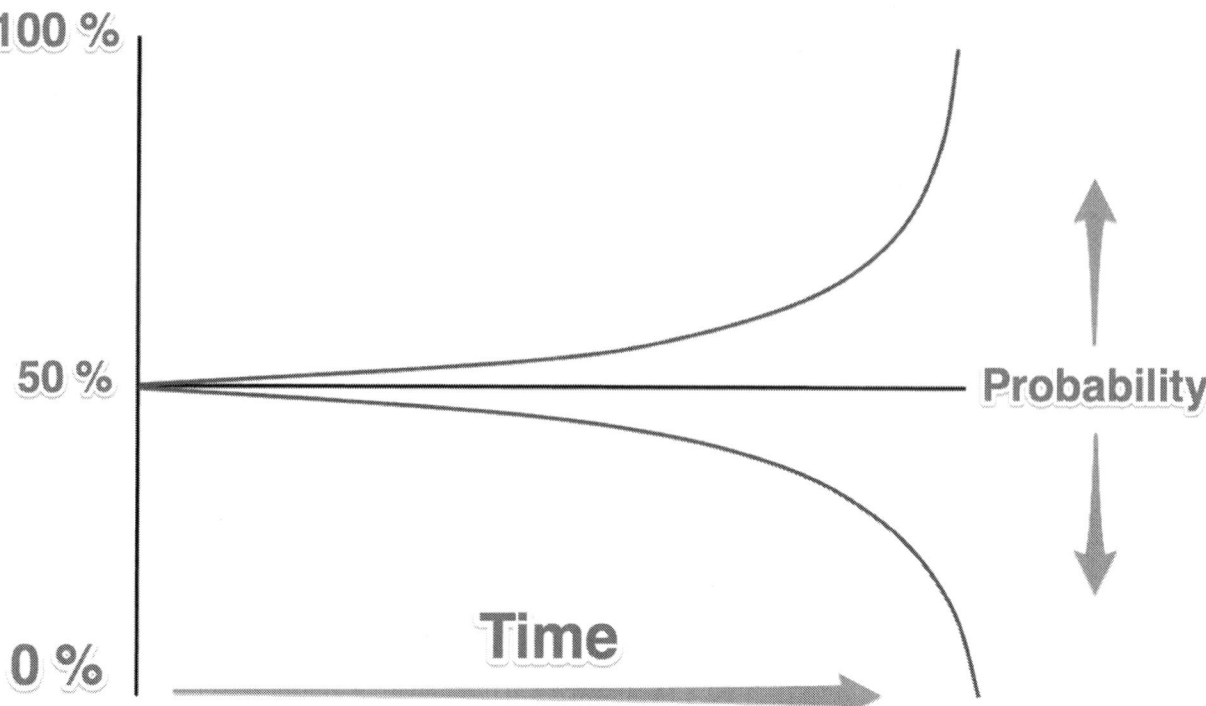

Fig 2.10 - The effect of time on probability

As you can see this is not a linear effect. The Y axis represents the probability the event will happen. In other words the probability from 0% to 100%, and the X axis represents the time available for the event to happen (or not happen). As the event starts, time has little impact at this point. Gradually as we approach the halfway stage of the event, time becomes increasingly important. Until in the last third of the event the erosion of time becomes exponential. As the event nears its conclusion, time is slipping away ever faster, with the probability of the event occurring becoming more or less likely. This relationship speeds up continually, until finally the event ends.

In some ways you can think of this as an old fashioned egg timer, but one with a hole that gets larger the longer the event. As it starts, there is plenty of sand still at the top of the timer, but as time wastes away so the hole in the middle becomes larger and larger allowing ever more sand to pass through increasingly quickly. The old maxim *'a race against time'* sums this up very neatly. This is precisely what is happening here - it is a race against time for the event to happen or not, before we run out of time.

Regardless of whether we are betting or trading in binary options or fixed odds, time is always draining away in one way or another, and if we are on the 'wrong side' of an event happening, then time moves ever faster against us. However, the converse is also true. If we are on the right side, time is working in our favor. This is one of the issues we have to overcome when trading such instruments, and as we saw above, one of the ways we can do this is by using the 'in running' feature which allows us to enter the event when we feel the probability/time relationship is more in our favor. Another is to understand volume and price and to use this knowledge to forecast future market behavior with confidence, of which more later.

In the world of vanilla options (those options quoted on a central exchange such as the CME), time is just as important, but here there is one critical difference. As a vanilla options trader you can buy **and** sell options. In the world of exotic or binary options you **only** have the choice to purchase the proposition, either to accept or reject the event. In other words select an option on an event happening, or not happening.

In the vanilla world, in selling an option you are getting time to work in your favor, and it is no longer working against you. This is absolutely fundamental and is why so many professional traders opt to sell options rather than buy them. Why? Simply because these traders understand time is a wasting asset, and as a seller they are using time to their advantage, and to the disadvantage of the option buyer on the other side. Furthermore, it is also generally accepted that between 80% and 85% of options expire worthless, and the reason is time works for the option seller, but against the option buyer. In the binary world we are option purchasers, agreeing or disagreeing with the proposition, and therefore need to be acutely aware of this and the immense power of time erosion.

This is not to say we cannot use time to our advantage when trading binary options - we can. As you will discover later, to get time on our side it is a question of timing and the associated probabilities. Think of this in terms of betting in running where the favorite in a horse race is well ahead in the final furlong of the race. Here we are putting time on our side since there is little time left before the end of the race. It is the same with a binary option. If we are prepared to accept a very small return on the probability of an event happening, time in this case is working for us as the event is near to expiry. And the same principle can be applied if we are betting on an event not happening.

Odds & Probabilities Explained

At this point I am very conscious of the fact that I have used the terms odds and probabilities as almost interchangeable, which strictly speaking they are not. Therefore, let me correct this now, so we can move on to look at some real examples, and explore the odds, probabilities and returns in more detail.

In some ways, in talking about odds and probabilities, this in itself also defines the crossing point between the fixed odds world of sports betting and the binary world of trading. Odds are more generally associated with racing and fixed odds, whilst probabilities are now associated with binaries.

But what is the difference?

In a sense very little, as they are both attempting to describe the chance of an event happening or not. Using odds, this is expressed in terms of success or failure. In other words, the number of **desired** outcomes compared to the number of **undesired** outcomes. Using probability this is calculated as the number of **desired** outcomes compared to the sum of **possible** outcomes.

If we start with probability, and take a simple example of rolling a dice. Suppose we want to know the probability of throwing a three on a dice. The maths are as follows:

- Number of desired outcomes = 1 (we want a three)
- Sum of possible outcomes = 6 (6 numbers on the dice)

The probability is therefore 1/6 = 0.1666666 recurring

This is then usually converted to a percentage and the probability becomes 0.16666666 x 100 = 16.67%

Another simple example would be the toss of a coin. Suppose we want to know the probability of the coin landing as a head:

- Number of desired outcomes = 1 (we want a head)
- Sum of possible outcomes = 2 (head or tail)

The probability is therefore 1/2 x 100% = 50%

To be precise, in this case there is a third outcome which we have ignored here. The coin could theoretically land on its edge. This is very unlikely, but nevertheless possible, and in the world of betting and binary options it happens. And it's called a dead heat.

I'm not going to explain the maths here, as it is not relevant, but my point is this. In sports betting dead heat rules generally pay out something. In binary options they generally do not, and this happens more than you would think. After all, no matter how many decimal places there may be on the quoted price, the closing price can often be identical to the open. A dead heat in other words. It happens, so you need to be aware of this and check the terms and conditions of your particular broker.

If we take the first example again, the probability of throwing a three of the dice, was 16.67%. But what is the probability of this event *not* occurring?

All the events we are looking at here are very simple and described as mutually exclusive. In other words, they cannot happen at the same time. In the coin toss you can only throw a head or a tail. There is no possibility of both happening at the same time. Before tossing the coin the probability of a head is 50%, and after the event there are two outcomes.

- If it landed as a head then the event happened and is 100%
- If it landed as a tail then the event did not happen and is 0%

The event therefore either happens, or does not happen. This is the binary notation of 0 and 1 simply converted to a probability percentage which is the way most binary options are quoted. So you will see 55, or 35 quoted which is simply 0.55 or 0.35 in the binary notation, and then multiplied by 100. You will not see the % notation, but simply round numbers as here.

Staying with the coin toss, if the probability of the event happening is 50%, and we know these are mutually exclusive events, the sum of the probabilities of all the possible outcomes must come to 100%. Therefore the probability of the event not happening is simply:

- 100% - 50% = 50 %

In other words, an equal probability in this case which is what we would expect as we only have two possible outcomes - a head or a tail.

If we take our other example using the dice. Here the probability of throwing a three was 16.67%. What are the probabilities of the event not happening? In other words of *not* throwing a three?

- 100% - 16.67% = 83.33%

This is intuitively what we would expect. After all, there are five other number on the dice which are not a three, so even with no knowledge of the maths behind the numbers, we would guess we have a better chance betting on the event not happening, rather than it happening - all things being equal.

If this event were being quoted as a binary option, it would appear something like this:

- Dice lands as a three 16.67
- Dice does not land as a three 83.33

Where we have mutually exclusive events, then the sum of the probabilities will always equal 1 or 100:

- 16.67 + 83.33 = 100
- 0.1667 + 0.8333 = 1

The above examples are very simple and designed to explain the basic concepts of probability. There is no influence of time or volatility here. We can toss the coin or throw the dice whenever we like. The event starts and finishes when we choose.

However, in binary options we have the additional factors of time, volatility, the underlying price of the derivative, and of course, in running betting. All of these will have a huge influence on the numbers being quoted, which change millisecond by millisecond, as the probabilities of the event ***happening*** or ***not happening*** are influenced by all the various underlying forces of the market, coupled with time.

Now let's move to odds.

In probability, we are looking at the number of desired outcomes against the number of possible outcomes. In odds, we are looking at the number of desired outcomes against the number of undesired outcomes. In other words, the chance *for* an event and the chances *against* the event. Success vs failure.

If we start with our coin toss example again:

- Number of desired outcomes = 1 (a head)
- Number of undesired outcomes = 1 (a tail)

The odds therefore would be quoted as 1:1.

If we take our dice example next:

- Number of desired outcomes = 1 (a three)
- Number of undesired outcomes = 5 (five other possible numbers on the dice, 1,2,4,5,6)

The odds therefore would be quoted as 1:5.

What the odds are telling us is simply this. In the first example, if we toss the coin and if we do this twice (1+1), we would expect a head to land once. In the second example, if we throw the dice 6 times (5+1), we would expect the three to land once.

One of the peculiarities of sports betting is that odds are quoted as the chances of losing not the chances of winning. A probability is quoted as the chances of winning. Odds are quoted as the chances of losing. A subtle but important difference.

In the second example above, the odds quoted for throwing a three would be quoted as 5:1 - five to one. In other words, five chances to lose against one of winning in every cycle of six throws.

To convert odds to probabilities is very simple. If we take our dice example again, then the probability is calculated as follows:

- Probability (%) = Number of desired outcomes/ (Number of desired outcomes + number of undesired outcomes) x 100
- Probability = 1/(1 + 5) x 100 = 16.67%

I hope the above gives you a very basic understanding of odds and probabilities in the context of the construction of the chances of winning or losing. However, odds and probabilities also play a major part in dictating the win/loss ratio you will need to achieve in order to succeed on a consistent basis, which in turn is wrapped up not only in the percentage returns, but also the broker or bookmakers profits. Again I will cover all of these in detail as we move deeper into this subject, and introduce them at the appropriate time. For now, that's enough of the maths, as it's time to move on to consider working examples.

And perhaps the place to start is with the first and most respected company to close the gap between sports betting and financial betting, a company which started life as BetOnMarkets.

I do accept that here in the UK spread betting also led the way, but the spread betting instrument and risk/reward profile is very different from the one we are considering here.

The name of the company BetOnMarkets really explains who they are and what they do. The company gives traders the opportunity to bet on the markets. It is licensed and regulated by two gaming authorities, the Lotteries and Gaming Authority in Malta, and the Gambling Supervision Commission on the Isle of Man.

However, the company has now changed its name to Binary.com and rebranded its platform and product offering.

The reason for focusing on Binary.com is that, in my humble opinion, they represent the gold standard for fixed odds instruments. The company is highly respected and has a long and established track record. In addition, it is one which is closely regulated and perhaps even more importantly one that manages its own book, its risks and also its own platform. Furthermore, they were voted best fixed odds broker in 2012, and have a proven track record going back to 2000.

But there is a further reason, which is even more powerful and fundamental to you as a trader. Binary.com are the only provider of a fixed odds instrument where you have the facility to select the starting time for your event. This is the point I alluded to earlier in the chapter.

To the best of my knowledge no other company offers this, and I cannot stress too strongly the control and power this places in your hands. This is the example I referred to earlier, where we want to run our race at a time of our choosing and under conditions favorable to us. You choose when to run your race, not the broker. This immediately shifts the odds dramatically in your favor. If you can read a chart and the market with confidence, using this simple but powerful feature puts you in complete control. It is a game changer in fixed odds and one you would be wise to consider and apply.

The proposition offered by Binary.com is very straightforward, and until just a few years ago, was referred to as fixed odds betting. This term has since morphed into fixed returns betting, and subsequently adopted into binary options as fixed returns options. The products are not quoted in probabilities, but in monetary amounts with the associated returns and it is not in running at present. However, as I stressed above, you do have the option to start the event at the time of your own choosing which is the game changer.

Below is a screenshot from the original BetOnMarkets trading window, which as you can see is very simple and clear:

Fig 2.11 - BetOnMarkets 15 minute trade on EUR/USD

In this example we have chosen a very simple proposition on the EUR/USD, the euro dollar currency pair from the forex market.

The proposition selected is a 'Rise/Fall' with a duration of 15 minutes. In other words we are going to speculate whether this currency pair is going to end higher or lower after this time period has elapsed. On the left hand side of the order entry window we can choose our payout, in other words the amount we want to win if we are right.

Here we have chosen £100 to keep the maths simple. You can also see the Start time is defaulted to Now*. This is where *you* start your race - no one else. You decide to take the offer or not and is one of the many advantages of this approach to the market. As already mentioned you are in complete control of the starting time of your race. You are the starter with all the horses lined up, and you are waiting to open the starting gates on your race.

Again I cannot stress to you how important this is.

You are not tied to a fixed event with a prescribed start and finish time. The event duration is set at 15 minutes in this case, but the starting time is your choice, as is the length of the race. Again this is an important differentiator. Not only are you defining your entry point, but also the length of the race. To use a horse racing analogy again. Now we are matching not only the conditions to our horse, but also the course length. All you need to do to move the odds in your favor is to start the race at the right time.

If you recall the analogy I used earlier where our horse preferred softer ground, we would wait until conditions are in our favor. It is exactly the same here. If you understand how the markets work, and how to forecast future price action particularly using volume, (and you will by the end of this book) to succeed, you simply wait until market conditions are in your favor. I'm sorry to labor the point, but it is vitally important you understand this.

Now, you are shifting the odds in your favor and away from the broker. With sports betting, this is far more difficult. In the financial markets it is straightforward, and something few traders ever take advantage of. Moreover, whilst there is no doubt time and volatility still play their part, as does the underlying price, if you can forecast future price action with any degree of confidence, suddenly the odds shift in your favor.

And perhaps this is one of the ironies of binary options and fixed odds instruments. They are ideally suited to the more experienced trader, but generally they are promoted to the novice. If you are a novice, the place to start is with an understanding of market behavior preferably based on leading indicators, and then to come to these instruments which are simple yet powerful. Rather like a stick of dynamite, in the wrong hands lethal, but used correctly has many advantages.

With Binary.com the time and length of the race are entirely your choice. This offers two distinct advantages. First, you can take advantage of market conditions, such as a pending news release. Second, this can free you from having to sit in front of your screen. The runners and riders have to wait until you are ready to start the race.

To return to our quote window.

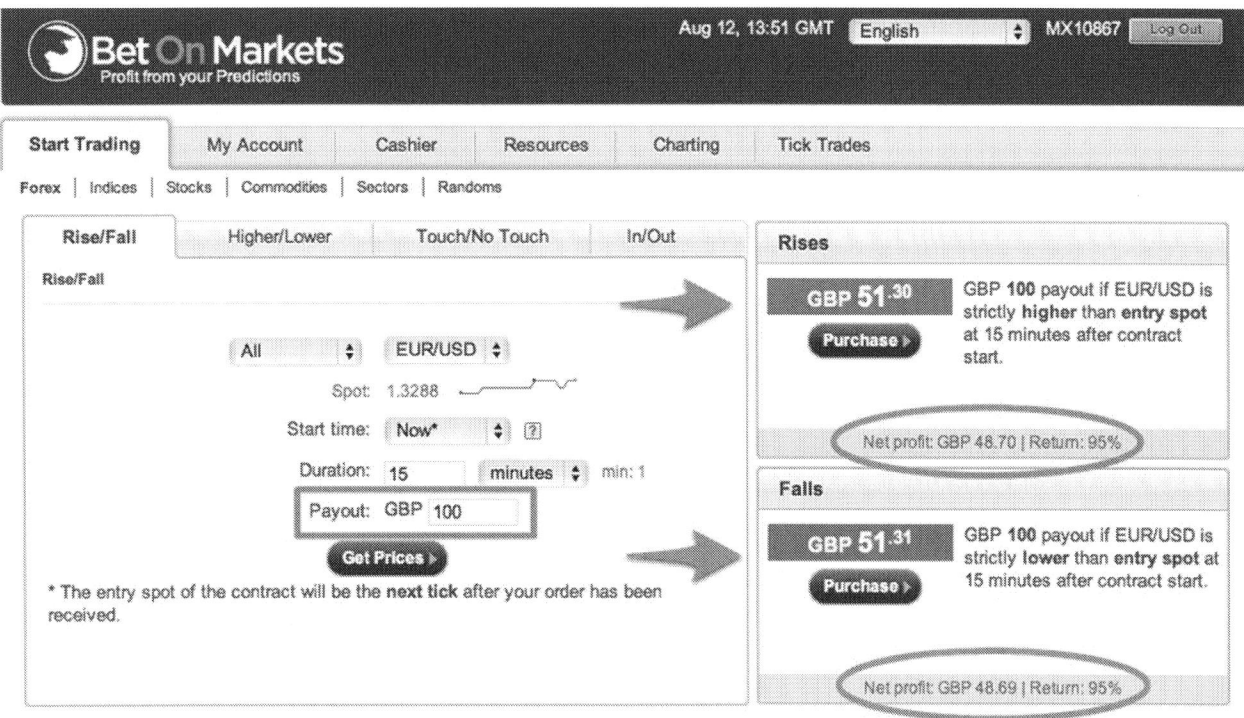

Fig 2.12 - BetOnMarkets 15 minute trade on EUR/USD

On the right hand side of the window is the quote from Binary.com. As you can see this is quoted as a cash amount in pounds, and the governing factor is the underlying spot market.

There are several points to note here which will help to explain how binary options differ from these fixed odds trades. In examining this trade in more detail, it will also help you to understand the very different role adopted by the broker in creating the binary options, odds and probabilities.

On the right hand side the order ticket is quoting £51.30 for a rise, and £51.31 for a fall. What does this mean? Again think of this in simple terms as a two horse race, which is actually what it is. We have two horses running here, and one is going to win, and the other is going to lose. In many ways we can think of Binary.com as a traditional bookmaker, making a book on a two horse race.

What is clear from the prices being quoted is Binary.com, at this precise point, has no idea which horse is likely to win.

But how do we know this?

In the first place the prices being quoted are almost identical. If they believed one or other of our two horses was a favorite, then the odds on that horse winning the race would be much shorter. They are not. In other words, at this point there is no bias. This lack of bias is reflected in the prices being quoted. If there were, this would be seen in the prices, which reflect the odds and the returns.

In fact, our bookmaker doesn't care who wins or loses. Just like any other bookmaker they will make money *provided* their book on the race is constructed correctly, and the trades placed are not heavily skewed one way or the other. This is always a problem for bookmakers, even more so in a two horse race. Because if all the money goes on the favorite, and very little on the other runner in the race, the bookmaker can make a loss. Bookmakers make their living from what is called the over-round, the percentage above 100% of the total odds on the race.

In our example above with our two horse race, this is very easy to calculate. If we assume we have 10 traders who believe the EUR/USD will rise over the next 15 minutes, and 10 traders who believe it will fall, then the maths is very simple.

Each bet is £100, so our bookmaker knows they will have to pay out 10 x £100 = £1,000. This payout to the winners will be funded by the bets placed, which is as follows:

- 10 x £51.31 = £513.10
- 10 x £51.30 = £513.00

The total in trades placed is £1,026.10

The profit for our bookmaker on this two horse race is therefore:

- £1,026.10 - £1,000.00 = £26.10

This is equivalent to an over-round of:

- £26.10/£1,000 x 100% = 2.6%

I appreciate this is a very basic example, and one which assumes everyone is trading the same size. And of course this figure can and does vary constantly, but at this precise moment, and making some very simplistic assumptions, the over-round is 2.6%.

As you will see later, this figure is very modest when compared to many other brokers in the market, and is one which impacts your percentage returns directly.

Returning to our two horse race. The bookmaker begins by offering odds of 5-6 on, on horse A and 5-6 on, on horse B. In both cases the 'on' simply means the horse has a higher probability of winning than losing. This means if the race is run eleven times, the horse is likely to win six times and only lose five times. If we convert these to probabilities:

- Horse A = 6/(6+5) x 100 = 54.55%
- Horse B = 6/(6+5) x 100 = 54.55%

The total probability is 109.10%. The bookmaker then pays out 100% leaving the 9.1% as his or her profit margin. This assumes an equal amount of money is bet on each horse, which is why the odds are constantly changing to reflect the 'weight of money' being bet, and to keep the profit margin in balance for the bookmaker. For the bookmaker the final book closes at the start of the race so his or her profit on that race is fixed. With the advent of betting exchanges, paradoxically many bookmakers now use this facility to hedge their book.

Many off exchange brokers also offer a fixed odds model both in terms of the instruments and quote protocols. However, as you will see later in the book, the over-rounds here are extremely high, and will have a direct impact on percentage returns. This is explained in detail in Chapter 5 when considering the maths of trading. In simple terms, as the percentage return increases so the break-even falls. As the returns fall below 100% so the break-even rises accordingly, making it ever harder to move forward with consistent profits.

For the on exchange options broker, their risk profile is much lower. Here the broker is simply providing the exchange as a market to match the binary option trades. The broker simply takes a commission for providing the exchange and matching the trades.

But let's go back to our two quotes and look at these in more detail.

The first thing to appreciate is the payout of £100 which we selected includes the return of our initial stake, if we are correct. This is the maximum amount we will receive back in our account if we are correct in our selection.

If we decide the EUR/USD is going to close higher in the next 15 minutes, and purchase this trade at £51.30, this is our maximum potential loss. Our actual profit is:

- £100 - £51.30 = £48.70

As soon as we click the Purchase button, £51.30 is deducted from our account. If we are subsequently proved to be correct, £100 will be credited to our account once the trade has expired.

This is how the odds are working here.

We have risked £51.30 to win £48.70, so the fractional odds here are slightly less than 1:1, which would be the case if there were no over-round. To convert this to odds, let us return to first principles:

- £10 bet at 3/1 if successful wins 3 x £10 = £30

Now let's add in our figures from above and solve for x:

- £51.30 bet at x/1 if successful wins = £48.70
- Therefore x = £48.70/£51.30 = 0.95

Our fractional odds are 0.95:1. This is what we refer to as an 'odds on' bet, as the probability of the event happening is slightly higher than 50% and we can calculate this using our formula from above:

- Probability (%) = Number of desired outcomes/ (Number of desired outcomes + number of undesired outcomes) x 100
- Probability = 1/(1 + 0.95) x 100 = 51.28%

The reason I chose £100 for the payout was simply these figures are also reflected in the quote window on the right.

Here we can see the return quoted is 95% alongside the Net profit of GBP 48.70 circled. If we convert our fractional odds to a percentage then we arrive at 95%:

- 0.95/1 x 100 = 95%

Finally we can see our probability of 51.28% reflects the reward of £51.30 if we are correct. The slight difference is due to rounding errors.

Taking another example, but this time we have moved to the new platform for Binary.com at http://www.binary.com.

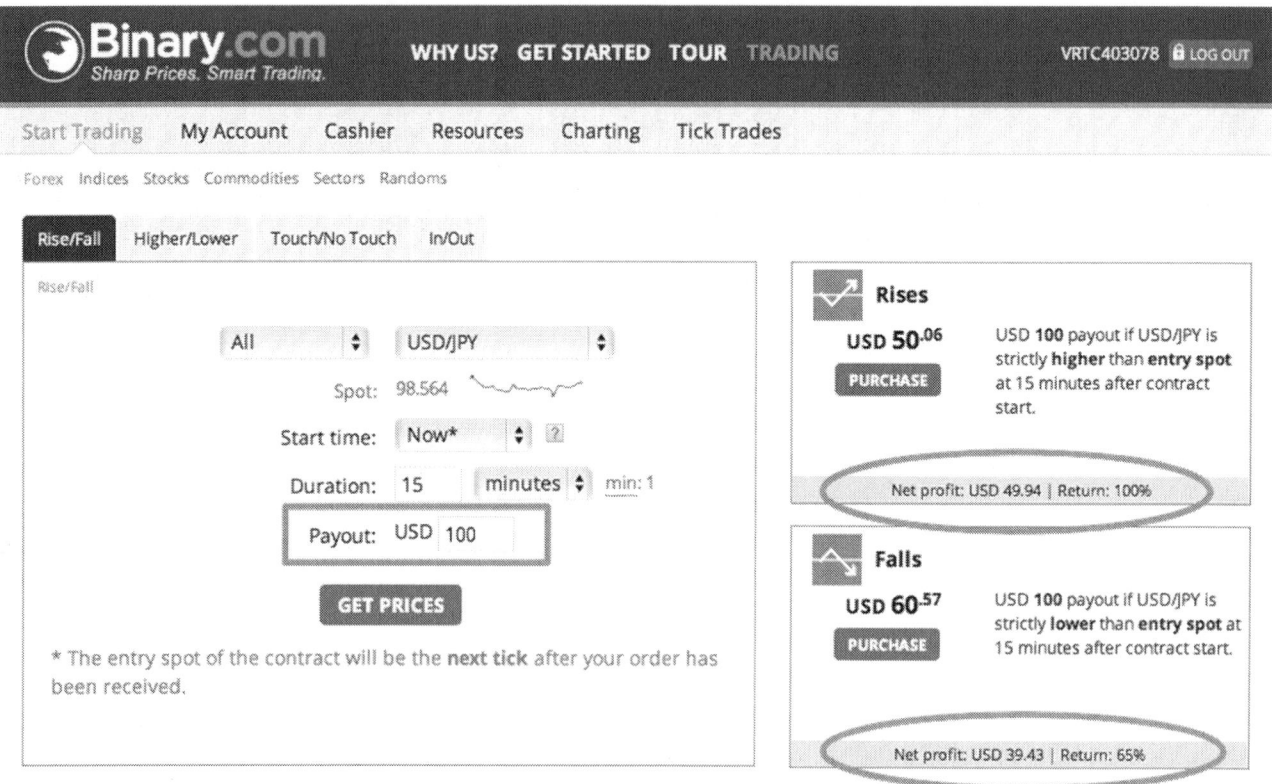

Fig 2.13 - Binary.com 15 minute trade on the USD/JPY

Once again we are considering a simple rise/fall trade so all we are judging here is whether this currency pair will close higher or lower in the next 15 minutes. The main difference is the default currency is now US dollars, but again I have chosen $100 to keep the maths simple.

What are we being quoted for the USD/JPY?

It is very different to our EUR/USD example, where the two trades were equally balanced in terms of the odds. In that example we had no favorite in the race. In this example we do, as we have the rising quote at $50.06 with a return of 100%, whilst the falling quote is currently $60.57 with a return of 65%.

The proposition that the market will rise is even money, 1:1 odds, or a 50% probability. The market to fall is favorite at $39.43 which is ($100 - $60.57)/$60.57 = 0.65/1.

If we convert this to a probability as before:

- Probability (%) = Number of desired outcomes/ (Number of desired outcomes + number of undesired outcomes) x 100
- Probability = 1/(1 + 0.65) x 100 = 60.60%

Once again this is as we expect, and is the equivalent amount in US dollars as the cost of the trade at $60.57 (allowing for rounding errors).

At this precise moment Binary.com believes over the next 15 minutes, the USD/JPY currency pair has a much higher probability of closing lower rather than higher. You can also see in this example the over-round is much higher at $110.63 or 10.63%, but bear in mind this changes all the time, and seconds later was much lower again.

So which option would you take?

And here it all comes down to risk, and without an analysis of the chart using volume price analysis, your guess would be as good as mine. All the broker will ever do is quote the odds on the book. If favorites won all the time the bookmakers or brokers would all be out of business very quickly. Equally, rank outsiders do win.

In the fixed odds world, the odds or the probabilities never vary greatly. However, there are some notable exceptions for certain products, which we will consider later in the book.

The example here is a two horse race, with two very similar horses. We do not have a donkey racing against a thoroughbred, which would be reflected in the odds being quoted. We are never going to see a rank outsider and a red hot certainty quoted at the start of the race. But will see this towards the end of the race as time exerts its powerful influence.

In accepting the odds we are using our skill and ability to forecast market behavior accurately and consistently, which will then provide the basis for our decision. To help us frame this decision, the questions we need to ask include:

- Are the odds in our favor, or are they against us?
- Is the risk high or low?

Without any meaningful analysis we may just as well flip a coin. With market analysis, and in particular using volume and price, we start to weight the odds in our favor, but always remembering we do have the complication of time. Time is the game changer. No longer are we forecasting whether a market will rise, fall or go sideways. Now we have to forecast **when** this is likely to happen, and that is the most difficult element of an option or bet.

One aspect we have not considered in this introduction to probabilities and odds, is the break-even ratio and profit margins - the maths of profitability if you like. This is where returns and your percentage of winners to losers becomes key. If the return on your investment is less than 100%, and often it will be much lower than this, you will have to achieve a better than 50% success rate just to stand still, viewed very simply. We are going to cover this in a later chapter, along with an explanation of profit margins and their importance. All will be explained in due course.

In the next chapter we are going to look at those platforms offered by off exchange binary options brokers, and see how they vary in terms of the quote window. This is where we enter the world of binary options and probabilities quoted from the start until the end of the race - or do we? Let's find out.

Chapter Three

Off Exchange Binary Brokers

The markets are the same now as they were five or ten years ago because they keep changing - just like they did then

Ed Seykota (1946 -)

Let me begin this chapter by trying to frame what you are about to read. And by framing, I am trying to put this chapter into some sort of context, and to provide what I hope will be a balanced view of the binary options market, as it is today. It is a new market, and one that is changing very fast indeed, driven by a variety of forces, some good, and some not so good. Once you have read this chapter, some of your perceptions of binary options brokers may change. Furthermore, what I am about to write may be seen as provocative, and indeed may even offend. However, this is the way I see things right now, and I make no apology for what comes next.

Perhaps I could begin with a paradox. A paradox or simple observation of life if you like, and it is this. In the 'real' world, when new markets are created, and new products and solutions delivered, the companies and individuals at the forefront are considered trailblazers, pioneers and true entrepreneurs. Some become icons with iconic brands. These markets then mature, develop and expand as products and services are enhanced over the years.

In the virtual internet world the opposite is often true. New markets attract the opportunist, the get rich quick brigade. What I call the 'cash and dash' merchants, eager to cash in on a generally unsuspecting and gullible public. The lifecycle generally runs for three to five years, and is repeated across all markets, but particularly in those where hope is the driving force, such as making money and weight loss. We have seen this cycle in the forex market which is only now starting to mature, but we are currently in the very early stages with binary options.

Let me give an example of what I mean by this paradox between the internet and the real world. Several years ago the betting industry was shaken up by the arrival of Betfair, who introduced a truly innovative approach to betting. Since then others have tried to emulate, what is in essence, a simple concept but one which changed the gaming industry forever. Was it a scam? No, most definitely not, and the company continues to hold its value and market share with an excellent reputation in the industry. Traditional bookies may hate the company, but the betting public love it.

By contrast the binary options market is in its infancy, and in its present iteration can only be described as the Wild West. It is a market populated by many cash & dash merchants whose only motive is to fleece the naive and unwary. This is usually done by promising unrealistic and unachievable returns. In many ways, it resembles the weight loss industry where ridiculous claims are made - acai berries being one of the more recent. However, this is not to tar every company with the same brush. It is merely to highlight a common trait whenever a new or innovative product or service comes to market.

In this section we are going to explore the underbelly of the binary broker world, and sadly it is not a pretty sight. Here we are considering that group of off exchange brokers who can best be described as 'bucket shops'.

In other words, they are quoting OTC (over the counter) products to you as the client. There is nothing inherently wrong with this model which is common in the forex world. However, it is the associated marketing tactics which define this group and is the common denominator. It is these tactics which have alarmed so many of the regulators around the world.

Therefore, let me begin with an explanation of how this group is generally structured in this market. And the first point to note it is a group dominated by what is known as 'white labels'. If you have never come across this term before, this means the broker is offering a platform supplied by another company, and is then rebranding it to make it appear unique. This is done by changing colors, fonts, and adding logos and minor cosmetic changes. However, the underlying product offering, the options quotes and settlements, will be identical to the originating platform. There is nothing wrong in offering such a platform, but it may surprise you to know, a large percentage of the 'bucket shops' currently operating in this space are a white label of just a handful of providers.

It is a relatively easy process for anyone or any group to set up a white label binary brokerage. All of the back end processing, risk and order management is handled by the white label provider. All the white label broker has to do is attract as many customers as possible to the platform. It is relatively inexpensive, and a white label broker can be up and running in a matter of weeks.

It is hardly surprising therefore there has been an explosion in the number of 'new' binary brokers joining the market. However, these are not 'new' brokers, but primarily rebadged platforms from one of the primary providers. You can check this for yourself very easily, by visiting several of the many binary broker websites, and very quickly you will begin to recognize the commonality of the platforms. You may be asking *'does this matter?'* The short answer is yes and for several reasons.

First, let's start with how the binary options are presented, and whether they are quoted as binary probabilities. The short answer is no. All of these companies quote a fixed proposition in terms of odds and time. And the reason for this is very simple to understand if we go back to our fixed odds horse race.

All bookmakers are well versed in managing risk. They adjust their odds constantly, and will lay off bets to hedge risk prior to the start of a race. Once the race begins all the bookmaker has to do is wait for the completion of the race and payout accordingly. This is a relatively simple process. Now imagine if the same bookmaker were managing the odds and risk 'in running'. This is a very different and complex process, with the odds changing second by second as the race develops. Small wonder therefore, this is not offered by such brokers as it is simply too complicated to manage the risk. Much easier therefore to offer a fixed odds model and market it as a binary option.

To continue the *'does it matter'* question, the second point concerns the 'in running' issue. At the time of writing, I have yet to find a white label broker who can offer early closure of a trade once underway. They do not have the in house expertise to offer this facility, because they are not managing their own risk or book.

Next on the *'does it matter'* question comes transparency, or should I say a lack of transparency. For you, as the client there is none. You have no idea what price is being quoted, and have no way of checking. And given many binary options are quoted over seconds or minutes to 5 decimal places, checking is impossible. A tick movement either way will push a position into loss, and it is remarkable how often this seems to happen just at expiry of the option. The transparency issue is a huge problem in the industry, and one that has yet to be addressed. And the issue is this.

Suppose you are trading the price of a stock using one of these brokers. You have the illusion of trading the actual movement of that stock, but have no idea if the price is settled based on the actual tick movement on the underlying, since no time or sale data is available to you as the client. The only information you have is the price quoted on your screen from your broker. Given these brokers are virtually all white label platforms, this problem is unlikely to be addressed anytime soon since it is the platform providers who will need to supply the data and charts.

Furthermore, there is a second and potentially more serious issue concerning transparency, and that is market manipulation. Whenever you take a position in an OTC contract, a conflict of interest arises. In the forex world many brokers have now moved to the STP (Straight Through Processing) or ECN model, where orders are routed directly into the interbank market pool for execution. However, many market making brokers still exist with a traditional dealing desk. Here they manage their A and B book clients accordingly, with the winning A book customers generally passed directly through into the interbank pool, whilst B book customers (the losers) are managed in house, and subject to the well know practices of stop hunting, re-quoting, and other sharp practices.

For white label binary brokers the opportunities for price manipulation are even more straightforward. In the forex market, brokers at least have to wait for news to create the required volatility. For these brokers time is the catalyst, and once a proposition approaches expiry, a simple change in price by fractions of a tick or pip is all that is required.

Maybe you believe this is all fanciful nonsense and I have an axe to grind with this sector of the industry. Nothing could be further from the truth, so let me include part of a press release from the CFTC which appeared in June 2013, in which they made the following comments:

'The third category of alleged fraud involves the manipulation of the binary options trading software to generate losing trades. These complaints allege that the Internet-based binary options trading platforms manipulate the trading software to distort binary options prices and payouts. For example, when a customer's trade is "winning," the countdown to expiration is extended arbitrarily until the trade becomes a loss.'

And what are the other two categories of alleged fraud alluded to in this release? The first is funds withdrawal, another major issue and one I will cover shortly, and the second is identity theft which is another growing problem.

But to continue with the '*so what*' question further.

If all these white label brokers are essentially the same, what other problems does this create? And the answer is in fact - several.

First, if everyone is attempting to market and sell the same service, how does one broker differentiate themselves from another? And here we enter the realm of what I refer to as 'desperate differentiation'. If the product offering is not unique, the platform has to appear to be different, and one of the simplest tricks is to rename the buy and sell buttons to call and put.

Next under the category of desperate differentiation comes funds withdrawal. Again this is a very simple marketing trick, but an extremely powerful one, and deployed with two initial objectives in mind. There is a third, of which more later. Here the white label brokers offer huge cash incentives with apparently no strings, to encourage clients to deposit further funds. Needless to say, if an offer is too good to be true it generally is, and this is the case here.

The first reason is to attract as much cash into the account as quickly as possible, since these brokers know this will ultimately be lost by the client. Second, these wild offers help to differentiate them from their competition. The mechanism here is very simple. The best ones usually are.

Here is an example from one of the many brokers I researched when writing this book. It is one of the less extreme examples, but I can assure you there are far worse.

The proposition is very simple. Deposit an amount with the broker, who in turn will top up your account to increase your trading capital which all sounds great. In my case, I suggested I was considering a deposit of $500, and they offered a sign up bonus of double this amount, in other words $1,000 thereby giving me a total of $1,500 in my account. We all know there is no such thing as a 'free lunch', and it is in the small print you discover why. The terms of this bonus are you will not be able to access any profits from your account until you have executed a minimum of 40, 50 or 60 times the bonus amount. In other words, you will only have access to any **profits** in your account, once you have achieved anywhere between $40,000 to $60,000 in profit - a staggering amount.

In the example above the lock in ratio was 40 times the deposit, but there are some much higher multipliers, with 60 currently the maximum. But what does all this mean?

Suppose we have decided to open an account offering such a deal, and we place our first trade with a maximum loss of $50. The trade closes as a loser and our initial deposit is now reduced to $450. Can we withdraw our deposit? In the above case I was told I could do so. But let's imagine our first trade is a winner. Can we withdraw the profit of $50? The answer is *no*. And here is the kicker. You will only be able to withdraw any profits once you have achieved the requisite trading volumes in dollars, as required under the terms of the bonus.

Any profits you make are effectively locked in by the broker. You **cannot** withdraw these until you have met the threshold of trading activity, as dictated by the broker in their terms and conditions applicable to the bonus on offer. In the case above I was told categorically I could withdraw my initial deposit at any time, and this was not subject to the terms of the bonus. However, I have my doubts and from my own research for this book I have discovered cases where legitimate deposits have been withheld as they fail to fulfill other minimum terms, such as duration of the account, number of trades, etc.

Given most traders lose in all markets, and not just in the binary world, the brokers know that few if any of their clients will ever achieve the threshold at which they can access any profits made. This is why the CFTC quoted the following in their recent press release, and which I alluded to earlier:

The CFTC and SEC have received numerous complaints of fraud associated with websites that offer an opportunity to buy or trade binary options through Internet-based trading platforms. The complaints fall into at least three categories: refusal to credit customer accounts or reimburse funds to customers; identity theft; and manipulation of software to generate losing trades.

The first category of alleged fraud involves the refusal of certain Internet-based binary options trading platforms to credit customer accounts or reimburse funds after accepting customer money. These complaints typically involve customers who have deposited money into their binary options trading account and who are then encouraged by "brokers" over the telephone to deposit additional funds into the customer account. When customers later attempt to withdraw their original deposit or the return they have been promised, the trading platforms allegedly cancel customers' withdrawal requests, refuse to credit their accounts, or ignore their telephone calls and emails.

Taking the ploy of the bonus concept a little further, and how it has a more subtle and corrosive aspect. This ploy is designed to lock you and your money into the account. Next it is there as a marketing tool to help attract new clients. Finally it is designed to provide you with leverage, a subtle but immensely powerful way to get you to trade in bigger positions. These brokers know their customers will ultimately lose, and in providing leverage wrapped up as a bonus, it simply helps them lose even faster.

What generally happens is the first trade is small and loses, and is then followed by increasingly larger trades, as the 'get even' mentality of gambling takes hold. The double or quits mentality finally takes over, and the client loses all their money, helped by the subtle leverage kindly offered by the broker. And if all this sounds a little cynical, sadly these are the facts and cannot be dressed up in any other way.

A bonus deposit is added to your account, but not to your balance, so it is available for trading matched by your deposit, but most definitely *not* available for withdrawal.

In summary, this type of bonus is rarely referred to as a leveraged bonus, but this in simple terms is what it is. It is a powerful marketing tool which locks clients and their money into the company, whilst simultaneously providing increased funds for trading larger positions.

There is another type of bonus which is a simple cash bonus, offered either as a 'loyalty bonus' for longevity or number of trades over time. There is nothing wrong with these offers, but they are few and far between, and again may come with strings attached. The moral of the story here is clear. There is no such thing as a free lunch, and if something sounds too good to be true then it generally is. This is certainly the case with the leveraged bonus. It is there for one reason, and one reason alone. To ensure you lose your money fast.

Another marketing ploy revolves around the demo trading account, or indeed the complete lack of a demo account. If you have come to binary options from the forex world you will be very familiar with the concept of the demo account. These are generally free, widely available and offered across virtually all platforms, and also within brokerage accounts.

White label brokers are very different. Most do not offer demo accounts at all. Those that do use the word 'free' in loose terms only. Others offer demo accounts only on approval from account managers, and finally if you do manage to open one they usually time out within a matter of days.

The reason demo accounts are generally not widely available is because these brokers know most clients will lose and lose quickly. This is not good for business. In order to overcome this problem brokers will offer what they call a '*free demo account*', but do not assume this is free. In the binary broker world free does not mean free. What this actually means is free, **provided** you make a deposit to the account. In other words open an account which will then give you access to a demo account.

Once again the approach here is to lock you in with your money, provide a very short term demo, and then get you trading live as soon as possible. The psychology is simple. If you have an account open with real money you are almost certain to use it at some point in the first few days, and from there you are hooked. In my research I even came across a free demo account which turned out to be a video of a demo account!

All of the above demonstrates a complete lack of faith in the product, balanced by a consuming desire to grab the cash as quickly as possible. In addition, this relentless pressure to get you, as the client, to provide your credit card details opens a much deeper issue which is that of identity theft. This is yet another of the growing problems in the industry. Setting up as a white label broker is relatively cheap and quick. The site can then be used to collect personal details and credit card information, which are then sold. This was another major area highlighted by the CFTC who said:

The second category of alleged fraud involves identity theft. For example, some complaints allege that certain Internet-based binary options trading platforms may be collecting customer information such as credit card and driver's license data for unspecified uses. If a binary options Internet-based trading platform requests photocopies of your credit card, driver's license, or other personal data, do not provide the information.

And from here, it is a short hop to the issues of security, regulation and control which are currently also blighting this particular sector of the industry.

The current situation is confused to say the least, as the regulatory authorities grapple with the problems the white label market has created. And the issues are not just whether this activity is considered to be betting or trading, but the complete package from transparency and conflict of interest, to capitalization and illegal marketing activities.

But where do we start? And perhaps the best place is with the current situation in the US.

Here, trading with a 'non US regulated' off exchange binary options broker is illegal in the US. The two principle authorities, the CFTC and the SEC have made their position very clear. They both consider this market to be akin to gambling, and as a result have banned every off exchange binary broker from accepting US clients as customers. Here is a quote from the Director of Enforcement for the CFTC, following a recent lawsuit against one such broker:

"It is against the law to solicit U.S. persons to buy and sell commodity options, even if they are called 'prediction' contracts, unless they are listed for trading and traded on a CFTC-registered exchange or unless legally exempt."

More importantly, both the CFTC and the SEC have cited the issue of transparency, or lack of transparency as a major concern. This has not stopped many white label brokers from continuing to target and accept US accounts, and in the last year several high profile cases have been brought against companies openly flouting the regulations. These have resulted in massive fines, and simply demonstrate the amount of money at stake for these companies, keen to penetrate one of the largest markets. Clearly the fines are worth the risks involved, and as competition increases no doubt many of these companies will try to find alternative ways to circumvent the US authorities.

With the US leading the way in regulation, Japan has also followed suit with the Japanese FSA and FFA introducing a tight schedule of rules and procedures which every binary options broker must conform to before they can operate within the jurisdiction. As you might expect, the Japanese authorities have cited the same concerns as other regulatory bodies. What is interesting is to delve deeper into the rules which now apply for Japan, which in turn may herald the future for binary brokers in other parts of the world.

First is the issue of transparency. Whilst the Japanese authorities will allow the off exchange OTC binary broker to operate, it is mandatory for the broker to provide transparent pricing throughout the trading period.

Transparency also requires brokers to advise clients on those instruments not being offered due to extreme market volatility.

The second issue concerns time, and here the FSA have implemented a ruling limiting products to a minimum of two hours duration, in an attempt to move the binary option product from a bet to a trade. Then comes the 'leverage offer', referred to as the 'cash back caveat', and here the regulators have imposed strict controls on what can, or cannot be said in any advertising or incentives.

Next on the list is client suitability, and just as in other markets, clients are required to provide, and binary brokers are required to obtain, proof the customer has the required knowledge and skills to trade in the binary options market. Based on the questions and answers provided, clients are then categorized accordingly and only offered products suitable to their level of trading knowledge and expertise. This is much the same as currently required in many other markets such as futures and options. In a further attempt to protect customers from themselves, regulatory rules now dictate the level of losses and trading volumes which once met by a customer, cannot be exceeded.

More significantly perhaps, the regulators have introduced major changes to the quotation system and payouts for binary options. Here the simple high/low price model has been banned as it is considered a bet, short and simple. Brokers are now required to provide a 'ladder' of strike prices available throughout the life of the option. In addition, and even more significantly, call and put options are priced in realtime, offering market based dynamic premiums, with live bid and ask prices also quoted.

Furthermore, the authorities have addressed the issue of capitalization and funding, and brokers are now required under the new rules to reveal their complete profit and loss position, including all trading activities of their clients.

Japan is a large and growing market. In the forex world, Japanese traders constitute over 40% of the retail sector, and the binary options market is now exploding in a similar way. As a result, binary brokers who wish to access this lucrative market have little choice but to embrace the new regulations, which should start to filter their way out into the other jurisdictions. Whilst the Japanese regulations are not perfect they are a start, as the regulators around the world attempt to manage this growing market.

Moving elsewhere, Italy has taken an alternative approach. Consob (Commissione Nazionale per le Societa e la Borsa) the regulatory body has applied for court orders allowing it to ban various IP addresses of those binary brokers it considers to be 'bucket shops'. Turkey has adopted a similar approach, whilst in Spain and France the authorities have issued warnings directly to several brokers to stop the marketing of binary options to their respective citizens.

In Europe, it is Cyprus that is the principle regulatory body under CySec (Cyprus Securities and Exchange Commission) which recognized binary options as a financial instrument in 2012, thereby attracting many binary brokers as a result. Whilst Cyprus has taken a relatively relaxed view of the industry, it too has been under pressure to tighten controls. It is symptomatic of the industry at present that in the space of just four weeks CySec first introduced, and then subsequently reversed a decision which would have banned regulated brokers from accepting non EU clients as customers. This followed vociferous lobbying from the industry with CySec reversing its earlier decision.

Whilst Cyprus remains the 'go to' destination for many binary brokers, Malta is now preparing to offer its services with the MFSA (Malta Financial Services Authority) having recently decided to designate binary options as a financial product. Prior to this, binary brokers came under the supervision of the Lotteries and Gaming Authority (LGA). The change in stance is seen by many as an opportunistic one, with the Maltese authorities keen to cash in on a growing market. And with a minimum capitalization of 730,000 euros required at the time of writing, no doubt many brokers will take this opportunity and set up on the island.

Moving to the UK, there are two regulatory authorities which have recently replaced the now defunct FSA. These are the FCA (Financial Conduct Authority) and the PRA (Prudential Regulation Authority). Both were created following intense criticism of the FSA following the financial crisis. Both organizations have a relaxed attitude to the binary options market at present, and companies are assessed for accreditation on their financial status and risk management, but not on the markets in which they operate.

The Isle of Man is another location with a long established track record for financial companies, with regulation here falling under the GSC (Gambling Supervision Commission). It is more closely associated with the gaming industry in much the same way as Malta.

Finally to Australia where the regulatory authority is the ASIC (Australian Securities and Investments Commission), who take a similar and more relaxed approach as with the UK.

Sadly this chapter does not make very pretty reading. Indeed as I was drafting it, I spoke to a friend in the industry, and his comment on the binary options world was this, and I quote:

'it is where the forex market was ten years ago'

And this really sums up the current state of affairs. As I said earlier in the chapter, the Wild West was a tea party compared to this sector of the binary options world. The reason for this is simple, and in many ways is like the old fashioned gold rush. Gold fever abounds, but the only people making money are retailers supplying the picks and shovels. In our case it is the binary option bucket shops.

The binary world is currently at an embryonic stage, and with the explosion of interest online money is simply pouring into this market. Many brokers are shooting fish in a barrel, and with a ready and willing supply of new customers, there is no need to worry too much about ethics or even the law. So, let me try to summarize where we are at present, and remember this is before we even consider the broader topic of break-even and profit margins, which are all part and parcel of the binary options package.

In chapter two, we began by considering the fixed odds trading proposition offered by Binary.com. They differ hugely. Binary.com has been in business for over fourteen years and the company is regulated in both the Isle of Man and Malta. Their platform is proprietary not white label, and risk management is all executed by the company. Over the years the company has won many awards, and with secure segregated funds your money is always safe. There are no 'extreme' offers, and you are free to trial their demo platform, with no requirement to fund the account. And all with the huge benefit of allowing you to select both the start time and duration of your event. In the next ten years others may migrate to this model, but at present there is only Binary.com.

Moving to the bulk of off exchange white label brokers, by all means approach some of these and ask them some simple questions as part of your due diligence.

Regulation is key and certainly the starting point. If a broker is not regulated simply walk away. There are one or two brokers who have made an effort to distance themselves from some of the worst excesses, but they are few and far between. This will change over the next few years and follow the same pattern we have seen in the forex market. Tightening regulations, a weeding out of the bucket shops, better products, greater security, and a great deal more education will all help the market to mature.

And my suggestion? It is very simple. If you are looking for a secure, straightforward binary broker with a solid track record, well regulated and with excellent products and a free demo account, then look no further than Binary.com.

And just to reiterate - I have no financial association with the company. All I am trying to do here is to highlight what I believe are the best of breed alternatives currently available as far as brokers are concerned.

To put this all into context, the market currently looks something like the schematic in Fig 3.10.

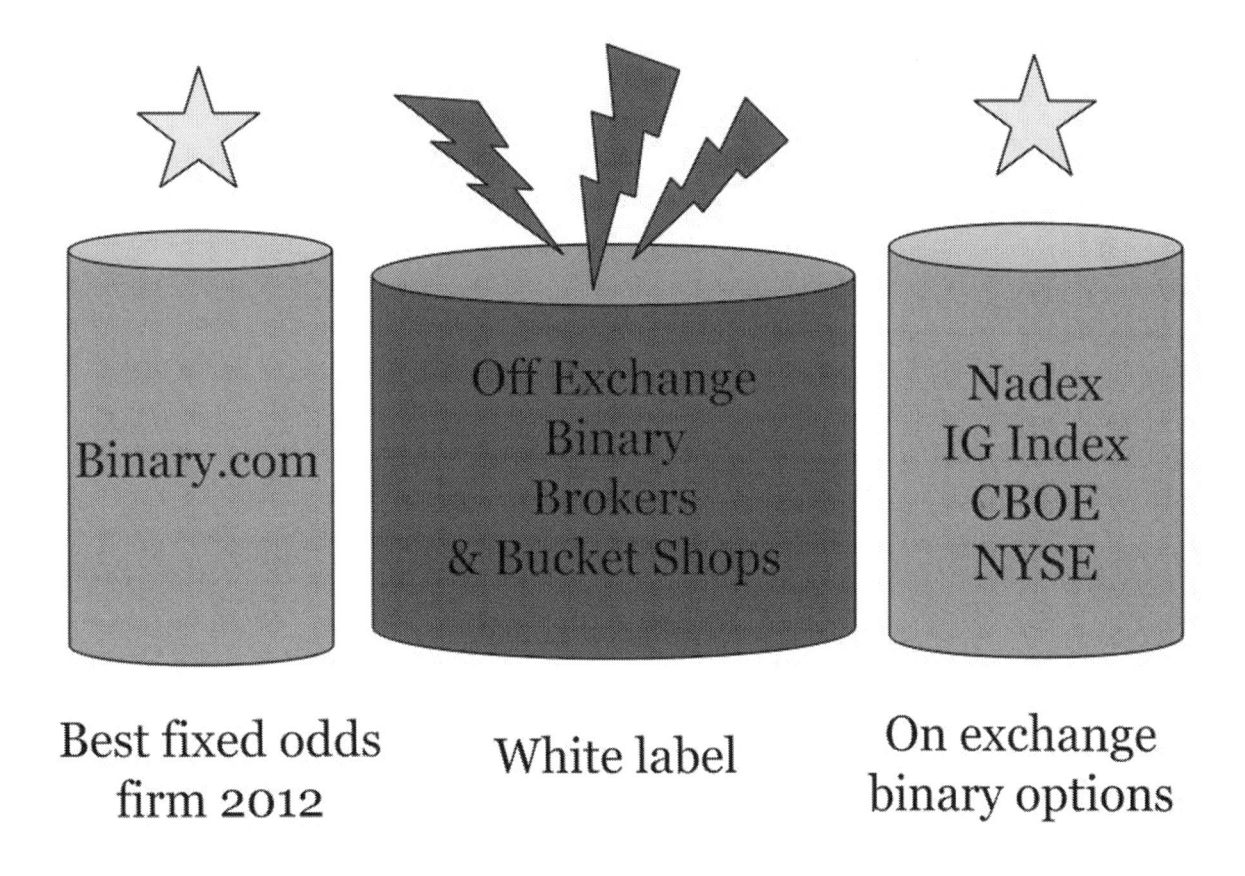

Fig 3.10 - The present binary ecosystem

This leads me neatly into the next chapter where we are going to move away from the off exchange brokers, and consider the on exchange brokers.

But just to round off this chapter, and to close with a warning note. In the last few months, a high profile off exchange binary broker closed and filed for bankruptcy. The broker in this case was a relatively large company with over 70 employees. What was perhaps more disturbing, was the broker had only recently been authorized by CySec.

As with all markets, authorization is no guarantee of financial stability and in such a crowded market we are likely to see more such failures. The warning signals were there with the forums full of messages from clients unable to withdraw funds from their accounts. In other markets this would be a red flag warning signal, but in the binary options world this is often routine.

Never has there been greater reason to conduct your due diligence, but sadly in the binary options market, even this may not be enough.

Chapter Four

On Exchange Binary Brokers

If past history was all there was to the game, the richest people would be librarians

Warren Buffet (1930 -)

If the previous chapter made rather depressing reading I hope this chapter will redress the balance a little. As you will discover in this, and subsequent chapters, an on exchange binary option is an entirely different instrument to those we have discussed thus far. This class of binary option moves towards vanilla options, and offers both the novice and more experienced trader, a variety of trading strategies with variable risk and increased flexibility.

Furthermore, an on exchange broker offers traders all the benefits of those available in the futures world.

Whilst binary options are relatively limited at present, and on exchange even more so, over the next few years this is likely to change, and I hope change very quickly. It needs to, if the instrument is not to be tainted by the bucket shops. As I mentioned in the previous chapter, one big broker has already gone to the wall, and others will follow. It is a crowded market, and despite the growth projections, there will be other casualties.

Before we move away from the world of fixed odds, let me just highlight the common thread that ties these two worlds together, which is this. Both approaches are premised on the fact that your risk is known and capped, but equally your profit is also limited. This is back to the horse racing analogy. You place a bet - your limited risk, and hope your horse wins the race for a limited profit. Your loss and potential winnings are both known in advance. You cannot lose more than you have staked on the race, and you cannot win more than the odds dictate.

And at this point you may be wondering how can one instrument be so different from another, if the risk and reward profiles are the same? A good question, and one I hope will be answered for you as we begin to explore on exchange binary options in more detail.

On Exchange Explained

First let me explain what I mean by on exchange, and why I believe it is so different. And by on exchange, I am simply referring to binary options which are bought and sold through a regulated exchange. If you have ever bought or sold a stock or a share, your order will have been transacted through a central exchange. In this case a stock exchange such as the New York Stock Exchange or the London Stock Exchange. Stocks are bought and sold with the process managed by the exchange. The same is true in the futures market. Here we have major exchanges such as the CME and the CBOE, which provide the meeting place where buyers and sellers can trade futures and options in a fair and transparent market, with the exchange matching buyers and sellers. This process is completely transparent and provides a level playing field to all participants, large or small. The exchange does not take positions, but merely matches the two parties.

The early days of commodity trading can be likened to the binary options world we have today. Before the establishment of a central exchange, buyers and sellers would meet, but with no central body to arbitrate, manage or standardize contracts, problems often arose in contract delivery. The creation of the CME, and other exchanges were fundamental in the establishment of a regulated and orderly market, and I believe the same applies to the binary options world today. The futures exchange is a true zero sum game. If one trader wins then another loses. Traders buy and sell with complete confidence in the full knowledge the playing field is level, the exchange is regulated and secure, and the process from start to finish is transparent. In my opinion this is the ideal.

In the remainder of this chapter I am going to focus on one company in particular. That company is Nadex, who I believe are the industry leader in offering on exchange binary options and whom I also consider to be best of breed at the time of writing this book. They have kindly allowed me to reproduce many images from their trading platform which I hope will help to explain why I believe an on exchange approach to trading binary options is one which provides many benefits and few drawbacks. As the market matures, I am sure others will also follow this model.

However, at this point let me make one thing clear. I am not affiliated to Nadex in any way and have no commercial relationship with them whatsoever. The reasons I have focused on them are as follows:

- They offer products which blend the best of off exchange instruments into a binary option which also draws in some of the characteristics from the vanilla world
- They operate as an exchange, so gone are all the issues of price manipulation, lack of price transparency, security of funds and information, access to funds, and clever marketing

Moreover, I believe Nadex offers a range of instruments, unmatched in the market at present. They are, what I consider to be best of breed. There are other companies who are looking to develop a similar model, and I will highlight these later. As you will also discover in this chapter, the CBOE (Chicago Board Options Exchange) also offer two binary options which again I will explain.

There is one issue with regard to Nadex and it is this - at present the company is only able to accept US clients. However, I believe this will change shortly, and indeed may have already done so by the time you read this book. In the last few months, Nadex has launched a product called Nadexconnect which allows other FCM (Futures Commission Merchants) brokers to offer the Nadex products to their own clients. So, some interesting developments on the horizon, but as you will see from the following short history these products are already available through their parent company IG in the UK, so they are slowly becoming accessible to a much wider audience.

Before moving to examine the trading instruments available, let me just give you a brief history of Nadex.

It is by a strange twist and irony that the foundations of Nadex lie in another pioneering company which attempted to change the face of the futures market. That company was Hedgestreet, and was created with one objective - to bring the world of futures trading to a wider retail audience. Trading futures requires significant margin, but the founders of Hedgestreet wanted to create smaller futures contracts, thereby offering retail traders the opportunity to trade the futures market with lower risk and smaller margins.

This approach has since been adopted by the CME and others who offer micro sized contracts on the most popular markets such as gold, oil and currencies. Hedgestreet was bought by IG Index (now IG) in 2007 who changed the name to Nadex in 2009. IG itself is a UK plc company publicly quoted on the London Stock Exchange and listed on the FTSE 250. Its own beginnings were in spread betting.

In 2013, IG also purchased all the back office software and systems from PFGBest which had collapsed in 2012, and these too have been incorporated into the Nadexconnect platform which is now being rolled out to the FCM brokers.

Whilst trading direct with Nadex is currently only available to US clients, Nadex binary options are available through their parent company IG in London, and I believe IG will take clients from many parts of the world, thereby opening up these instruments to a wider audience. You can find details on both Nadex and IG through the following links:

www.nadex.com

www.ig.com/uk/binaries-trading

The Nadex Binary Option

Let me start by outlining what I believe constitutes an on exchange binary option, which will then lay the framework for the remainder of the book. There are four basic characteristics I consider to be essential and these are as follows:

- A binary option is quoted between 0 and 100
- A binary option can be closed at any time
- The quote has multiple strike prices
- Returns, as a percentage are not capped

If we start with the quotation first, a binary option will have two numbers quoted between 0 and 100. Just like the fixed odds proposition, the binary option can only have two possible outcomes. The event either happens or it does not. If it happens the binary option will close at 100, but if it does not the binary option will close at 0. There are only ever two possible outcomes, and much like the fixed odds trade, you either win or lose.

Furthermore, like the fixed odds trade, your maximum loss on any position is known in advance, as is your maximum profit. But notice I have not used the word fixed, and this is one of the key differences between a binary option and a fixed odds trade. This difference stems from the fact you can close out any binary option position early either to reduce the maximum loss or to take some profit off the table. This is a key feature of a binary option, namely the ability to close out the position at any time during the life of the contract, and is one we are going to explore in a great deal more detail.

What is perhaps less obvious, is this in effect means you are in control of your percentage returns and these are no longer dictated to you by the broker. You set your own odds if you like and trade accordingly. In some ways, you can think of this as you being your own bookmaker. You decide on the odds, and then enter a position accordingly based on your own analysis of the market. This is a radically different proposition to the fixed odds trade. In addition, and perhaps more powerfully, you decide when to close the position. You do not have to wait for the end of the race, or in the option world what is called expiry. If you have decided on a target, which is subsequently achieved before expiry of the binary options contract, you simply close out and take your profit. You could of course decide to stay in for a further gain, or close out to minimize any loss.

Whatever your decision the key point is this. It is you who are in control at all times. You set the odds, you decide on your risk and reward profile, you decide when to close, and it is you who manages and controls your percentage returns. You can even decide what price you want to enter and exit the market. On exchange binary options have been designed for you, not for the broker. The on exchange binary options broker is simply there to provide the instruments and trading environment to give you this control. This is what Nadex offer.

I am going to explain all of these fundamental principles in greater detail. You will then start to appreciate why the fixed odds product is a good starting point, and a stepping stone into binary options themselves. I will also cover the maths later in the book as we consider break-even ratios and profit margins as these apply to you either as a fixed odds trader or a binary options trader.

If we start with the binary option quote itself, the easiest way to think of this is in terms of probability, and perhaps take the simplest example of the probability of an event happening or not such as the toss of a coin. There is a 50% probability of a head or a tail, and this would be quoted as 50/50 from which we would know immediately the probability of either event occurring was equal. And so it is when we look at the binary option quote.

Indeed when considering binary options and their notation, we can instantly think of price reflecting probability. In other words, it is the market's expectation of an event happening or not happening. As you will discover shortly, time has a huge impact on this simple statement. Therefore, let's start with a simple example, before gradually bringing in the other elements to build the complete picture.

Suppose we see a binary option being quoted as 22/26 for an event occurring or not occurring. What is this binary quote telling us? If we take the mid point of these two figures at 24, this binary option is saying the probability of this event occurring is low. Why? Because the probability being quoted is 24% of the event happening. The converse, is there is a 76% probability the event will not happen, since the sum of two mutually exclusive events must always equal 100. In this case it's 100 - 76 = 24. This is the basis of the binary option quotation. What you are seeing in a binary quote is the market's expectation of the event happening or not happening, at a particular moment in time. Moreover, since these two events cannot happen together, the sum of the two probabilities will always be 100.

Consider another example. In this case we see a binary option quoted at 92/96 for an event happening. Again taking the mid point of these two figures gives us 94%. A very high probability the event is likely to occur, and a low probability of 6% (100% - 94% = 6%) that it will not occur.

At a very simple level binary options show you instantly and quickly the market's view of an event happening or not, based on the current price action and the time left to expiry. As I've mentioned expiry and time on several occasions already, let's focus on these concepts now, and this is where perhaps it becomes a little more complex.

But perhaps before we move on, let me also explain a further facet of the binary options market which is this. The binary options quoted on a particular market and event are constantly changing. The probabilities are moving like shifting sands as various factors and forces come into play. Whenever you look at a binary option quote it will be moving, floating if you like, and constantly changing to reflect all the various elements which constitute the probability being quoted. This is what makes them so powerful. You choose when, at what probability level, and with which risk/reward profile of return you wish to enter the market - nobody else makes these decisions for you. You are in complete and total control.

Expiry & Time

Expiry and time are two of the fundamental concepts you have to understand as an options trader, whether in the world of binary or vanilla options. These concepts are very familiar to options and futures traders, but less so to those who have never traded these instruments. We did touch on these concepts in an earlier chapter, but it is at this point I want to consider them in much greater depth, so you can understand the nature of the instrument you are trading. Whilst binary options appear superficially simple, beneath that simplicity lies a web of sophistication and complexity, and it is these aspects we are going to cover now.

If you have already dabbled in the options market, you will know that many traders like to buy options which are cheap. But there is a reason they are cheap. It is because they have little or no chance of ever making money for the holder of the option. They are cheap for one reason, and one reason only. The probability of the underlying market moving in their favor is extremely low.

The difference in the binary options market is you will see these probabilities quoted, so there is no maths involved. Through the quote notation the market is giving you its verdict on whether the option has a high, medium or low probability of making money. But herein lies the danger. Far too many binary options traders take the same approach as in the vanilla options market, simply viewing a low probability option as a low cost/low risk proposition which has the potential to deliver a very high return.

Whilst probabilities can and do swing wildly from one extreme to the other (as you will see shortly), you have to understand the reasons why. On occasion this might be the right strategy to adopt, but it is one that has to be adopted for the right reasons. Understanding the effects of expiry and time will help you make logical decisions based on your analysis of the underlying chart, which is **always** the starting point.

In trading any option, whether binary or otherwise, you are essentially trying to forecast whether something will happen or not in a given period of time. In other instruments and markets this is not the case. As a spot forex trader you may have taken a long position in the GBP/USD, but you can keep that position open for as long as you wish, or until your stop loss takes you out. As a trader you would be managing that position, locking in profits and making discretionary decisions on staying in or closing out.

A binary option is very different. It has a physical expiry date and time. If the event has happened at expiry the binary option closes at 100. If it has not happened then it closes at 0. As you will see on the Nadex platform these expiry dates and times can be intra hour, hours, days or weeks, and this is one of the many advantages of trading options. If you are time limited in your life because of work or family commitments, you can trade the longer term options easily without needing to be in front of your screen all day, and of course any risk is both limited and known.

Let's examine the typical behavior of a binary option as it moves from inception to expiry, using the schematic shown in Fig 4.10. This could be in any market, as it is the concept I am trying to convey here.

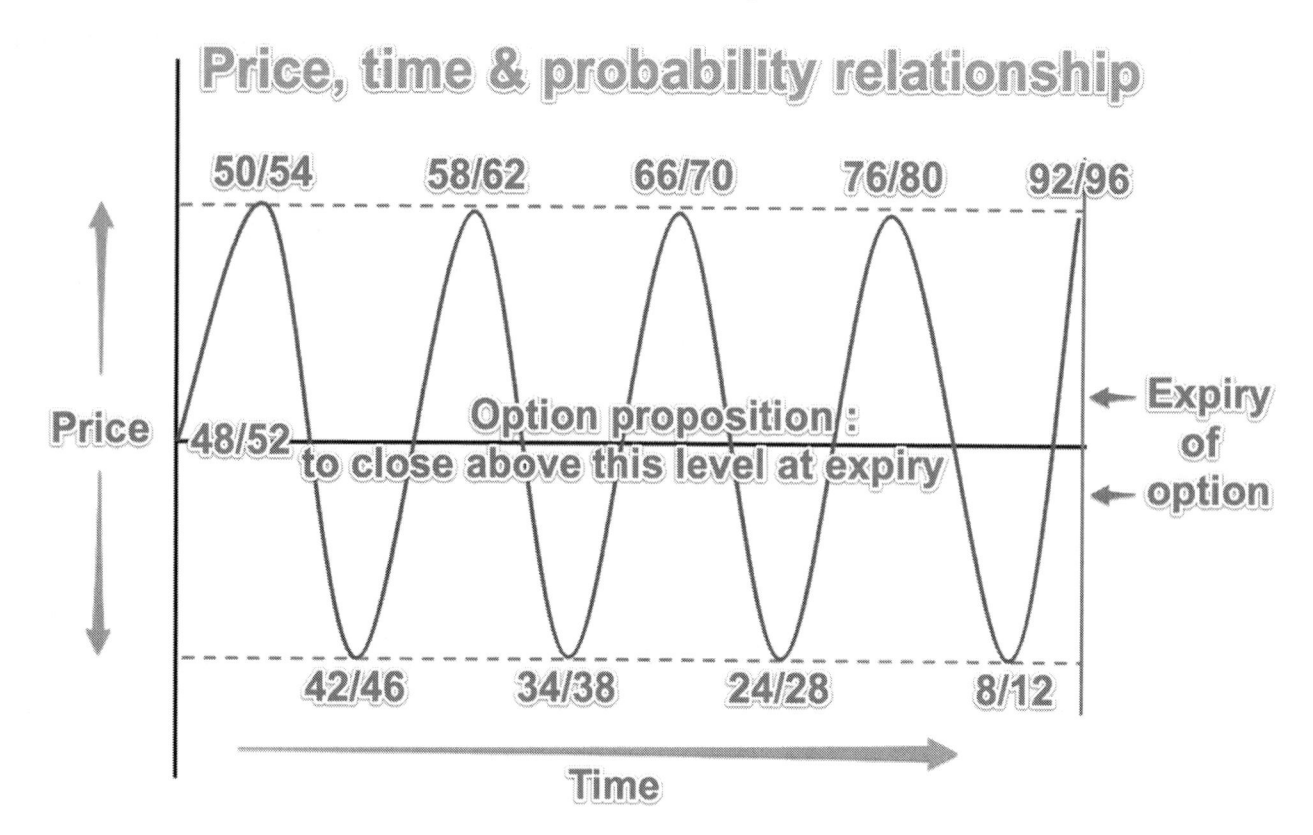

Fig 4.10 - The price, time and probability relationship

In Fig 4.10 I have created what I hope is a simple schematic to explain some of the key concepts you will need to be aware of when considering a binary option. The schematic is not perfect, but I hope conveys the essential elements in a simple and visual way.

The first point, which is perhaps self evident, is that every binary option quotation is based on an underlying market. This may be either the spot market, the cash market or the futures market, and this is always your starting point as a binary options trader. It is very easy to forget this in the rush to open a position based purely on the probabilities being quoted. This is completely the wrong approach. Your starting point should **always** be your chart analyzed in multiple timeframes. This is then backed up by the fundamental and relational aspects of your analysis, all of which are explained in my other books.

The schematic in Fig 4.10 is designed to show you the 'life cycle' of a binary option. The X axis is time, and the Y axis is price. The actual timeframe under consideration is irrelevant here as the relationships we are about to discuss will apply regardless of whether this is an intraday, daily or weekly binary option. The same fundamental principles will apply. In this example, the binary option has opened on the left and moves towards expiry on the right. The centre line is the axis around which the binary option oscillates. It is the fulcrum, the balancing point at which the probability of the event occurring or not is always 50%. In this case we are considering an option in which the proposition is that it will close above this level at expiry.

The figures you see here are the probability quotations which appear on the trading platform. Like any other market there will be a bid and offer, and this is why there is a 'spread' on the probability. This is an area we are going to focus on in greater detail once we start to consider open positions, order tickets and order placement. But for now I want to introduce the notion of seeing two numbers quoted for the probability. For the purposes of this example, I have assumed a 4 point spread in discussing the movement of the quote, and taking the mid point as the probability. For example where we have 58/62 the probability here is 60%. Now let me walk you through the price action, and highlight all the key points.

The market here is in sideways congestion, which is not uncommon since markets spend more of their time in consolidation phases than in trends. Here the price action first rises above the centre line (the event proposition) and then falls below, only to recover and move above once again, followed by a further fall below. This price action continues until finally the binary option approaches expiry on the right, and closes above the option proposition.

Now let's consider what is happening to the associated probabilities through this phase of price action. If we start at the left, and as you would expect, as the price moves through the centre line, the probability is quoted as 48/52 or 50%. The price then moves higher, so the probability of the event occurring rises, which is what you would expect. The price is now above the centre line and therefore has a higher probability of closing above on expiry. The market's expectation the event will occur at expiry (the option proposition is *true*) is now 50/54 or 52%.

However, the market then reverses and moves below the centre with the probability now quoted as 42/46 or 44%. The market's expectation has now changed and the probability has fallen below 50%, since there is now a lower probability of the price closing above the centre line at expiry. In other words, the option proposition is *not* true at expiry.

The market reverses again and moves back above the centre line and up to a similar price level as before, at the dotted line. As we would expect the probability of the proposition now being true at expiry has moved above 50%, and is now quoted at 58/62 or 60%.

However, the question you might ask is this. Given the market has moved to a similar price level, why has the probability shifted from 52% on the first 'peak' to 60% on the second? Shouldn't the probability be more or less the same? And the answer is no, because this is where time comes into play.

If you recall back in chapter two we looked briefly at the relationship between time and probability, and here I've included the same chart to explore this aspect in more detail. And the key point is this. The reason the probability, *at the same price point*, has risen from 52% to 60% is the influence time is now having on the associated probabilities. And again this is self evident once we start to think about time in this context. As an options trader time can be both your biggest enemy and your greatest friend. But time is a wasting asset. In simple terms, the longer the time to expiry, the more time there is available for the event to occur or not, and for the option proposition to be true or false.

As time dwindles away, if the option proposition is well away from the centre line, the chances of the event being true or false will move ever faster, and this in turn will be reflected in the probabilities being quoted. In racing terms, if your chosen horse is running last, with a furlong left to run, then the probability of your horse winning will be very low. However, if your horse is running last, but with a mile to run, the probability will be much higher. In both scenarios your horse is in the same place, last. But the probabilities of the outcome being true (your horse winning) have very different probabilities. The only reason for the difference is time.

I cannot stress the importance of time too strongly. It is vital you understand the role it plays, and the power it has, both good and bad. As I explained in chapter two, traders who understand the power of time will always sell vanilla options wherever possible. Time is then working for them and against the buyer, constantly draining away as expiry approaches, and this wasting effect is not linear. As expiry approaches, time dwindles away ever faster, and as you will see shortly, this is also reflected in the probabilities being quoted.

In the binary options market we do not sell an option in the same way as in the vanilla options market. In the binary world we purchase (buy) an option if we think the proposition will be true, and we purchase (sell) an option if we think the proposition will be false at expiry. This is very different as the 'sell' notation here is simply saying we believe the proposition will be false. And the question you might be asking is this. Is there a way in the binary options world to have time working for us, rather than against us? And the answer is yes, and we are going to look at that shortly. But let's continue with the example from Fig 4.10.

The underlying market has moved lower once again from the 58/62 high back to a new low at 34/38, and we can see the same principle at work. The probability of the event occurring has moved from 42/46 (44%) to 34/38 (36%) at the same price level. This pattern is repeated back and forth, and each time the price action revisits a similar price level above or below the centre line the probabilities change, and in the final stages of the price action the final low is 8/12 or 10% and the final high is 92/96 or 94%.

Time Erosion & Probability

This is a schematic representation of the image from chapter two which is repeated here as Fig 4.11.

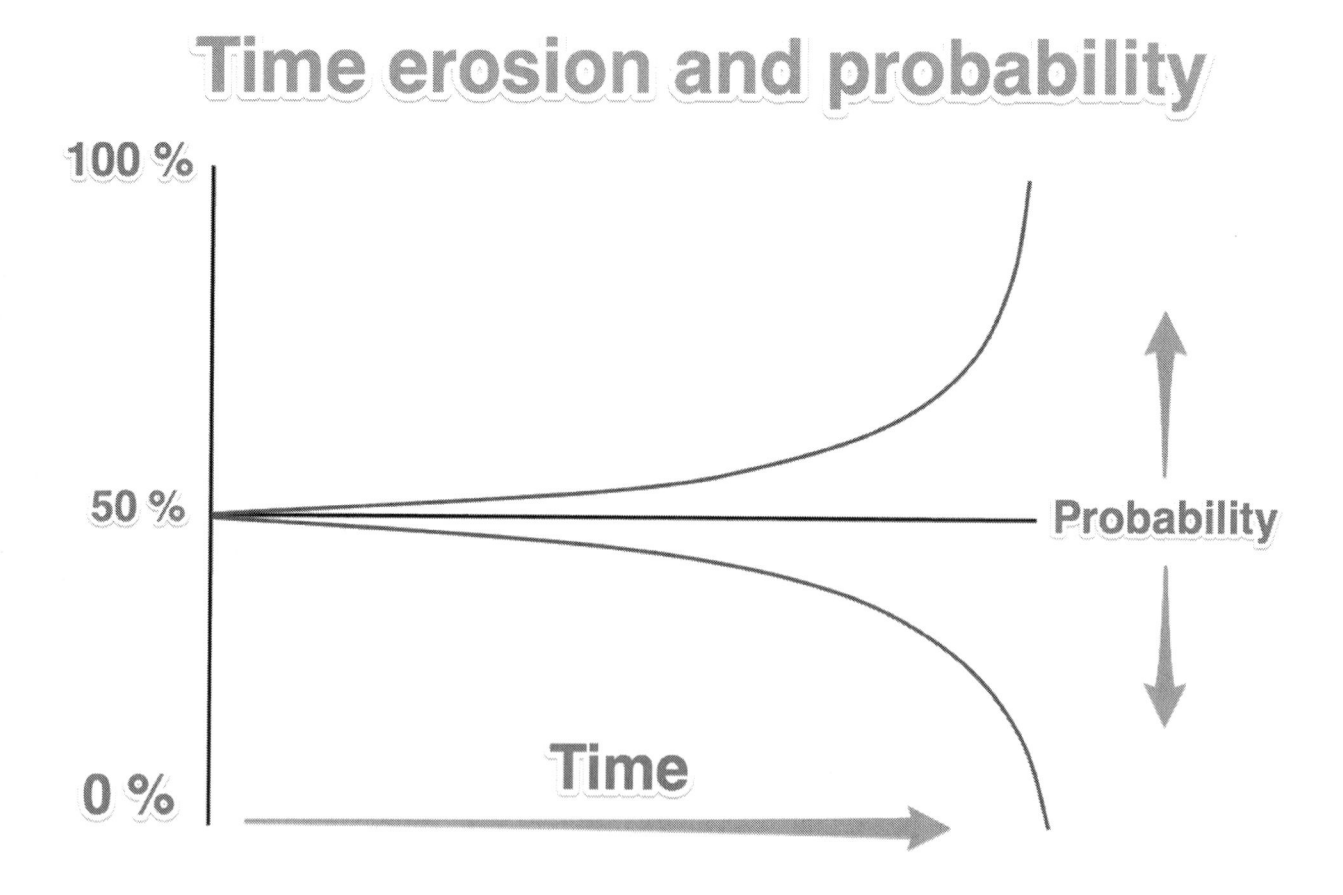

Fig 4.11 - Time erosion and probability

There are three simultaneous effects at work here.

First, time erosion increases exponentially. It is not linear as the effects increase dramatically the closer we are to expiry.

Second, as we move along the time axis, and towards expiry the probability of the event not being true tends to 0, and the probability of the event being true tends towards 100. We saw both of these effects in Fig 4.10. Each time the price revisited a similar price level the probability above the centre line was rising, and the probability below the centre line was falling. The exponential aspect was also reflected in this schematic and the associated probabilities as follows:

Option proposition: True

- Early in life 50/54 - 58/62 or 52% to 60%
- Late in life 76/80 - 92/96 or 78% to 94%

Option proposition: False

- Early in life 42/46 - 34/38 or 44% to 36%
- Late in life 24/28 - 8/12 or 26% to 10%

Early in the life of the option a similar move saw the probabilities change from a difference of (60% - 52%) 8% initially, then moving on subsequent price action to (94% - 78%) 16% for a true outcome at expiry.

For a false outcome again these have changed dramatically from (44%-36%) 8% to (26% - 10%) 16%. The change in probabilities is reflecting the increasing speed of time erosion on the probability of the event happening or not happening. In other words whether the outcome is ultimately true or false at expiry.

The third and final effect at work here is that of volatility, which we are going to consider in great detail and its relationship to the underlying price action. But the point I want to highlight here in relation to expiry and time is as follows.

Remember the nature of the instrument we are trading here. There can only ever be one outcome. The proposition is either true or false. It cannot be both. The binary will close at expiry at either 0 if false or 100 if true. This in turn means unlike other instruments, a tiny price move close to expiry can induce extremely volatility and fast moving changes in probabilities. Suppose the option is based on the price of an index to be above a certain level by 3 pm. It is 2.59 pm and the price is one point below, but then moves one point above and then back below. Within that simple price action, which would normally pass unnoticed, there will be massive spikes in the probabilities moving from very low through 50% up to very high, and then back again. All in the space of a few seconds. This is the power of time at its most devastating as the contract moves close to expiry. A tiny price move can have a huge effect on the probability since the option has to close at either 0 or 100.

And one of the key trading decisions you will have to make with every binary option is whether to hold until expiry. Of course, with an on exchange binary option this decision is made much easier for you, as you always have a choice when to exit the market. There is no requirement to hold until expiry. It is your decision. But remember if you do, and the option is very close to the proposition price, then you will see some wild swings in the probabilities on very small price moves.

There is a further aspect of volatility and it is where volatility is created from the underlying price action. Here it is much better news and is where on exchange binary options really come into their own, once we start to consider some simple binary option trading strategies.

In The Money - Out Of The Money

A concept which is very familiar to vanilla options traders, but perhaps less so to binary option traders is the notion of an option being in the money, at the money or out of the money. What does this mean? Once again let's start with a simple schematic as shown in Fig 4.12 where price is shown on the Y axis and time on the X axis.

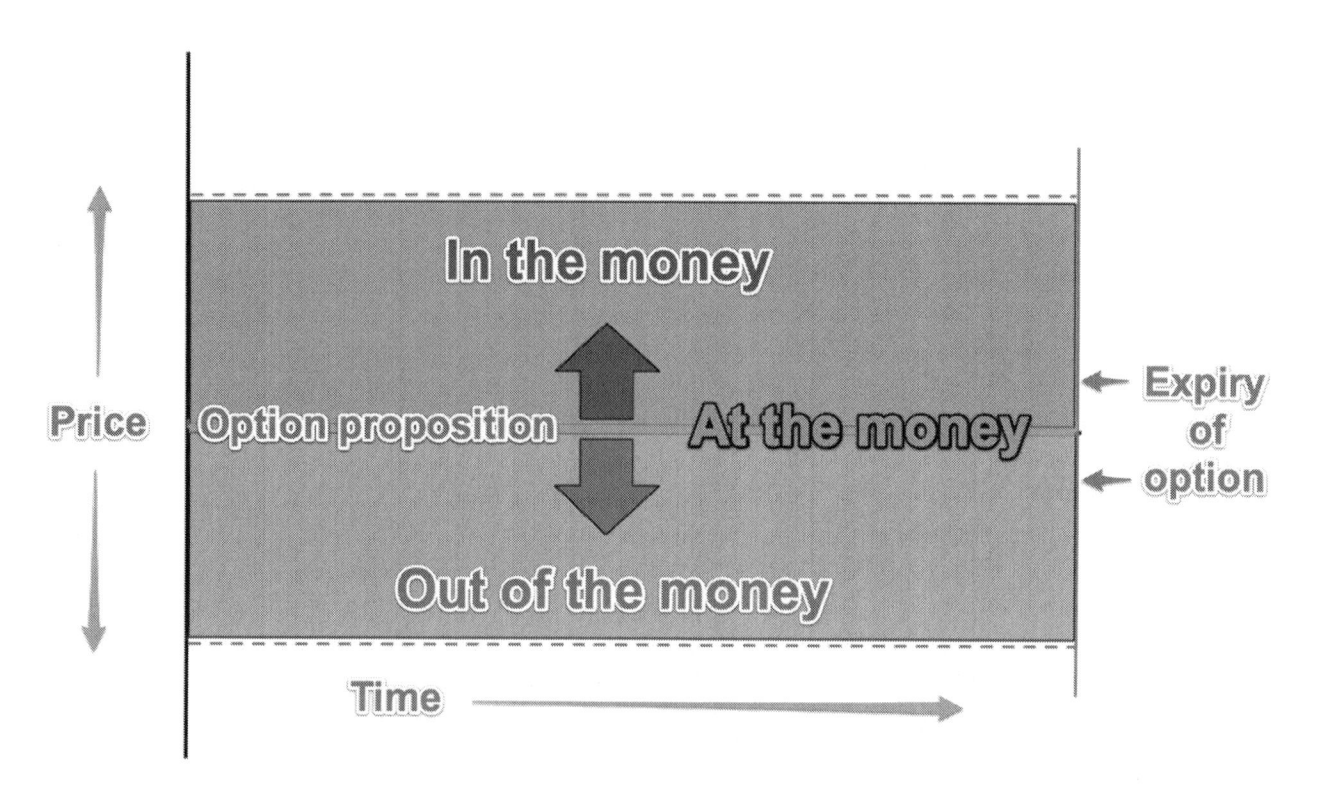

Fig 4.12 - Binary option ITM, ATM, OTM

There are only three 'states' an option can be in relation to the underlying instrument, and these are referred to as in the money (ITM), at the money (ATM), and out of the money (OTM). At any time in the life cycle of an option it is in one of these three conditions, and this applies to both binary and vanilla options although the interpretation in binary options is very different.

In the binary options world we are dealing with a single instrument, and only considering whether a proposition is true or false. In other words whether something is going to happen or not. In the vanilla options world we have a myriad of choice and associated strategies. For a binary option the state of an option will depend on whether we are agreeing with the proposition or are disagreeing. In the first case, an ITM option will be above the option proposition line, and in the second it will be below. In other words in Fig 4.12, we are considering an example where we are in agreement with the proposition of the binary option, and as the probability moves above the mid point, then it moves into the money (ITM) and below this line it is (OTM) out of the money. If we were considering this as not agreeing with the binary option proposition this would simply be reversed.

To recap in Fig 4.12 we are agreeing with the binary option proposition, and as such it is in the money as soon as the option moves above the option proposition. If the binary is based on the market being higher than a certain price level by expiry, then once the option has moved beyond this level it is considered to be in the money (ITM). It has some 'price value' by virtue of the option having a higher probability of closing with a 'true' result.

In this case if the option is below the option proposition it is considered to be out of the money or (OTM). A binary option which is at the 50% level is considered to be at the money or (ATM). Finally, one of the terms used a great deal when considering this aspect of options is to refer to them as 'deep in the money' - a high probability of being *true*, and conversely 'deep out of the money' - a high probability of *not being true.*

However, the question is this. Do probabilities and in the money or out of the money dynamics always go hand in hand? And the answer is no, most definitely not, and to find the reason why we have to go back and think about time.

If you recall from our example earlier with seconds to go to expiry, the probabilities were swinging wildly from deep in the money, to deep out of the money. In other words the probabilities would be swinging from 90% through to 50% and down to 5%, perhaps very fast. And the reason? Time and imminent expiry. In this case the high probability is not signaling a binary option that is deep in the money, but merely a high probability the option will expire as true at that second. This is very different from the concept we are discussing here.

In considering whether a binary option is ITM or OTM it is price we need to consider first. A binary option which has a high probability such as 90% and where the price is well above the option proposition can then be considered as deep in the money. In this case the option may be 50 or 60 points above the option proposition, and is therefore reflecting two things. First, a high probability the option will expire true, and second the option has price value as it is now in the money.

This is a key distinction. A binary with a high probability or a low probability **does not automatically mean** it is deep in the money, or deep out of the money. We need to check the price level as well. If the price is well above or below the option price proposition, then we can deduce the option has strong 'price value' or weak 'price value' which then confirms the probabilities being quoted on the binary.

I cannot stress this point too strongly. It is too easy to view the probability on a binary option as the only criteria for gauging whether the event will close at 100 or 0. It is not, and must always be viewed in the context of the underlying price. Consider the two examples here:

- 95% probability on an index with 2 minutes to expiry with a proposition target price of 2100 and with the index trading at 2101
- 95% probability on an index with 2 minutes to expiry with a proposition target price of 2100 and with the index trading at 2120

The probability being quoted is the same, yet the first has virtually no price value, since the high probability is as a result of the time and expiry relationship. The probability in the second is a deep in the money option with high price value. The only difference between the two is the underlying price and its relationship to the proposition target price.

In summary, never assume the probability reveals the complete picture for a binary option. It may not for the reasons explained above.

This is a concept you need to be aware of as a binary options trader, and why trading binaries is far more complex than simply deciding whether a market is likely to rise or fall. The 'value' of the option as dictated by the time to expiry and the price will be an important one along with several other factors.

A further notion which moves on from the above, is the relationship between probability, time and price and is one many option traders struggle to grasp. And perhaps the easiest way to explain this relationship is with two simple examples.

In our first example, suppose we have agreed with the binary option proposition which is deep in the money and is now at 85%. There is still some time to expiry, and the price of the underlying asset is well above the option proposition expiry price. The question is this. Does the market have to move for the binary option to close at 100%? The answer is no, **it does not**. All we have to do is wait, and time will do the rest for us.

If the market didn't move at all, we already know time is a wasting asset, and as we approach expiry works exponentially. This is what I was referring to earlier when I explained the power of time. Time erosion can work both for us as option traders, and against us. In this example we are using its power to 'run down the clock' on the option to expiry.

In our second example, suppose we have agreed with the binary option proposition once again, but is deep out of the money, and is now at 5%. We entered this trade because it was cheap and potentially offered a great return. The question is this. Does the underlying market have to move for us to make money? The answer here is yes, it does. And perhaps even more importantly it has to move a long way. The option is deep out of the money with the underlying price a long way below the binary proposition price, and here we have two factors working against us. Time is eroding fast, and in addition the probabilities will be tending to 0% as we saw in Fig 4.11. Unless there is a major news announcement before expiry or some other catalyst, the probability is the option will close at 0%. And here the point is this:

A binary option that is deep in the money **does not** require the underlying price to move. A binary option that is deep out of the money **does** require the underlying price to move, and significantly as well.

I do not want you to run away with the idea I am suggesting you only trade binary options which are deep in the money with price value. I am not - far from it. What I am suggesting is when we move to considering the various approaches and strategies, understanding the pivotal relationship of probability time and price is vital in your decision making process. It is a balance, and the starting point for any analysis is always the chart. It may well be from your analysis you believe that a big move is likely, but as always in the options world it is timing the decision which is paramount.

Before moving on, let me clarify one further point. If you have disagreed with a proposition which is then tending towards 0, this is also considered to be an option which is deep in the money, assuming it also has price value.

Strike Prices & Option Chains

I am very conscious that in the descriptions and explanations thus far I have referred to the 'binary option proposition' and the 'option proposition' as I wanted to introduce the various terms and terminology in logical steps, and so avoid overwhelming you as the reader. However, I feel it is now time to introduce two further option terms, namely the strike price and associated option chains. If you feel at this point we are moving further and further away from fixed odds trading, you would be correct.

Let's start with the strike price, which is very simple. The strike price is the price which must be exceeded for the binary to close at 100 or not achieved for the binary to close at 0. This is the point at which the probability tips over the 50% line. As with vanilla options, so binary option providers offer a range of strike prices, which in turn gives you the opportunity to select your own risk and reward profiles, as well as a choice of those options which are already in the money, at the money or out of the money.

This is often referred to as an options ladder or an options chain, but you can think of it rather like a menu in a restaurant. Some items on the menu are more expensive, others are cheaper. It is for you, as the customer, to decide what you would like and the same applies here with the options ladder. If you think of it as a ladder this may be easier, with the 'rungs' on the ladder usually set out in equal increments. For example on a EUR/USD binary option, the increments might be in 20 pips. On an index such as the YM, the increments might be 25 points, and each rung of the ladder will have its own strike price with the current binary option quote alongside. In Fig 4.13 I have created a simple schematic which I hope explains these basic principles.

Binary option ladder

Market & underlying contract	Strike price	Date & time of expiry	Bid	Offer
S&P 500 Dec	> 1855.0	20/12/2013 @ & 4.15 pm ET	8.00	11.00
S&P 500 Dec	> 1852.0	20/12/2013 @ & 4.15 pm ET	12.50	15.50
S&P 500 Dec	> 1849.0	20/12/2013 @ & 4.15 pm ET	17.50	21.00
S&P 500 Dec	> 1846.0	20/12/2013 @ & 4.15 pm ET	26.00	29.00
S&P 500 Dec	> 1843.0	20/12/2013 @ & 4.15 pm ET	43.50	46.50
S&P 500 Dec	> 1840.0	20/12/2013 @ & 4.15 pm ET	51.00	54.00
S&P 500 Dec	> 1837.0	20/12/2013 @ & 4.15 pm ET	59.00	63.50
S&P 500 Dec	> 1834.0	20/12/2013 @ & 4.15 pm ET	71.50	74.50
S&P 500 Dec	> 1831.0	20/12/2013 @ & 4.15 pm ET	79.50	82.50
S&P 500 Dec	> 1828.0	20/12/2013 @ & 4.15 pm ET	84.00	87.50

Fig 4.13 - A typical binary options ladder

In this example there are several key points to note, and perhaps the first is whilst this is a 'static' schematic, if you were looking at this in real time the probabilities on the right hand side would be changing constantly, reflecting the constant changes in the underlying contract. And, if this looks a little complicated it is in fact very straightforward, and more so than its equivalent in the vanilla options world. In vanilla options we have calls and puts which can be both bought and sold, in effect two ladders side by side. In the binary options world we only have one ladder, but many of the techniques and strategies you will learn here can also be applied to vanilla options. I hope in discovering binary options, you will then be keen to learn more about vanilla options. I will be publishing a book about trading vanilla options in the near future, as I have always found options a fascinating subject and instruments which can offer traders a huge amount of flexibility in their trading. However, I digress. Back to our binary options ladder, and please remember this is only a hypothetical schematic and the ladder may differ depending on the platform you are using. We will take a look at the Nadex platform shortly, but the essential elements will be the same.

Starting on the left we have the market being offered, which in this case is the S&P 500 index, and also specified is the underlying contract. This is important. If you remember when we looked at off exchange bucket shops, one of the many issues was that of price transparency. As a trader you have little or no idea of where or how the broker is delivering the price, and more importantly how much these prices are likely to be manipulated at expiry. In trading with an on exchange broker these issues do not arise. Here you know precisely what price is being quoted, and the instrument. In this example it is the underlying futures contract for December. I will also explain how the price is calculated at expiry from the underlying, once we start to dig a little deeper into the Nadex platform and consider the entire process from start to finish.

Next comes the strike price. This is the price which defines the yes/no outcome of the binary option. The symbol > is simply a mathematical symbol meaning 'greater than'. It is short hand for writing the binary option proposition. Here you can see we have a range of strike prices in the ladder, which are stepping up in 3 point intervals from 1828 at the bottom to 1855 at the top. These intervals are set by the exchange, and will generally be equal increments, reflecting the market and instrument being traded. By contrast, it would be unrealistic to have a spot forex ladder moving higher in 3 pip increments as this would make the ladder unwieldily.

The increments reflect the average range for each instrument in the timeframe being quoted, and are set accordingly, to provide a balance of deep out of the money, deep in the money, and at the money options. Perhaps you can begin to see how elegant options can be as a trading instrument. No longer are we considering the simple prospect of a market rising or falling. Here we have a range of contracts which we can trade according to our risk appetite, and even more important, gives us the ability to construct various trading strategies.

The strike price is the defining price for our option. If the strike price quoted for that option is > 1840.0 (to close greater than 1840.0), then the index must close *above* this price at expiry for the option to settle at 100. If it is at or below this price the option will settle at 0. The strike price is the fulcrum of the option, and is the point at which the probability is 50. If you are agreeing with the proposition, above the strike price the option is moving into the money, and below the strike price the option is moving out of the money. Conversely, if you are disagreeing with the proposition, then below the strike price your option is moving into the money and above the strike price is moving out of the money.

Next comes the date and time of the expiry. This specifies the precise time and date at which the option expires and settles either at 100 or 0.

Finally on the right hand side we have the bid and the offer, the spread of the probability if you like. And as we have done before, by simply taking the mid point this will give us an overview of where the underlying market is trading. By looking at the bid/offer column on the right we can see immediately the index is probably trading around the 1840 price level, since this is around the 52.50 mid-point probability.

In the context of this example, the following explanation is based on an assumption we are viewing the ladder on the premise of a proposition being true. What the ladder is telling us is that at the extremes we have a deep in the money option at the 1828 strike price, and a deep out of the money option at the 1855 strike price. And remember, options are cheap or expensive for a reason. The option with a strike price of >1828 has a very high probability of closing at 100 as it is very unlikely the underlying index would move 12 points in the remaining time available. There is always a chance of course. The market could react suddenly to an unexpected event.

Anything is possible. This is why a binary option is quoted in probabilities. But on balance this option is deep in the money with the index trading well above the strike price of 1828, and with a current probability of 85.75. However, with time eroding fast this option will increasingly tend to 100, *even if the price does nothing* and simply remains where it is at present.

At the other end of the binary ladder, we have a deep out of the money option with a strike price of >1855. With the index trading around the 1840 price level the underlying futures contract would have to move a considerable way, 15 points or more and quickly, for this option to have any chance of closing above this price. This is why the probability is being quoted at 9.5. First, it is very unlikely the market will move this far in such a short space of time. Second, time erosion is working against the binary. Third the binary is already tending to zero as these factors increase their effect as expiry approaches.

These are the two extremes on the binary option ladder, but as you can see there are other propositions to choose from, all with varying degrees of risk attached, as defined by the probability being quoted in the bid and the offer. These will be changing constantly as the underlying market moves accordingly.

Throughout the above example we have considered the ITM and OTM notation through the prism of agreement with the proposition. If we viewed the ladder through the prism of disagreement with the proposition, the statements above would be reversed. Here for example we could disagree with the proposition the strike price of >1855 will be achieved, in which case this would then be considered an in the money option viewed from that standpoint, not greatly in the money, but in the money nevertheless, since the probability of the event happening is very low.

Before we round off on the ladder, it is also important to realize your binary options broker will offer a huge array of option ladders for each instrument with a variety of expiry dates and times. Some will be hourly, or even shorter, whilst others will be longer intra day, end of day, weekly and even monthly. Ultimately the choice of which options you choose will be dictated by your strategy, time available and the sophistication you wish to apply to your own trading. At their most basic level, binary options are a simple and low risk way to trade market direction. And with an on exchange broker such as Nadex, you will be trading in a safe, secure and transparent environment. But in my humble opinion binary options can offer so much more.

Before moving on to look at the bid and offer in more detail, along with how we trade these options, their associated risk and reward ratios and how they are priced, let me introduce one further notion. When considering an options ladder we are also viewing the market's opinion of the probability of strike prices being achieved higher or lower in the chain. This may sound obvious, but it can be useful when considering risk and return, as well as setting take profit targets of which more later.

Here is an example using the ladder from Fig 4.13, and taking the mid point probabilities, as we are going to cover the bid and offer relationship in the next section. If we take the six strike prices from >1843 and below and their associated mid point probabilities, these are as follows:

- > 1843 - 45.00
- > 1840 - 52.50
- > 1837 - 61.25
- > 1834 - 73.00
- > 1831 - 81.00
- > 1828 - 85.75

Assume we want some idea of how the probabilities on our options are likely to change if the underlying market were to move higher by 3 index points. In other words move to the next strike price level. Let's assume the underlying future is trading around the 1840 strike price level, and we want to have some idea of what would happen if the index moved to 1843 in a relatively short period. As always time will have a major influence on the probabilities being quoted. What we are considering now is a 'what if' scenario of the market possibly moving higher to 1843 in the short term. In simple terms the ladder 'steps up' one level as follows:

- > 1843 - moves from 45.00 to 52.50 = 07.50
- > 1840 - moves from 52.50 to 61.25 = 08.75
- > 1837 - moves from 61.25 to 73.00 = 11.75
- > 1834 - moves from 73.00 to 81.00 = 08.00
- > 1831 - moves from 81.00 to 85.75 = 04.75

What we are considering now is the comparative shift in probabilities if the index moves a full strike price in the short term. It is the market's view of the future probability at this price level - *in the short term*. We can use this information in one of two ways. First it gives us a perspective on which options *may* offer the best returns, *should* the market move this far. In this example we can see the most significant shift in probabilities is on the 1837 strike option, with the least significant move on the 1831 strike option. This is as we would expect.

A short term move from an at the money option, to an in the money option, will have a greater effect than the equivalent price move on an option which is already deep in the money (viewed as the proposition being true). In looking at the options ladder in this way, and when we begin to look at risk and return, this will help to guide us in our decision making. However, a word of warning. Time is eroding and this is only ever a guide. Any decisions you make regarding where a market is likely to move to in terms of price must always be based on sound analysis of the chart using a primary methodology such as volume price analysis. If your analysis of the chart, and associated markets, is suggesting a possible strong move higher (or lower), then this is an excellent way to judge what *may* happen to the associated binary option probabilities as a result.

The second little nugget of information that is revealed by the binary ladder, is it provides a sense of what is likely or unlikely. What do I mean? First of all consider the steps in which the strike prices move. In this example they are moving in 3 index points which suggests this is perhaps the average move to expect under normal circumstances and in short periods of time. A currency contract for example, may have 20 pip increments, which again provides a perspective on the market's view of that contract.

This helps with defining take profit targets, as in binary options you can exit the market at any time. You do not have to wait until the option expires. We are going to look at this in more detail, but for now just remember this fact. The binary ladder gives us a wealth of information of which take profit targets, and the best options to trade from a return perspective, are just two. There are other factors to consider which will help to frame your decision making process. But I am going to repeat this again - we *always* start with the chart.

And now here are the mechanics of trading binary options and the associated risk and reward profiles.

Bid & Offer, Risk & Reward

As we already know, the binary option only has two outcomes. It is either true and closes at 100, or it is false and closes at 0. This is all dictated by the strike price. As a binary options trader we therefore have only one decision to make as follows, and on the Nadex platform:

- If we believe the strike price will be exceeded at expiry then we *buy*
- If we do not believe the strike price will be exceeded at expiry then we *sell*

However, just to reiterate the above buy and sell is as follows:

We buy (purchase) if we agree with the statement, and sell (purchase) if we disagree. The buttons on your trading platform may say many things. They may say, buy and sell, call and put, purchase and purchase, agree or disagree. However, in all these cases you are in effect buying - buying to say yes, and buying to say no. The Nadex platform uses buy and sell, but it is the above context of agreement or disagreement. *Buy to say yes, and sell to say no.*

Just as in the futures market where buyers and sellers are matched by the exchange, so the same occurs here. For every buyer there is a seller and for every seller there is a buyer. This instantly removes the issues associated with many bucket shops where you are often trading directly against them. In an exchange traded binary option this never occurs. The exchange simply matches buyers and sellers, and every option is fully collateralized by the two parties in cash. Unlike some futures, binary options are always cash settled so there is never any physical delivery to worry about. How this works is explained in schematic example Fig 4.14.

Buying & Selling

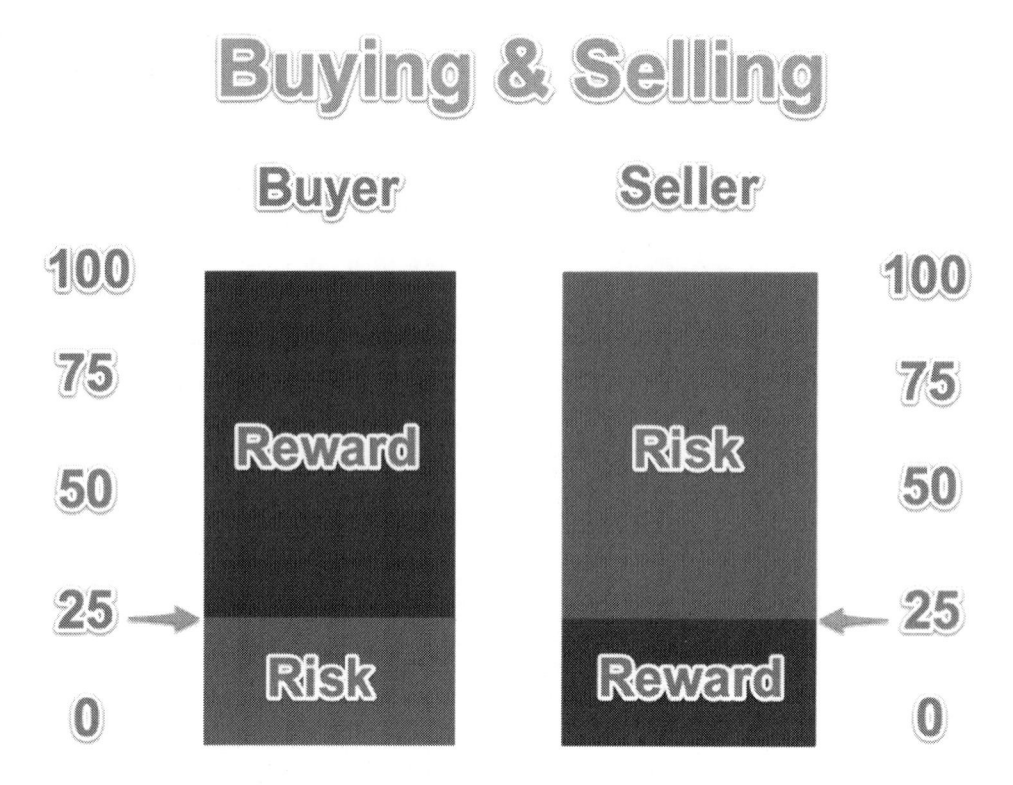

Buyer — 100, 75, Reward, 50, 25 →, Risk, 0

Seller — 100, 75, Risk, 50, ← 25, Reward, 0

Fig 4.14 - Buying or selling a binary option

Here we have a binary option with a 25% probability (we will get to the bid and offer in a moment) with a buyer on the left and a seller on the right. You will be pleased to know on the Nadex platform each 1% of probability is equivalent to 1$, so every contract is $100 which makes the maths nice and simple.

We decide to buy this contract as we believe the market will close above the strike price by expiry. The cost of the binary is $25 (25 x $1). This is our total risk. We cannot lose any more than this on the contract. Our reward here is the difference between 100 and our risk, in other words $100 - $25 = $75. In buying this binary we are taking a 1:3 ratio of risk to reward which seems attractive, but the underlying price has to move for this to finish above the strike price. This is an out of the money binary option, and for it to move towards 100, the underlying price has to move. Risk and reward go hand in hand in all forms of trading and investing, but in binary options this has to be balanced by the time to expiry and the underlying analysis.

Now if we look at the opposite side of the position. We have bought at 25, so the exchange has matched a seller, who has sold at 75. Their risk/reward profile is the inverse of ours as the buyer. As a seller their risk is $75 and their profit is $100 - $75 = $25. Their risk to reward ratio is 3:1. You may wonder why anyone would want to trade with a risk to reward ratio of 3:1. This is similar to backing an odds on horse, and the reason is simply the probability. The seller has sold the option at 75%, as they believe there is little prospect of the option closing above the strike price. The same principles that work for the option buyer, also work for the option seller. Let me explain by taking two extremes of the binary option. The first at 90 and the second at 10 and assume both are relatively close to expiry.

In the first example, suppose we have a binary option trading at 90. The probability is very high the option will close at 100 and as an option buyer we are prepared to risk $90 to make $10. We are buying this binary option as we believe the proposition will close as true.

In the second example the binary option is trading at 10, and once again is close to expiry. The probability here is very low the proposition will close as true, so we are a seller of the binary option. As before we are risking $90 to make $10. The risk and reward profile is the same, but in one we are a binary option buyer, and in the other a binary option seller. However, in both cases our potential profit is $10 and our risk is $90. In both of the above examples we will be matched on the other side of the position with a seller in the first example and a buyer in the second. And just for completeness these examples are based on the assumption the underlying market is well away from the strike price and deep in the money.

If we return to our example in Fig 4.14, here the option buyer and option seller are matched and the exchange will hold the funds from both parties as the collateral for the contract. In total this will be $25 + $75 = $100. On expiry of the contract one party will receive $100 and the other will receive $0. If you think of the binary option on Nadex in these terms it makes the whole process very simple to understand. Buyer and seller are matched, and the total risk exposed by both parties comes to $100 per contract. You can of course buy or sell multiple contracts, but the same basic mathematics still apply.

One of the many beauties of trading on exchange binary options is there is no need to wait until expiry to close a position. Indeed many option traders will close once the option approaches an extreme, as there is always the very slight chance of a sudden reversal, and any additional profit to be gained from 3 or four points is not justified in holding the contract until expiry. This is one of the many decisions that you as a binary options trader will have to make, but the decision is yours. You have complete control over your positions, and once open these can be closed out at any time, either to reduce the risk further or to take profit early.

Before moving to the Nadex platform itself, I want to tackle the thorny issue of the spread and the cost of trading, because as always in trading there is no such thing as a free lunch.

As traders the spread is something we all tend to focus on. It is a topic we all have an opinion on, and is the sole marketing focus for many brokers particularly in the world of forex. For a scalping trader this is a huge issue both in terms of the percentage cost of the trade, and more importantly perhaps, in the context of any return. If we take the spot forex market as an example, the currency pair the majority of forex traders focus on is the EUR/USD for several reasons. First, it is the most liquid and heavily traded. Second, it generally offers the tightest spreads, and third the majority of spot forex traders adopt a scalping approach to this market. Scalping by its very nature is high speed. The average pip target for scalping traders is between 5 and 7 pips, with positions open for seconds or minutes.

Active traders will often execute tens, if not hundreds of trades a day which makes having a tight spread vital. The difference between a 1 pip spread and a 2 pip spread is huge in percentage terms, when looking for a target of perhaps 5 or 6 pips. This is one of the reasons why it is almost impossible to trade the cross currency pairs using a scalping approach, as the spreads here are so much wider. The maths simply does not work. As a scalping trader you are constantly battling a large spread. On the EUR/USD for example we may have a 0.5 pip spread, but move to the EUR/NZD and the spread may be 6 or 7 pips, or more.

In addition, in times of market volatility many of the spreads quoted in the forex market will widen dramatically.

The final point I want to stress on this issue is as follows. When we are trading in a cash, futures or indeed spot market, there is a linear relationship in place. This means if we open a position with a 2 pip spread, and assuming there is no volatility expected in the short term, this spread will remain much the same as the price moves higher and lower in whichever timeframe you are trading.

In the world of binary option spreads, price is not the only force which dictates the speed binary bids and offers will move. As we have already seen this is not a linear relationship, since time and the proximity to any strike price will also play their part. Whilst the spread may indeed remain much the same throughout the life of the option, the rate of change in terms of recovering the spread and moving into profit will be very different. As we saw earlier the price does not need to change to trigger a change in the option quote. It's very easy to forget this aspect of binary option pricing as we move from traditional instruments, where the spread is linear in its relationship to price, to an instrument where this is no longer the case.

I am not suggesting the spread is not important, far from it. What I am saying is try to keep it in context in two ways. First the relationship is not linear. A spread of 4 or 5 points on a binary option is very different to a 4 or 5 point spread on a traditional instrument because of the different forces involved. Second, my personal view is that longer term strategies work extremely well with binary options, and as a result the spread, as with all longer term approaches, becomes less relevant.

What is crucial is the starting point which is always an analysis of the underlying chart, supported by the fundamental and relational aspects. So please don't become too focused on the spreads. Yes they are greater, but these are very different instruments with a non linear profile. I should also make the point that Nadex is a relatively new exchange, and the liquidity provided by the market makers is increasing all the time, which in turn will no doubt be reflected in tighter spreads over the next few years.

Here are a couple of examples from the Nadex platform to show how the spread is quoted.

Contract	Expiry	Bid Size	Bid	Offer	Offer Size	Update
US 500 (Mar) >1806.0 (4:15PM)	30-DEC-13	10	97.00	-	-	03:00:07
US 500 (Mar) >1809.0 (4:15PM)	30-DEC-13	10	97.00	-	-	03:00:07
US 500 (Mar) >1812.0 (4:15PM)	30-DEC-13	10	97.00	-	-	03:00:07
US 500 (Mar) >1815.0 (4:15PM)	30-DEC-13	10	97.00	-	-	03:00:07
US 500 (Mar) >1818.0 (4:15PM)	30-DEC-13	10	97.00	-	-	03:00:07
US 500 (Mar) >1821.0 (4:15PM)	30-DEC-13	10	97.00	-	-	03:12:09
US 500 (Mar) >1824.0 (4:15PM)	30-DEC-13	10	96.00	99.50	10	09:46:01
US 500 (Mar) >1827.0 (4:15PM)	30-DEC-13	250	91.50	95.50	250	09:46:20
US 500 (Mar) >1830.0 (4:15PM)	30-DEC-13	250	82.50	86.50	250	09:46:20
US 500 (Mar) >1833.0 (4:15PM)	30-DEC-13	250	67.50	72.00	250	09:46:20
US 500 (Mar) >1836.0 (4:15PM)	30-DEC-13	118	47.50	54.00	156	09:46:20
US 500 (Mar) >1839.0 (4:15PM)	30-DEC-13	250	30.00	34.50	250	09:46:20
US 500 (Mar) >1842.0 (4:15PM)	30-DEC-13	250	15.00	19.00	250	09:46:20
US 500 (Mar) >1845.0 (4:15PM)	30-DEC-13	250	5.50	9.50	250	09:46:20
US 500 (Mar) >1848.0 (4:15PM)	30-DEC-13	10	1.00	4.50	10	09:46:20
US 500 (Mar) >1851.0 (4:15PM)	30-DEC-13	-	-	3.00	10	09:33:56
US 500 (Mar) >1854.0 (4:15PM)	30-DEC-13	-	-	3.00	10	03:00:07
US 500 (Mar) >1857.0 (4:15PM)	30-DEC-13	-	-	3.00	10	03:00:07

Fig 4.15 - Nadex index option ladder - bid and offer

The binary option ladder in Fig 4.15 is displaying a selection of options contracts on the US 500 index. On the left in the Contract column you can see the various strike prices in the ladder moving down in 3 index point increments, from 1806 at the top to 1857 at the bottom. At the time of writing the index was trading in the 1835.50 area with several hours left to run. The underlying futures contract is shown in brackets (March) and the expiry time for all these contracts is the end of day when the physical exchange closes at 4.15 pm ET. Alongside is the expiry date for the contract in the Expiry column. For the time being don't worry about the Bid Size column as we will come back to that later. Then we come to the Bid and Offer column where our binary option prices are quoted and we buy and sell as follows:

- We *buy* on the *offer*
- We *sell* on the *bid*

As you can see here the spreads vary, moving from a minimum of 3.50 at the extremes of the ladder, to a maximum of 6.50 towards the mid-point and this is the typical profile of spreads - a bell curve of spreads if you like. As I have stressed above and throughout this chapter, these will move extremely quickly and even more so if the markets are volatile, which is good news for option traders.

In Fig 4.16 we have a further selection of contracts, this time on gold. The contracts here are a mixture of those closing in a few hours (11AM) and those closing at midnight (12PM) (ET). Here you can see strike prices for gold move in $1.5 per ounce increments and the spreads between the bid and the offer are a little wider on these contracts, owing to lower liquidity. These vary from 5.50 to 7.0.

Contract	Expiry	Size	Bid	Offer	Size	Time
Gold (Feb) >1199.3 (11AM)	30-DEC-13	1	96.00	-	-	10:13:35
Gold (Feb) >1199.7 (12PM)	30-DEC-13	1	93.50	-	-	10:46:10
Gold (Feb) >1200.8 (11AM)	30-DEC-13	1	96.00	-	-	10:41:30
Gold (Feb) >1201.2 (12PM)	30-DEC-13	20	87.00	93.50	20	10:46:10
Gold (Feb) >1202.3 (11AM)	30-DEC-13	1	94.00	-	-	10:44:17
Gold (Feb) >1202.7 (12PM)	30-DEC-13	20	73.00	79.50	20	10:46:10
Gold (Feb) >1203.8 (11AM)	30-DEC-13	20	75.00	82.00	20	10:46:21
Gold (Feb) >1204.2 (12PM)	30-DEC-13	20	53.00	59.00	20	10:46:10
Gold (Feb) >1205.3 (11AM)	30-DEC-13	20	21.00	28.00	20	10:46:19
Gold (Feb) >1205.7 (12PM)	30-DEC-13	20	30.50	37.00	20	10:46:10
Gold (Feb) >1206.8 (11AM)	30-DEC-13	-	-	6.00	1	10:45:53
Gold (Feb) >1207.2 (12PM)	30-DEC-13	20	13.00	19.50	20	10:46:10
Gold (Feb) >1208.3 (11AM)	30-DEC-13	-	-	4.00	1	10:38:43
Gold (Feb) >1208.7 (12PM)	30-DEC-13	2	3.50	9.00	20	10:46:10
Gold (Feb) >1209.8 (11AM)	30-DEC-13	-	-	4.00	1	10:35:02
Gold (Feb) >1210.2 (12PM)	30-DEC-13	-	-	6.00	1	10:38:43

Fig 4.16 - Nadex gold binary options ladder - bid and offer

And here is a longer term ladder for the EUR/USD on a weekly basis, giving another example of spreads. This is shown in Fig 4.17.

Contract			Expiry	Bid Size	Bid	Offer	Offer Size	Update
EUR/USD >1.3425 (3PM)			03-JAN-14	10	97.00	-	-	04:45:27
EUR/USD >1.3475 (3PM)			03-JAN-14	10	97.00	-	-	08:00:20
EUR/USD >1.3525 (3PM)			03-JAN-14	10	96.00	-	-	07:25:29
EUR/USD >1.3575 (3PM)			03-JAN-14	10	96.00	-	-	10:00:02
EUR/USD >1.3625 (3PM)			03-JAN-14	200	94.00	98.50	200	10:59:24
EUR/USD >1.3675 (3PM)			03-JAN-14	200	88.00	92.50	200	10:59:49
EUR/USD >1.3725 (3PM)			03-JAN-14	200	77.00	82.00	200	10:59:49
EUR/USD >1.3775 (3PM)			03-JAN-14	200	61.00	67.00	200	10:59:49
EUR/USD >1.3825 (3PM)			03-JAN-14	200	42.50	48.50	200	10:59:49
EUR/USD >1.3875 (3PM)			03-JAN-14	200	25.50	31.00	200	10:59:49
EUR/USD >1.3925 (3PM)			03-JAN-14	200	12.50	17.50	200	10:59:37
EUR/USD >1.3975 (3PM)			03-JAN-14	200	4.50	9.00	200	10:59:36
EUR/USD >1.4025 (3PM)			03-JAN-14	-	-	4.50	10	10:59:49
EUR/USD >1.4075 (3PM)			03-JAN-14	-	-	4.00	10	10:23:39

Fig 4.17 - Nadex EUR/USD weekly options ladder - bid and offer

Here the spreads vary from a minimum of 4.50 to a maximum of 6.00 at the mid-point with the strike increments in 50 pips.

Just to end on the bid and the offer. There is an easy way to remember what your profit and risk on expiry will be, and this is as follows:

- when you are *buying the offer,* this is showing your *maximum risk*
- when you are *selling the bid*, this is showing your *maximum profit*

If you recall you do not have to take the bid and offer that is being quoted. This is a further benefit of trading an on exchange binary option. You simply place an order outside the current quote range and wait for the order to be filled or not. This is executed on the Nadex platform using the Limit Order. When the probability ladder moves outside of a quotable range, the exchange will not offer a price hence these will remain blank. In addition when these move close to expiry you may also find prices are not quoted.

Moving to an order ticket from the platform here we can see how it all comes together. In addition to the spread there is also a commission charged by Nadex on each contract which is 0.90 cents per side or $1.80 per round turn. To open and close a position will cost $1.80. Whilst this is not a significant cost in dollars it can be significant if you are scalping, and perhaps even more so, if you are only trading single contracts. As you increase the number of contracts traded this becomes increasingly less significant as Nadex do offer a cap of $9 per order for multiple contracts.

And here is an example of an order ticket from the Nadex platform. In Fig 4.18 I have selected a weekly contract for the USD/CHF.

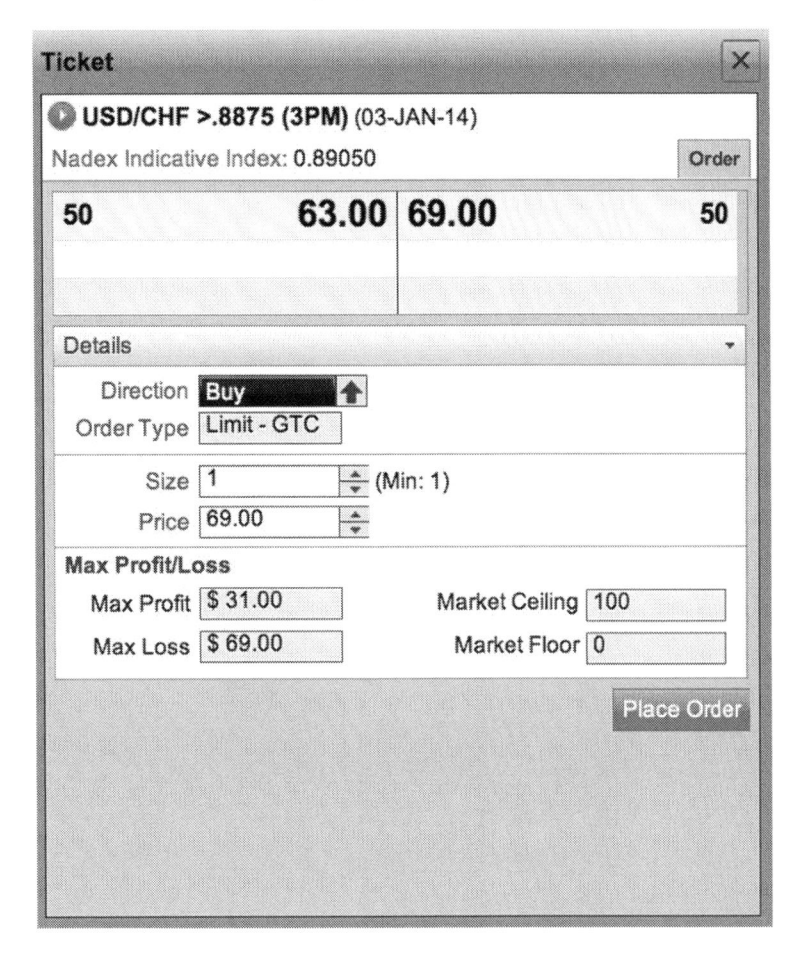

Fig 4.18 - The Nadex order ticket

If we start at the top of the ticket, here you can see the contract we are trading is the USD/CHF currency pair. It has a contract strike price at expiry > 0.8875 at 3PM ET on the 3rd Jan 2014. Immediately below we can see the current quote for the underlying which is trading at 0.89050.

Next comes the quote window, and here you can see the binary option is trading at 63.00 on the bid if we want to sell and 69.00 on the offer if we want to buy. The two figures to the left and right (50 & 50) are simply displaying the latest bid and offer sizes to go through the market.

Moving down the order ticket, the next selection is whether we want to buy or sell - the **Direction**. Click the arrow on the right to change the order from a buy to a sell. If we buy we are agreeing with the proposition the market will close above 0.8875 by the expiry date and time. If we sell we are disagreeing with this statement. In this case we have selected a buy order as we believe the market will close above this strike price by expiry.

Next comes the **Order Type**. All Nadex orders are Limit orders which I will explain shortly. There are no market orders on Nadex, just Limit orders. The GTC alongside stands for Good Till Cancelled and again I will explain this shortly.

Then comes *Size* and *Price*.

The size is simply the number of contracts. The minimum is 1 and the maximum will depend on the cash balance in your account. Here we have chosen 1. Next comes the price which in this case is 69 or $69 at $1 per point on the exchange. Finally in the window at the bottom of the ticket is our profit and loss summary. In this case we are buying at $69, which is our maximum potential loss, and our maximum potential profit on the order is $31, and these two numbers always total $100 per contract. The right hand side of the order ticket simply confirms the option closes at either 100 or 0. If we are happy with our order we click the **Place Order** button on the right hand side of the ticket and the order will be filled.

If we are correct, and the market does close above the strike price at expiry, we will have made a profit of $31. If we are wrong we will lose $69. However, we do not have to wait until expiry to close out either to take a profit early or to reduce a loss. The figures quoted in the summary window are always the maximum. The maximum profit and maximum loss, but with an on exchange binary option we are always in control of our positions. The choice of when to close out is up to us, or we can simply wait until expiry.

Limit Order & GTC

Many traders are familiar with the market order and the stop loss order, but perhaps less so with a limit order.

A limit order can be used in two different ways on the Nadex platform. First as an order to get us into the market at a better price than the one being quoted, and second to set a take profit order to close out before expiry. This gives us complete control over where and when we get into the market, and also in setting the automatic take profit targets, if required. On many occasions the market will reverse on minor pullbacks on a longer term trend, but using the limit order offers the flexibility to set our own entry price based on the analysis of the underlying chart and associated price action.

Here is an example of another order ticket to see how this works in practice.

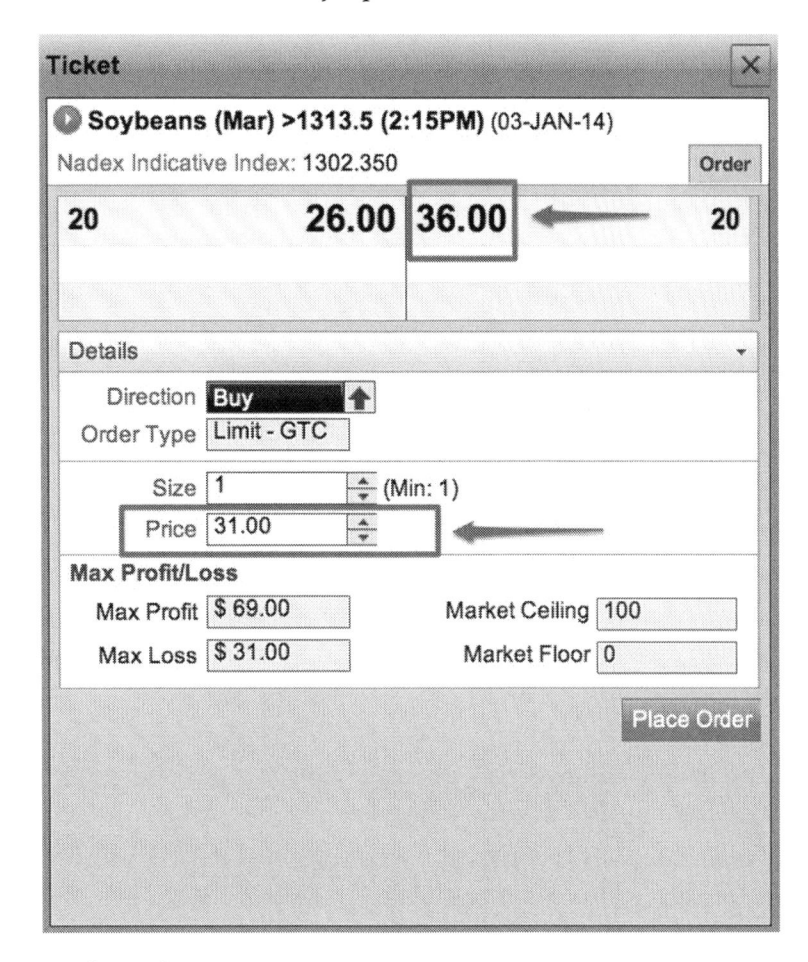

Fig 4.19 - Placing a limit order to buy

On this ticket we have a weekly contract for Soybeans. The underlying market is currently trading at 1302.35, but we believe this is a good probability trade given the technical picture and the time to expiry. The quote on the offer is currently 36, but we would like to enter the market at a better price. Having looked at our charts we believe that whilst the longer term is bullish, the price action and volume analysis is suggesting short term weakness. Rather than enter at 36 we decide we would like to enter at 31, allowing us to get into a stronger position and generate a higher return. In the price window we enter 31.00. The profit and loss window now reflects this change with a maximum loss of $31, and a maximum profit of $69.

However, when we place the order this does not become an Open Position live in the market, but instead is known as a '*Working Order*'. A working order is one that is waiting for a limit order to be hit. This order will now be triggered when the market reaches our desired price point for entry. You can think of the limit order as a 'pending order', waiting for the market to touch the price you have set.

You can apply the same approach to creating a 'take profit' order. Suppose the above order has been live for a few days, but we see some longer term weakness now appearing on our charts, or perhaps some fundamental news has resulted in a slow down of the bullish momentum. We still believe the option will close above the strike at expiry, but want to close the position completely at a certain level, or partially close the position. Again this is done using the limit order. All we need to do here is the reverse. We place a *sell* order at say 85, and click the **Place Order** button. This becomes a working order, and will only be triggered into a 'take profit' order when the option hits the sell order price level. The take profit order would then close the position. The main points to note are these:

- We do not need to close the whole position. If we have 10 contracts we could place a limit order to close 5 at one price and leave the remainder to expiry. Alternatively, we could create two or more take profit orders to close out in steps as the market moves higher
- The process is identical if we have opened with a sell order
- We have to make sure we sell or buy **the same contract** to close or take profit. In the futures and options world to close a position requires placing an order opposite to the open position. An open buy position is closed with a sell order, whilst an open sell position is closed with a buy order. We are then square the market. With so many contracts in the option ladder, it is very easy to select the wrong contract to close a position

Using limit orders in this way is an elegant approach to managing any position in the market. And in the binary options world a stop loss is redundant.

The other term which we came across on the ticket was GTC, which is simply **Good Till Cancelled**. All this means is exactly what it says. The order will remain a working order until it is either cancelled or becomes a live position in the market when triggered by the price hitting the limit order price specified on the order ticket.

Let me try to summarize the binary options marketplace at present, and also point you to another exchange which has been offering these instruments for some time.

As I explained in my introduction this is an extremely fast moving market. In writing the first few chapters I have tried to outline in an unbiased way, what I believe are some of the pros and cons of trading using a fixed risk approach. We are going to consider the whole business of risk/reward ratios and percentage returns in the next chapter, but the point I want to make is this.

Whilst there is certainly a place for the fixed odds trade, and we will look at some of the products on offer shortly, my belief remains the on exchange offering has much to recommend it.

This chapter is not a pitch for Nadex. It is simply they are leading the way in this market at present. No doubt others will follow, and the choices for you as a trader will increase dramatically. Having said that, I can wholeheartedly endorse the company for its dedicated support and for the trading platform which is simple, straightforward and easy to use.

Just to prove the point regarding other exchanges, let me highlight the CBOE (Chicago Board Options Exchange). At present, they offer two binary options products as follows:

- BVZ - a binary option based on the VIX
- BSZ - a binary option based on the S&P 500

These are the only two binary option products currently available, and are traded through the CBOE. They trade in a very similar way to the Nadex products, with each contract equivalent to $100 and settling at either 0 or 100. The option chains are described using puts and calls and expiry dates are generally longer. The only issue however, is these instruments can only be traded if you have an account with a broker authorized to offer vanilla options. If you do these are two great products to investigate further, particularly if you are an index trader on the S&P 500. In addition to these, the NYSE also offers binary options of which more later in the book.

This is one of the unique aspects of Nadex. You are trading directly with the exchange and you have no need of a broker. Your money is safe, and with no leverage or margin requirements, you cannot lose more than the capital in your trading account.

In the next chapter we are going to move on and consider the risk/reward issue as we look at the maths of trading returns.

Chapter Five

Risk & Reward Ratios Explained

Remember the clever speculator is always patient and has a reserve of cash

Jesse Livermore (1877 - 1940)

I hope in the first few chapters I have managed to explain in a clear and unambiguous way, the background and companies which currently fall under the umbrella term 'binary'. For the newcomer it can be a confusing picture with claims and counterclaims, endless marketing hype and the inevitable dash for cash from the less scrupulous. As we have already seen the regulatory authorities are desperately running to catch up in this fast moving market.

In this chapter we are going to look at another hugely contentious issue which surrounds this market, and concerns the central trading tenet of risk and reward. But before we start let me restate.

There is nothing wrong in trading using a fixed odds approach provided it is coupled with a sound analytical methodology such as volume price analysis. This will help shift the odds in your favor and away from the broker. Bookmakers and bucket shop brokers have been around for many years and have survived for one simple reason. The odds are always in their favor not yours, and I hope by the end of this chapter you will understand why.

My objective here is to explain the maths of odds, probabilities and returns, as they apply to the instruments we have considered thus far, namely off exchange and on exchange binary options.

As you will discover the 70% to 85% returns marketed by the bucket shop brokers are not as good as they would have you believe. This is one of the less desirable aspects of the binary market at present. It is awash with headline grabbing claims which, when considered logically are highly misleading. The same applies to sign up incentives. It's just clever marketing. The maths explained here will reveal the truth behind these claims.

The Maths Of Break Even

Let's begin by considering break-even from the traditional standpoint of a trader in a conventional market, before moving to consider how it applies to both off exchange and on exchange binary options.

The generally accepted wisdom for growing a trading account longer term is premised on keeping losses small and profits large. Trading is not, and never has been, about the simple ratio of winners to losers. It is about the relative size of those winners to losers.

Many people outside the trading world believe it is a 50/50 business. It is not.

When trading binaries it is very different. Here we are dealing with an instrument which is capped both to the downside and the upside. Our risk is capped which is great, but then so is our profit. This creates a unique profile and one which undermines the perceived wisdom of trading, which is premised on an entirely different risk and reward profile. I have created two simple schematics in Fig 5.10 and Fig 5.11 to explain this principle graphically.

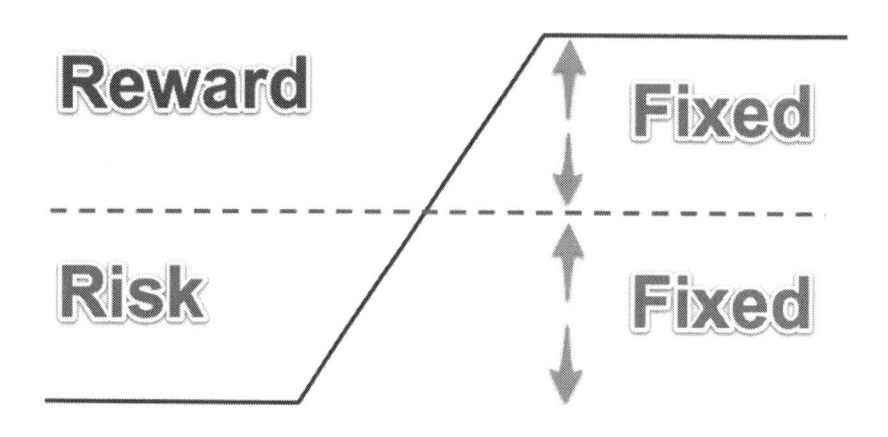

Fig 5.10 - Binary profile of risk and reward

Conventional profile

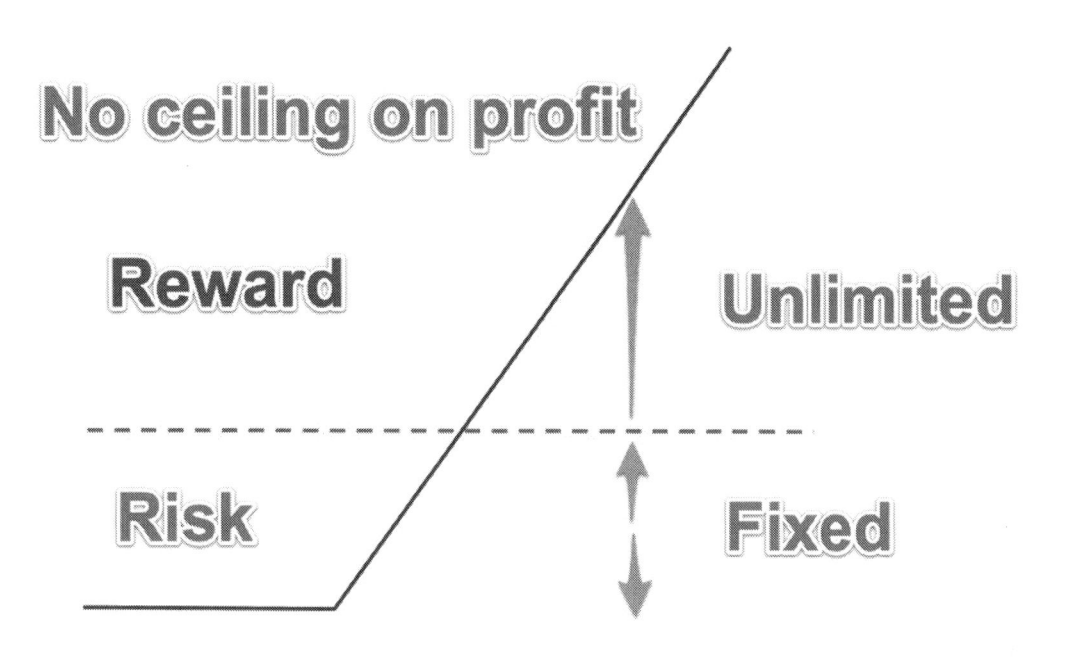

No ceiling on profit

Reward — **Unlimited**

Risk — **Fixed**

Fig 5.11 - Conventional profile of risk and reward

In Fig 5.10 you can see the schematic representation of risk and reward. The risk is fixed and known, but so too is our reward.

In the conventional world of trading, and assuming we are using a stop loss, the risk reward profile is represented in Fig 5.11. Here we have limited risk, but our profit potential is unlimited. The profit line can continue higher for as long as we have the position open in the market. Our risk is still defined and capped at a maximum, but the profit potential is unlimited. It is this simple fact, that sets binary options apart from the more conventional approach to trading, and herein lies the central issue.

As mentioned, long term success in trading is premised on keeping losses small and letting winners run. In a sequence of ten trades, seven could be negative and three positive. However, provided the three positive trades are relatively large, and the seven negative trades small, overall the trading account balance will increase. This is how the maths of trading has always worked. The reason why many traders struggle to move forward is they allow losses to build and cut profits short. This has been confirmed to me by a number of brokers over the years.

Getting in is easy, it is staying in and then holding to maximize any profits which are the most difficult things to do. But, they are the foundation stone of success, and is why the maths of trading is often counterintuitive. If this ratio can be improved to four in ten or greater then so much the better.

We do have to differentiate between on exchange and off exchange binary options. In the binary options model, whilst the risk to reward profile is the same, there are two major differences. First, you have the ability to set your own entry and exit points in on exchange binary options. Second, this in turn allows you to define your own risk reward parameters for the mainstream products. But let's just stay with the off exchange example.

There are several issues here so let's consider them one by one.

In the above scenario in conventional trading I suggested that three positive trades to seven negative trades could still produce positive results. In other words 3/10 or a 30% success rate. Reduce the number of negative trades to 6, and the ratio moves to 4/10 or 40%. Does this sound reasonable and achievable? Four correct and six incorrect, and the maths still works for us as our losers are small, and our winners outweigh these.

Moving to the off exchange model where our profits are now limited, the question to ask is as follows:

How long would we survive with a 30% success rate? And the answer is not very long, and it's easy to see why with some maths. Let's assume that we work on a 1:1. We risk $1 to win $1. For every $100 we would be winning $30 and losing $70.

With a 40% success rate we would last a little longer perhaps, winning $40 and losing $60 for every $100 in our account.

Moving to a 50% success rate we finally achieve break-even, neither moving forwards or backwards. For every $50 we win, we also lose $50. An oversimplified example I accept, but we have to start somewhere.

The next point is this.

Few off exchange brokers offer 100% returns. The returns are generally anywhere between 70% to 85%, and as we saw in chapter two Binary.com comes close at times, and in Fig 2.10, the return being offered was 95%. These can go higher and above 100% with this company, even for the mainstream products.

There is an exception. For one product group in particular, namely the one touch/no touch, returns here offered by all off exchange brokers will be dramatically higher. However, the quid pro quo for these higher returns, is greatly reduced flexibility in the instrument. In the case of the white label brokers there is zero flexibility, and these returns will be marketed as 500% and more. This is the equivalent of a very low probability event occurring. Yes the returns may be amazing, but the prospect of achieving this level of return is remote.

For mainstream products, any percentage return below 100% is pushing the mathematical break-even point ever higher and above the 50% level.

Moreover, we have the all encompassing aspect of time to consider. To achieve a success rate of better than 50% or five in ten consistently is difficult enough. It is harder still when we are being asked to consider not only *if* the event will happen, but **when**. This is what makes a fixed odds proposition a weaker offering from a purely mathematical perspective, and why brokers will always have the odds on their side.

Let's just stop and think what we are being asked to do here:

- We **have** to be right more times than we are wrong - no ifs, no buts, no maybes. We cannot drop below 50% and we have to be closer to 60%, ***just to stand still***
- Not only are we being asked to forecast price action correctly, but also **when** this is going to happen. Does this increase or decrease the odds of success? It is hard enough to forecast when a market is

strong or weak, harder still to say what level it will be at in a few minutes, an hour, a day or a week. Yet this is what we are being asked to do in a binary

In the table below I have created some typical percentage returns currently being offered by the white label brokers, with the associated break-even percentage you would need to achieve just to stand still. Calculating these is very simple, and uses the following formula:

- Break-even = OTM%/(ITM% + OTM%)

Here is an example:

- OTM% - this is always 100%
- ITM% - this is generally somewhere between 70% and 85%, and here we are using 70%
- Break-even = 100/(70 + 100) = 0.58 or 58%

If we are trading a binary that is offering a 70% payout if we are correct, and zero if incorrect, we have to be right almost 60% of the time. Six times in 10, to make money and move our account forward. In fact I would suggest seven would be nearer the mark. The question then is this. Given that we are also being asked to say *when* this is going to happen, are the odds in our favor or against us?

I will leave you to ponder that question, but it is no wonder why there are so many white label brokers in this market. There is simply too much money to be made, and the odds are all in their favor. Let's look at the table in Fig 5.12:

ITM vs Break-even

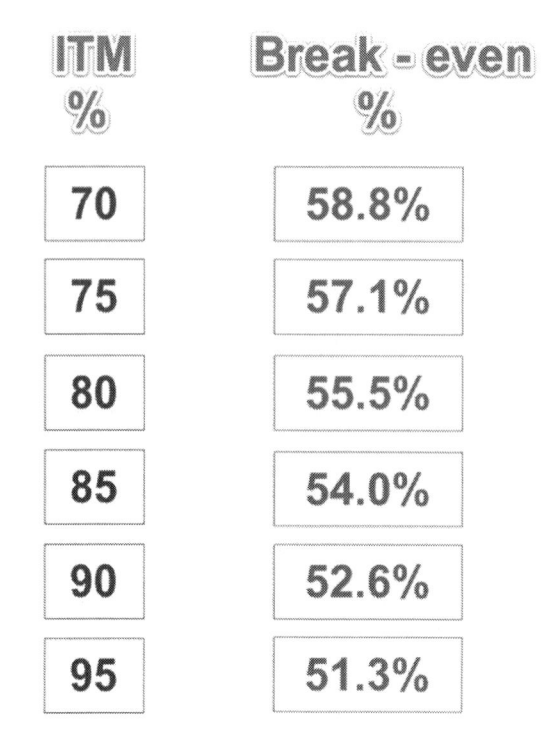

ITM %	Break-even %
70	58.8%
75	57.1%
80	55.5%
85	54.0%
90	52.6%
95	51.3%

Fig 5.12 - ITM% converted to break even %

All things being equal it goes without saying, the higher the percentage being offered for an ITM binary, the lower your break-even needs to be, and as the returns approach 100%, the closer we move to 50% for break-even. This is still only break-even. If you achieved this consistently your account would remain flat. Furthermore, it is not only a question of being right or wrong, but you also have to be right or wrong before expiry. I fully accept the above figures are based on some simplistic assumptions, and are far from perfect. Nevertheless, I hope these basic principles do convey the underlying issues surrounding the maths of returns and break-even.

Now some general comments concerning the timeframes of the products on offer in this market. There is everything from guessing the next up tick or down tick, to forecasting price moves over the next few seconds or the next few minutes. My own view on this type of product is as follows.

At this end of the spectrum it is nothing more than betting, and like all forms of betting it can be fun. It is not trading, and never can be. And with the odds stacked so heavily against you, you will lose your money fast. As I have said many times already, time is the game changer with options, and to succeed you need to have time on your side, and get it working for you. If you want to bet that's fine - but if you want to trade then consider the schematic in Fig 5.13.

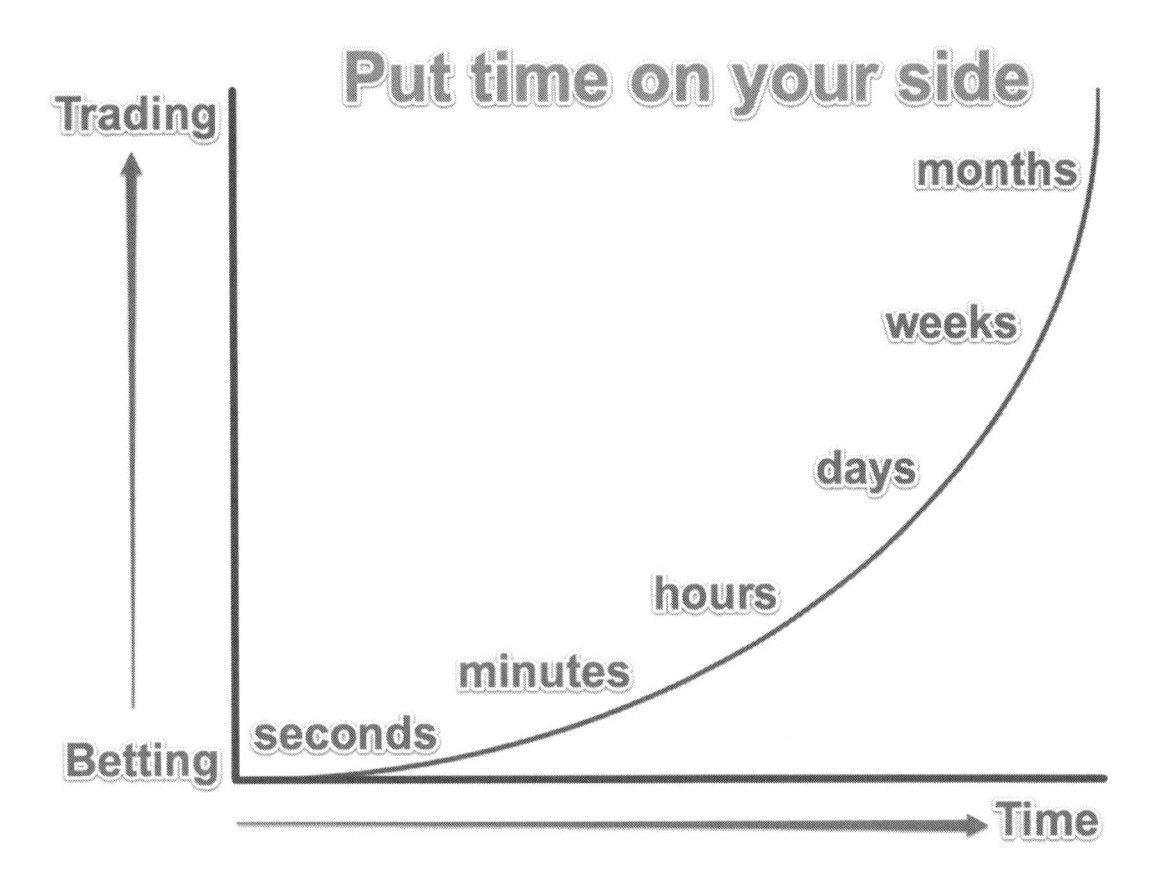

Fig 5.13 - Betting vs trading

The Maths Of Risk & Reward

The concept of risk and reward is very straightforward. It applies to every aspect of our lives, and even more so in the financial market. It is in fact the primary driver of market sentiment. Money is constantly moved to seek higher returns, which is then reflected in risk sentiment. Higher yields come at a higher price with more risk, lower yields carry less risk. The hot money flows into high yielding currencies are a classic example, but as soon as sentiment changes, the money flows out just as quickly. But how do we apply the idea of risk and reward in the binary options world?

In the binary world, we have to consider risk and reward in two different but related ways. The starting point as always is the chart, and the binary option quote second. I will keep stressing these points throughout the book as it is very easy to be seduced by the probabilities or odds being quoted. These are being quoted on the underlying markets coupled with time. Therefore, the chart must always be your first port of call.

If you have read any of my other books on trading, and in particular the aspect of setting risk and reward targets, you will know I hold very strong views on this subject. Many trading books, particularly those for spot forex traders, will advise you set a risk and reward target before entering a position, based on nothing more than mathematics. In other words they urge you take a position using a 1:3 or 1:4 risk to reward profile. I am sure you have come across this approach. The author suggests that if you are prepared to risk 5 pips, then you should have a target of 15 pips. My response to this is always the same. Why should the market give you anything, let alone some arbitrary target that *you* decide upon in advance, simply to make the maths work for *you*. The market does not care about you, or what you think. The analogy I use here is of a shop. Do you open your shop every day and say 'today I am going to make $1,000'?

The short answer is no. Every day is different. It may be raining, it may be hot or cold, other shops in the area could be holding a sale. It may be the end of the month when people have less money in their pockets, or there could be repairs being carried out in the road making access to your shop difficult. There are all sorts of reasons why your daily takings will vary. It may be a good day, an average day or a bad day. And the same is true in trading. You cannot approach the market with a predetermined risk to reward ratio, simply because it supports the maths of trading. As I have said in my other books, the market will set these target levels for you, and it does so by defining the support and resistance levels on the price chart. This is one of the fundamental tenets of volume price analysis which is covered in the next chapter.

Support and resistance (or accumulation and distribution as it is also known) is one of the building blocks of the underlying primary methodology of VPA (Volume Price Analysis). It is a key analytical approach I use, not only for judging where a market may pause and reverse, but also in placing and managing any stop loss. In the binary options world the stop loss is redundant, so the role for support and resistance is in identifying those key areas where we believe the market may struggle in an uptrend, or find support in a downtrend.

When considering the risk and reward relationship, the starting point has to be the chart. Here we consider all the analytical aspects of volume and price, support and resistance, coupled with a multiple timeframe approach. From our analysis, we can arrive at an assessment of the risk on the trade. Is it a high risk, medium or low risk trading opportunity? Are we trading with the dominant trend in the longer term, or against it? When I refer to a dominant trend, this could be over minutes, hours, days or weeks. It all depends on your time horizon on the proposed position. But a dominant trend on an hourly chart is as valid as the dominant trend on a daily or weekly chart, they are all relative. Again I explain this in the next chapter as we explore VPA in more detail. But the point is this. Based on our analysis of the chart, and all the various aspects of price, volume and time, we are now in a position to consider whether this is likely to be a good short, medium or longer term position. And from our analysis of the charts we can also then infer the associated risk and reward relationship on the position.

Now let's consider the issue of risk and reward in the context of the odds and probabilities of the instruments for both on exchange and off exchange brokers.

If we start with off exchange we have no choice but to accept the odds being quoted. With Binary.com these do vary and will certainly come close to the 1:1 region at 100%, and exceed this on occasion. But Binary.com is the exception. The white label brokers offering binary options, will be quoting between 70% and up to 85%, sometimes with a sweetener of a small percentage return for a losing trade.

You either accept the odds or not. You have little control over these or the associated risk to reward profile. However, with an on exchange binary option instrument you do. And the reason you do is because with on exchange binary options, not only can you set your entry price, you can also close your position when you choose. This gives you complete control over your position, and more importantly in determining your own risk and reward profiles for every trade based on the binary probabilities being quoted. As I have said before this is akin to you being your own bookmaker.

You are setting your own odds for you own position, based on your own analysis of the underlying chart. I cannot stress this aspect too strongly, and is a further reason for considering the on exchange binary option as your instrument of choice. Using this instrument not only puts you in complete control of your position from a trading perspective, but also from a percentage return perspective, a fact which many traders fail to appreciate. The example in Fig 5.14 is an order ticket from the Nadex platform.

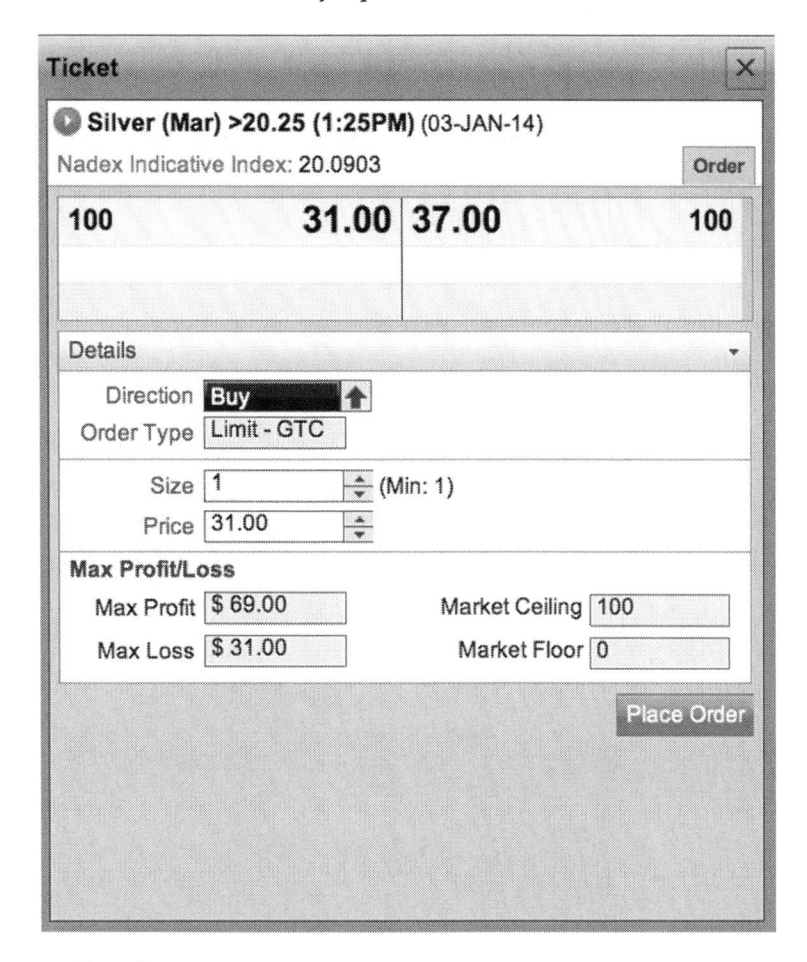

Fig 5.14 - Weekly contract for silver

In Fig 5.14 we have a binary option being quoted for silver with the March futures as the underlying market. The strike price is >$20.25 per ounce and the current binary price is 29/35. We have studied our charts and believe the longer term outlook for silver is bullish. We are therefore looking to buy this option at 35 with a maximum profit at expiry of 65. If we buy one contract then our profit at expiry is $65 if the strike price is achieved.

But what is our risk and reward and potential percentage return in this case?

- Our risk is : $35
- Our reward (at expiry) if true is : $65
- Our percentage return is : $65/$35 x 100% = **185.7%**

However, this is not the end of the story as we have two other mechanisms here with which we can control our returns. Suppose in a few days time, and following further analysis of our charts, we believe the bullish trend for silver may be over in the short term, and rather than wait until expiry we decide to close out early and take any profit. For simplicity let's assume the option being quoted at this point is 70/75. If we sell at this price, our percentage return has now reduced, and is as follows:

- Our risk is still : $35
- Our reward is now : $70 - $35 = $35

- Our percentage return is : $35/$35 x 100% = **100%**

Even though we have closed our position early, and well before expiry, we have still managed a 100% return. But the more important point is this - we have chosen to close this position. We did not have to accept this risk profile from the start, nor wait until expiry. We are in complete control from start to finish, and this is reflected both in the risk to reward ratio we adopt from the start, and the consequent return during the life of the option. If we choose to wait until expiry, the option settles at our original risk to reward ratio, but we also have the choice to close out early, foregoing further potential profits in exchange for a lower percentage return.

There is a further way we can set and manage our own risk to reward profile, and this is done at the initial open. And here is an example in Fig 5.15. This is where we become our own bookmaker.

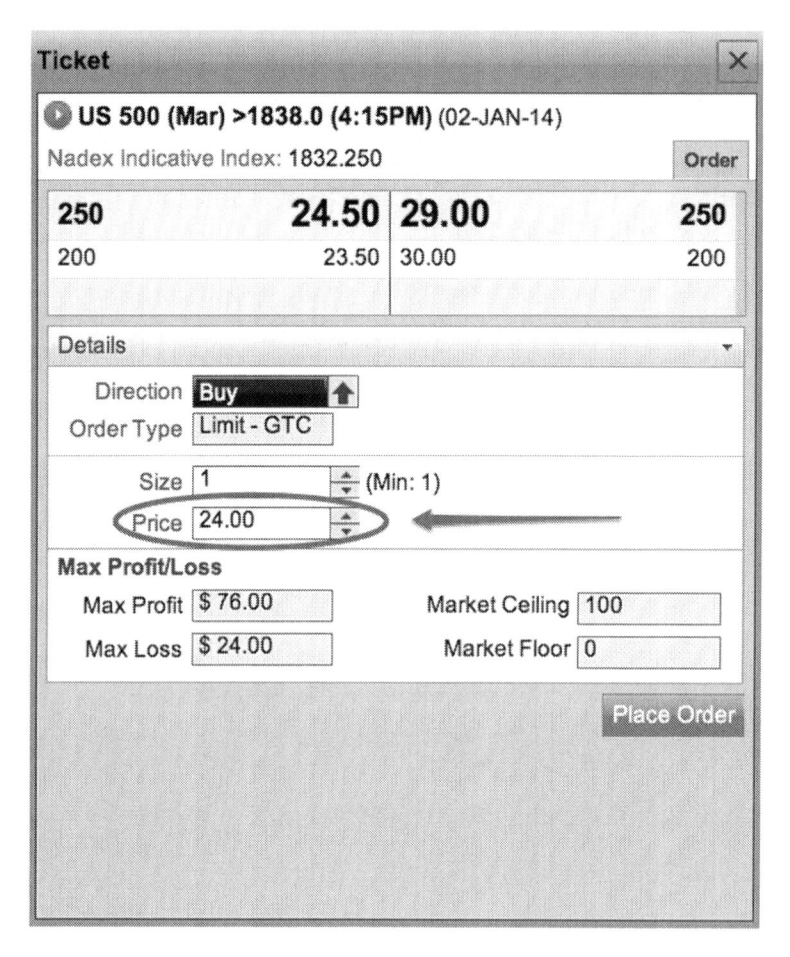

Fig 5.15 - Setting our own odds

Here we have an order ticket from Nadex for the S&P 500 index on a daily contract with an expiry of >1838 on the March contract. The underlying is currently trading at 1832.25. The binary quote is currently 24.50/29.00, so our risk reward profile if we accept this offer price is:

- (($100 - $29)/ $29) x 100 = 244.82%

Suppose we believe the index is due for a short term reversal, but the outlook for the day is still bullish. We can either accept this quote, or place a limit order to be triggered if we are correct. In Fig 5.15 you can see we have entered a quote of $24 rather than the $29 currently being offered. Our risk and reward profile has now changed to:

- (($100 - $24)/$24) x 100 = 316.66%

Next let's look at a sell order where the same approach can be applied. In Fig 5.16, this is an intraday quote on the AUD/JPY with an expiry of less than an hour. The strike price is >172.37 and the underlying spot market is trading at 172.223, and with time eroding fast there is a strong probability the position will close at 0. However, the risk to reward profile is very low. At the current quote of 6.00/12.50, we are being asked to risk $94 to make $6 - perhaps not the most attractive return despite the fact this has a very high probability of closing deep in the money with price value. However, in trading there are never any guarantees, and even though the probabilities are heavily in our favor as a seller of the option, we want to improve them if we can. Once again we use the limit order, and as you can see in Fig 5.16, we have entered a price of 14.00 rather than the quoted bid price of 6.00.

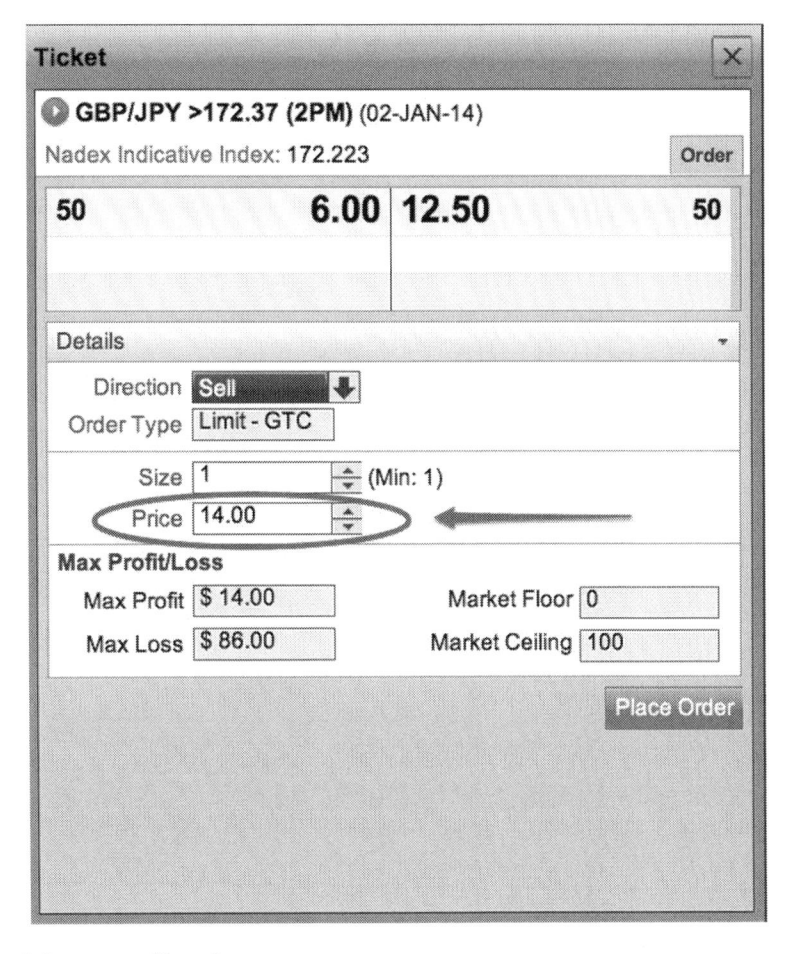

Fig 5.16 - Setting our odds on a sell order

Our risk and reward profile has now changed as follows:

- At bid of 6.00 - 6/94 x 100 = 6.38%
- At bid of 14.00 - 14/86 x 100 = 16.27%

This is perhaps not a percentage return you would want to repeat time and again, but every trading decision is always based on the underlying price action, and if your analysis confirms the probability, this is a perfectly acceptable position to take with the associated risk and reward profile.

If you think of this in horse racing terms you are backing an odds on loser here (your horse is running last with a furlong left to run). In other words to make a small amount of money you have to risk a large amount of money. If you wanted to consider the reverse of this option and buy it, you would be risking a small amount of money to make a large amount. Here you are backing your horse which is currently last, to move to the front and win the race in the final furlong. This is very unlikely to happen, but is always possible. It is a matter of judging the risk, not only in terms of the probabilities and consequent returns, but also in pure monetary risk. In other words the cash amount you are going to win or lose. Backing 'racing certainties' (either as a buy option or a sell option) comes at a price. Sometimes they don't win, and when they don't this is when they become an expensive loss.

In this chapter I have tried to explain the importance of understanding the idea of break-even, and the equally important concepts of risk and reward with the consequent returns. I do understand there is a degree of maths involved in the above, which I hope I have managed to explain clearly and concisely. I also accept the examples are illustrative to portray the essential aspects.

Nevertheless I believe it is imperative you understand these concepts if you are to succeed in the binary world, not least because it will help you to understand the uphill struggle you are likely to face in trading any fixed risk/fixed reward instrument. We can level the playing field a great deal in the next chapter, but nevertheless the odds are stacked against you. This is the world of fixed odds bookmaking which has worked for many years and will continue to do so. The house always wins because the maths is working for them, and not for you.

In the sports betting world it was Betfair who changed the rules of the game, introducing in running betting to allow players to back both winners and losers and to facilitate peer to peer bets. In a sense one could say Nadex is in the same vein. They are offering an instrument which is unique, but more importantly one which changes the game, and in many respects levels the playing field. And none more so than in the risk and reward relationship.

It is perhaps ironic that whilst both the off exchange and on exchange instruments are premised on the fixed risk and reward methodology, they can be so different in the returns offered to the trader. This in turn has a profound impact on the simple break-even relationship. In the fixed odds environment you are hostage to the simple maths of positive and negative trades. While for on exchange binary option this is no longer the case. Ultimately of course, your longer term success will depend on your chart reading skills, and in having an underlying methodology which will help to shift the balance in your favor.

This is what we are going to tackle in the next chapter as we move away from maths and into the world of technical analysis using the only two leading indicators we have to forecast market direction accurately - namely volume and price.

Chapter Six

Shifting The Probabilities Using Volume Price Analysis

Only when the tide goes out do you discover who's been swimming naked

Warren Buffet (1930 -)

If you are approaching binary options with the idea these are simple instruments, with a simple yes or no outcome then please think again as this is not the case. Whilst it may be the marketing message at present, this will undoubtably change as more traders begin to appreciate the complexity that lies beneath.

In many ways an on exchange binary option has a great deal more in common with the options traded on the major exchanges of the CBOE and the CME. Binary options are sophisticated instruments, with sophisticated risk and reward profiles. The proposition may be simple, the instrument itself is not, and as with any form of speculative trading the starting point is always an understanding of the instrument itself.

Once we understand the forces driving them, the next step is to apply our analytical techniques to shift the probabilities in our favor.

If you have never traded an option before, understanding the impact of time is essential. It lies at the heart of any wasting asset such as an option. As I often say in my training rooms and seminars, in trading and investing you are never really wrong, it's all a question of timing. Whilst I may say this a little 'tongue in cheek' there is a grain of truth in this statement. After all, in the world of forex, a currency never goes to zero and will eventually return to revisit a price. This may take days, weeks, months or even years, but if you have enough money and time, a losing position will eventually move into profit. And the key word here is eventually. You have no constraints of time, and this does also assume you have no stop loss in place.

Many traders approaching binaries fail to appreciate the question being asked. It is no longer good enough to be right, we have to be right within a certain period of time. If the first is difficult, the second makes it even harder. And if perhaps you may be having second thoughts about trading binaries, just remember the wasting aspect of time can work for you and against you.

As a binary trader if the probabilities of the proposition are heavily weighted in our favor, time is working for us but against the trader on the other side. The underlying price can do one of three things and we can still remain in profit. The price can do nothing, move higher or lower (provided it does not move back to the strike price) or just move sideways.

On the opposite side, the trader has only one hope of salvation - the price **has** to move, and quickly. As time erodes ever faster, the probability of this occurring diminishes until ultimately the option expires at zero.

Equally of course, we can put time on our side as a binary option seller, as here we are selling on the expectation the event will not happen. Again if the probabilities of the proposition are heavily weighted in our favor, the faster time is eroding towards our target of zero. Understanding the importance of time and using it wisely in binary trading is therefore crucial.

In the remainder of this chapter I want to share with you the tools and techniques to help you forecast future price action with confidence. The approach you are going to learn here is the one I have used for almost twenty years, and have applied to all markets and instruments. It is the approach that has worked for me, and I hope in this introduction to the subject you will begin to understand why. It is one based on sound logic and common sense, and can be applied to any market provided that market reports volume. It is what I refer to as volume price analysis, and I am going to introduce and explain the broad ideas and concepts. I have written a book on the subject called **A Complete Guide To Volume Price Analysis**, which you can find on Amazon, and I do hope that once you have read this chapter you will become a volume believer too.

Volume price analysis is premised on some straightforward principles. The first and perhaps most important, is that both volume and price are leading indicators. They are the only indicators we have with which to forecast future market price action based on what is happening at the live edge of the market. Every other indicator we use is lagged in some way, and is considering past price action to forecast the future. The second point is this - volume and price on their own are just that. One reveals the activity as a volume bar, and the other reveals the price action, again in a bar or candle. On their own this is all they reveal, but put them together in volume price analysis, our charts explode into life. Suddenly, using the analytical power of volume and price, we can forecast where the market is heading next, and even more importantly for binary trading the associated strength of any move.

Volume is the fuel that drives the market. It is the power behind the price action. A market needs volume to move, both higher and lower. If there is weak or low volume the market is not going to move far. Equally, if a market is moving firmly on high and rising volume, we know this is a strong and solid move and likely to have some momentum behind it. All of this can be seem through the simple prism of volume price analysis, which utilizes two indicators freely available on every trading platform.

Finally, every market is manipulated to a greater or lesser extent. Volume reveals the truth behind a market move. It signals valid and false moves. It reveals every aspect of price manipulation, whether in the cash, spot or futures markets. Volume cannot be hidden from view. Understand the power of volume and what it is revealing when considered with the associated price action, and your confidence in forecasting future market direction will grow exponentially.

My starting point is a simple schematic, which explains the underlying philosophy and methodology of volume price analysis.

Trading on three levels

- Time
- Tertiary indicators specialist
- Secondary indicators SMA, Gann, Fibonacci etc
- Primary trading methodology volume price analysis

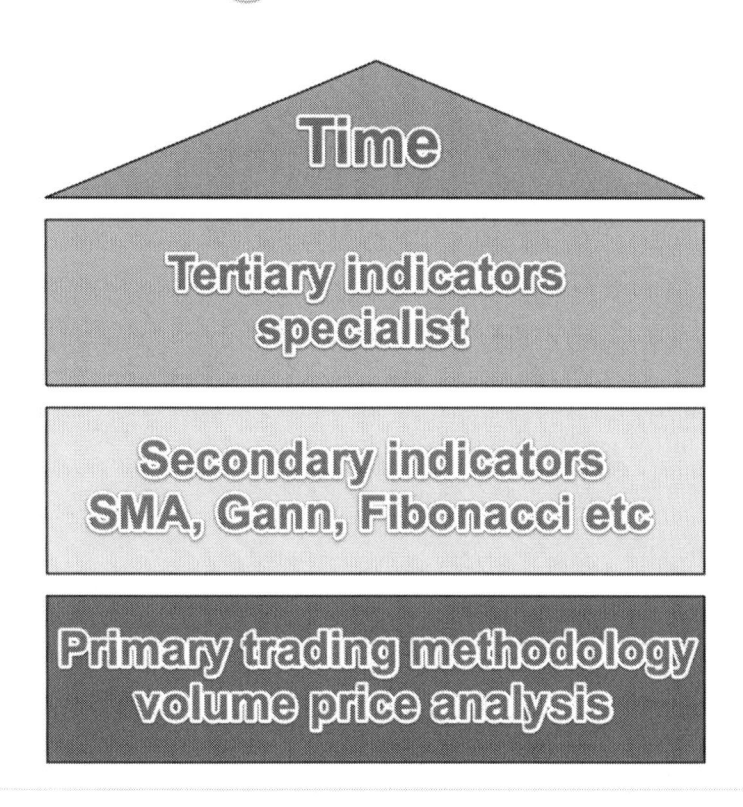

Fig 6.10 - Trading on three levels - the foundations of success

Fig 6.10 encompasses the principle reason most traders struggle with technical analysis. I use the house analogy as I believe it makes the point clearly.

Imagine for a moment our house has no foundations.

We are a new trader, and like virtually every other trader we are approaching the market from a technical perspective, using the freely available indicators on our platform. Indicators such as simple moving averages, MACD, Gann, Fibonacci, and many more. We try them for a while, and perhaps even have some limited success, but then they start to fail us. We have no idea why. Our approach is the same as before, and yet our trusty indicators are no longer working. Eventually we give up and move on, until we come across another indicator or indicator strategy, and start to apply this to our trading. Once again, the same pattern is repeated. This too works for a while, and we believe we have found the holy grail to trading success. But our joy is short lived. Once more our indicators fail us and we start to struggle. We give up and move on, disillusioned but determined to find the answer. If all this sounds familiar to you, the first thing to say is, this is not your fault, because no one has ever explained the reasons why.

And let me make this clear from the start. There is nothing wrong with lagging or, as I call them secondary indicators. And I must stress that by secondary I do not mean second best. The problem is these secondary indicators work well under certain market conditions, and less well in others. In a trending market for example, a moving average crossover strategy will work well. In a congestion phase of price action any crossover strategy will take you out of the market time and time again. This is why the patterns of success and failure are repeated. All of these indicators are based on historic data and attempt to forecast future price action based on history.

Whilst a moving average crossover strategy will work well in a trend, a trend for most traders is not clearly identifiable until it is over. It is very easy with hindsight to look at a chart and draw a trend line or consider two moving averages which confirm the trend.

Other indicators work well in congestion phases when price action is trading in a narrow range. But at the time, does the trader have the tools and techniques to recognize when a market is about to trend, or is in a congestion phase? The answer is no, and perhaps to make things even more confusing the trader sometimes adds several other indicators which only deliver conflicting signals. For confirmation of this we don't have to look very far. Fig 6.11 is a classic example from Fxstreet.com who provide this information to all their visitors and is freely available.

	RSI (14)	STOCH (13,3,3)	MACD (26,12,9)	CCI (14)	MOMENTUM (10)	ROC (10)	WILLIAMS %R (14)	ADX (14)
EURUSD	28.1712 Neutral	0.0000 Buy	0.0022 Sell	-147.4382 Sell	-0.0053 Sell	-0.3882 Sell	-89.8550 Buy	23.3200 Neutral
USDJPY	43.3744 Neutral	0.0000 Sell	0.1097 Neutral	24.3109 Buy	0.1100 Buy	0.1054 Buy	-23.0166 Neutral	17.3807 Neutral
GBPUSD	42.3230 Neutral	0.0000 Neutral	0.0017 Neutral	-65.8962 Sell	-0.0030 Sell	-0.1823 Sell	-67.1643 Neutral	17.3549 Neutral
AUDUSD	60.4185 Neutral	0.0000 Neutral	-0.0020 Neutral	-3.8698 Sell	0.0002 Buy	0.0223 Buy	-48.3868 Neutral	18.3638 Neutral
USDCHF	72.4764 Neutral	0.0000 Sell	-0.0017 Buy	142.9140 Buy	0.0040 Buy	0.4442 Buy	-9.6772 Sell	39.1376 Neutral
USDCAD	36.8822 Neutral	0.0000 Buy	0.0008 Sell	-91.8289 Sell	-0.0045 Sell	-0.4223 Sell	-93.7514 Buy	17.6062 Neutral

Fig 6.11 - The problem with secondary indicators

I'm sure you recognize some of these indicators such as MACD, RSI, CCI and Stochastics. All very well known and yet here on six currencies pairs there is no agreement. Worse still every pair has a range of signals from buy to neutral to sell. Is it any wonder, as traders we end up confused and disillusioned, and constantly searching for an answer to the problem of wanting to know where a market is heading.

The problem in a nutshell is this.

With no primary methodology in place to define the market conditions as they unfold, it is impossible to use secondary indicators with any degree of confidence. However, by using volume price analysis you will know when the market is in a congestion phase as it will be apparent from an analysis of the price action and associated volume. You will know when a market is trending because it will be clearly signaled and confirmed using VPA (Volume Price Analysis). The VPA methodology is one based on using leading indicators, and in using this approach we are able to both interpret market conditions as they unfold, and as a result forecast future price behavior. This is the power of having volume price analysis as the foundation of your approach. Moreover, it also works on several different levels.

First, it is the only way to forecast future price action with any degree of confidence as it uses two leading indicators - the only two we have as traders. Second, it describes the market state in real time at the live edge, and in doing so the most appropriate secondary indicators can then be applied with confidence. In other words, in market conditions for which they were designed. Finally, volume price analysis works in all timeframes and in all markets.

And this is probably the sole reason many traders ultimately fail. They do not have a primary methodology as their foundation. Their house has no foundations. What they are trying to do is trade with secondary indicators in market conditions for which they were never developed. If the market is moving sideways, one group of indicators will work better than others. And conversely in a trending market a second group will come into play.

Finally, at the top of our house we have our tertiary or third level indicators. Our proprietary indicators which you either buy or have built. These are specialists indicators and fulfill precise requirements. For example, a currency strength indicator would be one here - essential in my view for trading forex markets.

At the top of our house we have the roof. The over arching element which applies universally is time. Time is the key component of our binary option, but is also a key element in our trading approach. Time gives us our trading perspective, our horizon if you like. Trading and using indicators in multiple timeframes is a further key element to which we apply volume price analysis.

Volume price analysis is the foundation stone of my trading. I was lucky as my own introduction to trading began with volume and price trading index futures. Since then I have used it in every market and with every instrument. I hope you will to. Therefore, let me begin and explain the essential principles of volume price analysis or VPA for short.

Why Volume?

To answer the question, let me start with some simple analogies, and perhaps the place to begin is by thinking what we mean by 'volume'. Volume to me is the same as activity. Activity is represented by volume and volume by activity. When the sales begin after the Christmas holidays, there is a great deal of activity. Shops are busy as eager shoppers rush to snap up bargains at a discount. This 'buying activity' would be represented both in terms of the sales revenue and profit for the day, but also in the number of transactions. Compare this perhaps to a quiet day in the middle of summer.

Sales are likely to be low, coupled with a low number of transactions on the day. Volume then gives us our yardstick of activity. In the context of a shop, volume is the number of transactions which we can compare one day against another. That volume of activity will be reflected in the sales figures for each of those days, which would tend to correlate relatively closely. In other words, on days when volumes were above average we would expect the sales figures to be above average too, and when volumes were low or below average, we would not be surprised to see our sales decline as well.

Volume then is a very simple comparative tool. It is one of the most basic yardsticks used throughout industry in terms of the volume of units sold. Think of volume in terms of a warehouse for a manufacturer or wholesaler.

It describes in a simple, quick and visual way whether sales of a product are above average, below average or simply average. It tells us how many items have left the warehouse that day, week or month. If we divorce volume from price all it is telling us is precisely that, no more and no less. We could infer higher volumes leaving the warehouse must mean higher sales due to the correlation. However, higher volumes may be as the result of a promotion at a lower price, which could in turn lead to lower revenue and smaller profits.

Volume on its own is just that. It reveals the number of units sold, the activity in the shop, the number of transactions at the tills, but without the associated prices is simply giving us some limited information. Volume only becomes meaningful when associated with price. The classic example from the world of economics is when considering the elasticity relationship of goods and services. Here price and volume go hand in hand and generally fall into one of three categories as shown in Fig 6.12.

A product is considered to be perfectly elastic if any minor change in price, either higher or lower has a huge impact on volume. There are few perfectly elastic examples in terms of products or services. This is the horizontal line on the chart. A perfectly inelastic product is one that continues selling at the same volume, whatever the price. In real life the closest examples here are those services and products which we have to have i.e. gas, electricity and water. The curved dotted line represents the most common type of relationship. As price increases so volumes decreases, and as price decreases so volume increases. This is the traditional relationship in the world of economics, the elasticity curve.

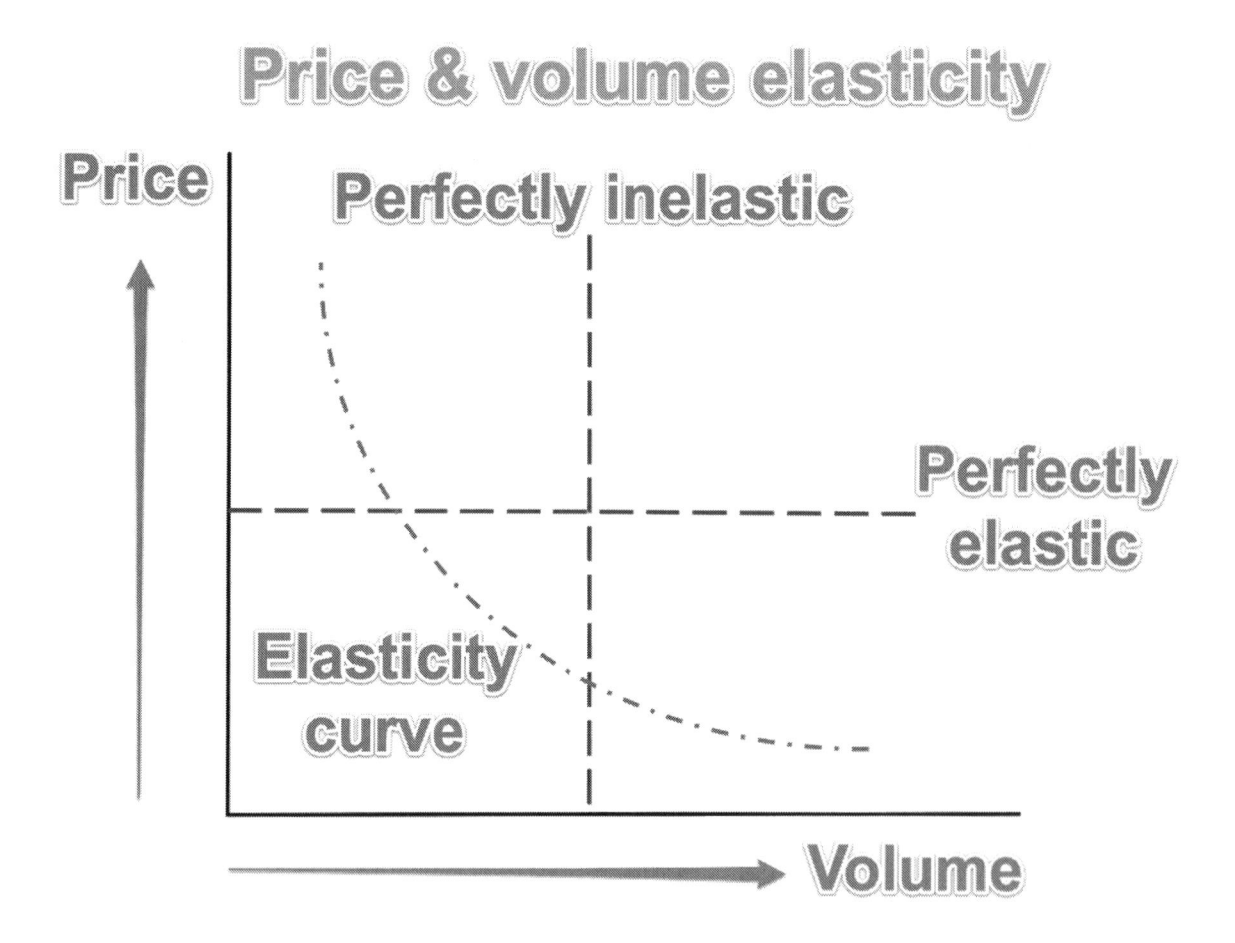

Fig 6.12 - Price and volume elasticity

My point however is this. Considering volume in isolation is meaningless. It is simply a statistic from which little information can be gathered other than in a comparative sense. We can compare this week with last week, or today with yesterday for a sense of whether volumes are higher or lower, but little else. It is only when we begin to analyze volume with price that its immense power is revealed.

Finally, there is one further aspect to volume, and it is this. It is a leading indicator. It reveals activity in real time. If we have a shop we can see the cash register ringing up the sales. A coffee shop will be busy in the morning, then quiet, then busy at lunchtime with queues of people waiting to be served. Volume is activity and activity is volume. It is visible, simple, instant and when combined with price action, is the catalyst for volume price analysis - an explosive combination.

Now let's consider price, the second part of our chemical reaction.

Why Price?

To answer this question, price is once again a leading indicator. For a split second it represents every aspect of risk and market sentiment before moving on again. The price represents all the buying and the selling, the economic news, the balance of fear and greed, risk and reward and of course, consequent returns. Technical analysis and the study of price action is premised on this fact, and is a fundamental tenet of trading. Over the last few years we have seen a strong move towards price action trading or PAT. In principle this sounds a perfect way to analyze market behavior. After all if we believe a price chart displays all this sentiment why not simply trade using price alone?

And to answer the question let me create a visual picture for you with the following analogy. It is not perfect, but I hope it will make the point.

Imagine for a moment you wish to buy an item at auction, but cannot attend on the day of the sale. Instead, you contact the auctioneer and agree to bid by phone. The bidding starts and the price begins to rise. You start to bid, but have no idea whether you are bidding against one person or several people, as you cannot see the auction room. Indeed, you have no idea whether the auctioneer is taking bids 'off the wall' - false bids - to drive the price higher, which does happen. Suppose the price is moving higher quickly. You would assume, possibly correctly, it was being driven higher by the number of bids in the room. But there is no way you could be sure. The only way you could be certain is if you were in the room, and able to see the number of bids. This would give you the confidence to know the price was being bid higher by genuine bids.

Price on its own is just that - a price. The market may be higher or lower than it was a few minutes ago, and indeed the analysis of historical price patterns and candles is an important part of the volume price methodology, but without volume it is weak. Price validates volume and volume validates price. In my humble, opinion trading on price alone is akin to bidding blind. You cannot see whether the price is being driven by genuine bidding or by false bidding, and this is why VPA can be the key to your success.

Every market is driven by insiders, the professional money, the smart money, the big players. Call them what you like. In equity markets it is the market makers, in the futures markets it is the big operators, in the forex market it is the banks in the interbank liquidity pool. These are the major players who manipulate and move the markets using a variety of mechanisms including the media. The constant flow of news, stories, economic statements and releases, gives the insiders the perfect tool. Every opportunity is taken to shake traders out of the market through the manipulation of price, both large and small, and for evidence of this we need look no further than the monthly NFP (Non Farm Payroll) release. This follows a similar pattern month in and month out. The news is released, and the market reacts strongly in one direction. Minutes later, the market reverses and moves in the opposite direction. Why?

The reason given by the media (as they cannot think of anything else) is the market reacted first to the headline numbers. The subsequent reaction is as a result of a more considered view of the detail buried deeper in the report. The real reason is the insiders are using this release as an opportunity to trigger stops.

The insiders of course will always attempt to hide their activities, but there is one indicator that reveals everything, and it is volume. Volume reveals activity. It reveals the involvement of the insiders. If the price is moving on good volume, this is telling us immediately it is a genuine move. The insiders are joining in the move, and so can we - with confidence. Equally, if a market is moving on low or falling volume - what is this telling us? It is revealing to us this market is not going far, since the insiders are not joining the price move.

This is why I am perplexed by traders who embrace price action trading methodology. It is only half the story because in effect they are trading blind. As I say in the introduction to my book, **A Complete Guide To Volume Price Analysis**, there is nothing new in trading. Volume price analysis is not a new concept, it has been around for over 100 years. It was adopted by all the iconic traders of the past, who used tape reading as their primary trading methodology. And what were these great traders looking at when considering the ticker tape? Volume and price. If a stock or commodity price was rising fast, and the volumes on the ticker tape were confirming the move, they would buy. Equally, if the prices were falling fast and volume confirmed the move, they would sell. Imagine saying to a Charles Dow, a Jesse Livermore, a Richard Wyckoff, or a Richard Ney, they could no longer have volume on the tape but just price. How do you think they would have reacted?

If it was good enough for them, it is good enough for me, and I hope you will embrace it too. For trading binary options I believe it is the only approach to take, not only for the reasons outlined above, but also because of the time aspect which is so important. A price move which is confirmed with strong volume, will then reveal the likely extent of any trend. Price action alone will never offer this insight. Combining price and volume will reveal many things such as the strength of any move, its validity, the trick moves by the insiders, and finally market states which are so important when using secondary indicators.

I hope I have made a case for volume price analysis, and the best way to see VPA is in action. And here I want to walk you through some examples and explain the methodology.

The VPA Methodology

The central core of the VPA methodology is the analysis of volume and price, which is then combined with three other powerful elements as follows:

- Candles
- Candle patterns
- Support and resistance

Volume price analysis sits at the heart, with candles, candle patterns and support and resistance then completing the circle.

And to boil VPA down to its core essentials, what we are trying to do in any analysis is to answer two simple questions as follows:

- Is the volume and price in agreement?
- Is the volume and price in disagreement?

From these two questions, we can begin to determine precisely what is happening in the market and see what the insiders themselves are doing. After all, it is the insiders we want to follow all the time. And again these are very simple principles:

- If the insiders are buying we buy
- If the insiders are selling we sell

It sounds straightforward. And it many ways it is, provided you understand, and can interpret the volume price relationship.

There are many ways to represent price action on a chart, but the one I was taught and have used ever since is based on Japanese candlesticks. This was introduced to the West in the early 1990s and has now become the 'de facto' standard on charts. For me, and I suspect for most traders, candlesticks are highly descriptive, but when coupled with volume even more so. There are many good books on the subject of candles and candlestick patterns if you would like to discover more. In this book I am only covering the basics in case they are new to you. So briefly let me explain the basic elements of the candlestick nomenclature.

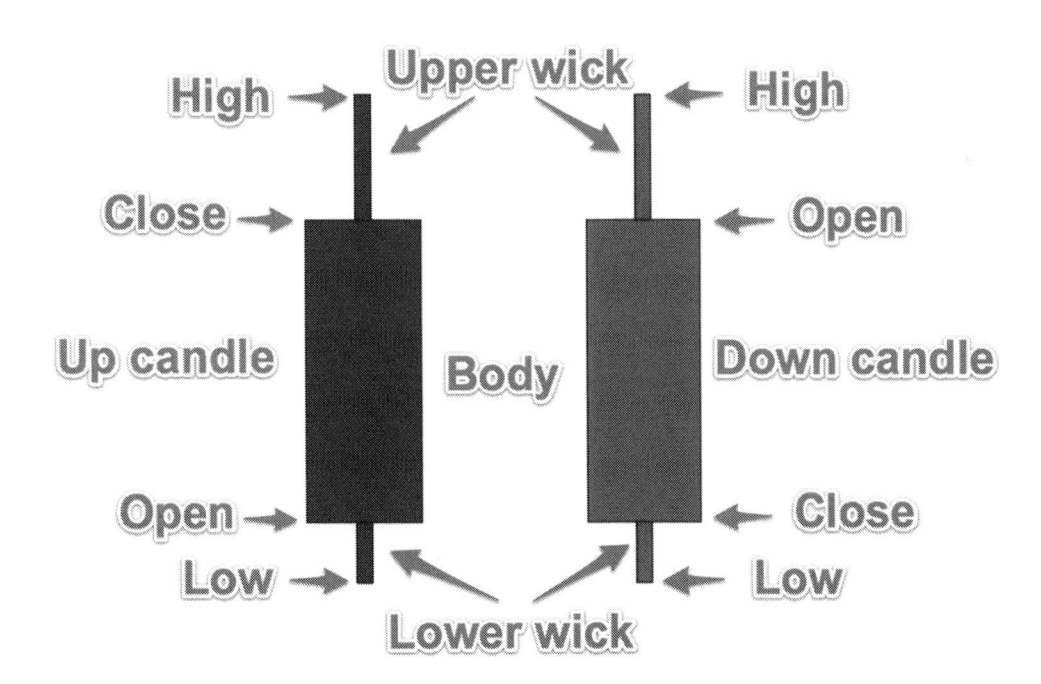

Fig 6.13 - Candlestick terms explained

In Fig 6.13 we have the price action described with two candlesticks which I will refer to as candles in the rest of the book. Here we have two candles, the one on the left is an up candle, and the one on the right is a down candle. In the price action on the left, the price opened, touched a low during the session, then climbed higher to touch a high of the session, before closing at the close price.

The difference between the opening and closing price is then filled, and becomes the 'body' of the candle. To the top and bottom we have 'wicks', hence their name. These are generally referred to as the upper wick and the lower wick.

The candle on the right is a down candle, but the terms used to describe it are the same. In this case the price opened, climbed a little higher, then moved lower to register the low of the session, before recovering and closing off these lows. In this case, the closing price is well below the opening price, thereby creating the down candle. The colors of the candles are a personal choice. Generally up candles are either blue or green, whilst down candles are usually red.

The two most important aspects of the candle are the body and the wicks. The body of the candle represents the 'battle' between the bulls and the bears. This gives an instant visual picture of two aspects of the price action. First, it reveals the 'strength' of the momentum in the candle by the height of the body. A tall body suggests strong momentum, a short body weak momentum or a lack of interest by the market. However, as you will see shortly, this is where volume becomes an important element in confirming this for us. The second component is the wick.

A long wick, either to the top or bottom of a candle is sending a clear signal, simply from the price action alone. If we consider the upper wick to the up candle in Fig 6.13, here the market has been rising, hits the high of the session before closing lower. The height of this wick represents a short term change in sentiment. After all, if the buying momentum had continued, then the candle would have closed at the high of the session. It hasn't and has closed off the high. The wick is therefore signaling some short term selling pressure in the market. In other words, the buyers have been unable to maintain the upwards price move, as selling pressure has come it at this level. Moving to the lower wick this is relatively small, confirming an attempt to move lower has been overcome with buying pressure which has taken the market higher.

The same principle applies to the down candle on the right. The upper wick here was an attempt to rise, but the sellers were clearly in control of the market sending it lower. The lower wick is relatively small, suggesting some weak buying and taking the price marginally higher.

I cannot stress too strongly the significance of understanding what the wick and body are revealing from the price action, which is then brought to life with volume. The body of the candle is revealing price momentum, the wicks are revealing possible changes in sentiment, either minor or major depending on the shape of the candle.

Now let me touch on the two most important candles in volume price analysis, namely the hammer and the shooting star. These candles are descriptive in their own right, but when combined with volume will signal both major and minor reversals in trend depending on the strength of volume associated with each. They are the 'premier' candles and in many ways, if you simply focused on these two candles and no others, they would set you well on the road to success. Like all candles they appear in all timeframes and in all markets. So let's take a look at both, before bringing volume into our analysis.

Two premier candles

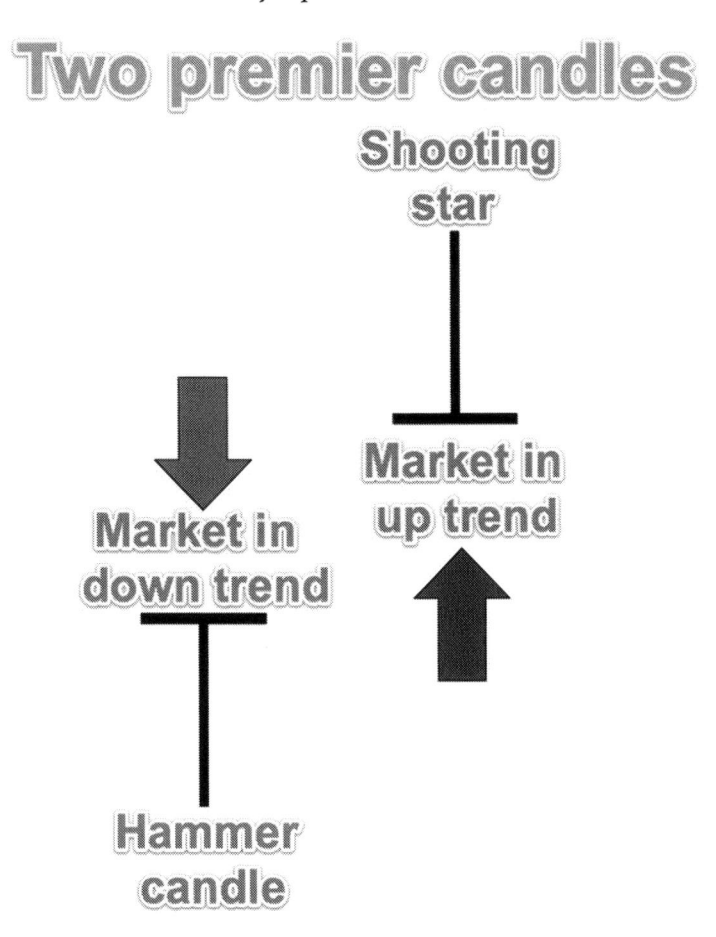

Fig 6.14 - The hammer and the shooting star candles

On the left in Fig 6.14 is the hammer candle, and on the right is the shooting star. The hammer candle appears after the market has been in a downtrend, so called as it is 'hammering out' a bottom. It is the first possible signal of a market reversal from this price level. The candle should have a narrow body and a deep lower wick, and this is what gives the candle its power. In the session of this candle, the market has opened, then fallen sharply only to reverse at some point to close back near or at the opening price. The selling pressure that was evident for part of the session has been completely absorbed as buyers have come into the market, overwhelmed the sellers, and 'bought the market'.

You can think of this price action as an old fashioned tug of war. Two teams are pulling on the rope, and initially one team is stronger pulling the rope further and further to one side. Then gradually they start to tire, and the opposing team finds the strength to pull them all the way back to the centerline again, recovering all the lost ground. This is what is happening here in terms of the price action. It is the first sign of a potential reversal in trend from bearish to bullish, and therefore sending a clear signal to 'pay attention'.

The shooting star is the hammer in reverse, with the same principles applying, only in this case it is the buyers who are overwhelmed, as they struggle to take the market higher. The sellers come in at this price level and take the market back to the open. Again, the shooting star is sending a strong signal of a potential reversal, this time from bullish to bearish. With both these candles we then apply volume price analysis in order to validate these signals. The insiders love playing tricks trapping traders into weak positions, and using these price moves is a classic one. If the insiders are buying on a hammer candle we can see it in the associated volume, and should consider buying with them. Equally, if the insiders are selling on a shooting star candle, again we will see it and we should be thinking about selling too.

What we are constantly looking for when applying volume price analysis, is either to confirm that volume and price are in agreement, or they are in disagreement. From there we are able to interpret what the insiders are doing and to follow them accordingly. Here are a couple of examples to demonstrate this.

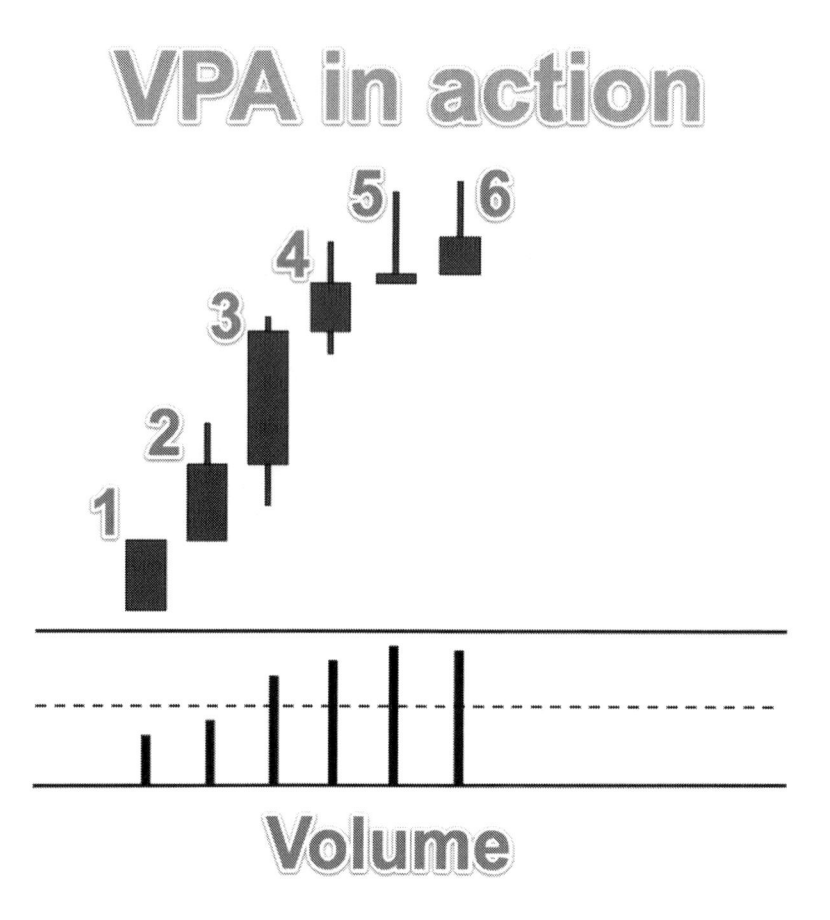

Fig 6.15 - VPA in action in a market moving higher

In Fig 6.15 we have a market which is moving higher from candles 1 to 6, and beneath each candle is the associated volume. The horizontal dotted line is simply to show the average volume for the session. It is not essential, and as you will see from the following explanation of the volume and associated price, when comparing volume we are always considering what has gone before and assessing whether volume is high, medium or low as a result.

At this point let me introduce Richard Wyckoff - one of the founding fathers of volume price analysis. Wyckoff enshrined this relationship in three laws as follows:

- The law of supply and demand
- The law of cause and effect
- The law of effort and result

The first law maintains that when demand is greater than supply prices will rise to meet this demand, and conversely when supply is greater then demand, prices will fall with this 'over supply' being absorbed. All of this is reflected in the associated volume.

The second law states that in order to have an effect you must first have a cause, and furthermore the effect will be in direct proportion to the cause. In other words, a small amount of volume activity will only result in a small amount of price action. This law is applied to a number of price bars, and will dictate the extent of any subsequent trend. If the cause is large then the effect will be large as well. If the cause is small the effect will also be small.

The simplest analogy here is of a wave at sea. A large wave hitting a vessel will see the ship roll violently, whereas a small wave would have little or no effect.

Wyckoff's third law is similar to Newton's third law of physics. Every action must have an equal and opposite reaction. In other words, the price action on the chart must reflect the volume action below. The two should always be in harmony with one another, with the effort (volume) seen as the result (consequent price action). This is where, as Wyckoff taught, we start to analyse each price bar using a 'forensic approach' to discover whether this law has been maintained. If it has, the market is behaving as it should, and we can continue our analysis on the following bar. If not, and there is an anomaly, we need to discover why, and just like a crime scene investigator establish the reasons.

So let's begin our forensic analysis of Fig. 6.15.

The first candle in the sequence forms and is a narrow spread up candle. The associated volume is below average which is what we expect to see. In this case, the price action is narrow so the volume should not be high. Volume is validating price and price is validating volume. The two are in agreement, and we can expect to see prices move higher.

Candle 2 then forms. The price spread here is a little wider, and the candle has a small wick to the upside, but it is of little concern at present. What about the volume? Is it in agreement? And the answer here is yes. The first step here is to compare the price action between candle 1 and candle 2. The price spread on candle 2 is a little wider than on candle 1, so we should expect a taller volume bar, which is what we see. As with the first candle the law of effort and result is being met, and this tells us the insiders are joining this move higher, and therefore we can join in with confidence.

The market continues higher and candle 3 is formed. This closes as a wide spread up candle. Our focus is now on the price. The spread of candle 3 is wider than candle 2. If we follow Wyckoff's third rule we should expect to see much higher volume on this candle than on the preceding one. After all, as we can see the price action on candle 3 is approximately twice that of candle 2, so we should expect to see this relationship represented in the volume bars, which is precisely what we have here. The volume associated with candle 3 is significantly higher than that associated with candle 2, so once again all is in agreement. More importantly, we now have a short term yardstick with which to judge volume as we move forward. Once again, all is in order. The insiders are continuing to buy as the market moves higher.

And now we come to candle 4 and taking the price action first. Here we have a narrow spread candle with small wicks to the top and bottom. Nothing unusual. These occur frequently in all timeframes. But take a look at the associated volume. What do we see here? The first thing that strikes us is the volume which is very high, and well above average. Second, when we compare the volume with the previous, it is higher. This seems very odd. After all, if the volume on candle 3 resulted in a candle with a wide body, why has even higher volume (more effort) resulted in a very narrow bodied candle (result)?

What we are seeing here is a clear anomaly between volume and price. In volume price analysis we are only ever looking for two things. Either agreement or disagreement. If there is agreement, then Wyckoff's third law is being maintained. The effort (volume) is in agreement with the result (price action). If there is disagreement, this is an anomaly and sending us a clear and unequivocal signal something is wrong, and we therefore need to pay attention.

In this case, effort and result are in disagreement. We know from the previous candle this level of volume should have resulted in a similar price spread. It has not, and is now signaling an anomaly. Clearly if there is a great deal of effort with little result the market is starting to struggle at this price level. If this were not the case, the price action in candle 4 would have been tall, it is not, it is short. The market is now signaling potential weakness and a possible pause or reversal.

The insiders are already aware of this weakness, and indeed would almost certainly have started to sell out at this level, conscious of the weakness ahead, and selling into any continued buying demand. What tends to happen here is that nervous traders, who have missed the initial move higher, are now regretting not taking a position earlier. They jump into the market fearing they are about to miss out on a further leg up in the move higher. The insiders happily sell to these willing buyers. But how do we know the insiders are selling? Because if the insiders were buying, the market would be moving much higher. It isn't, so we can deduce most of the volume here is selling volume for two reasons.

First it is high, and therefore likely to be the insiders moving in large volume. Second we are at the top of a small bullish trend. The insiders will always sell at the top of a bullish trend and always buy at the bottom of a bearish trend. Retail traders do the opposite. They sell at the bottom and buy at the top. This is why volume price analysis is so powerful. It makes you think like an insider. No longer do you have to guess when the insiders are buying or selling - you see it all reported in one simple indicator - volume. When this is then compared to the price action, this reveals when and where they are starting to buy and sell, which ultimately develops into a buying or selling climax for a major reversal.

Candle 5 is even more descriptive. Now the selling by the insiders is in full flow.

Candle 5 is one of our premier candles, a shooting star. The price action alone is telling us this market is weak. But when we add volume, suddenly we have the complete picture. Now we can actually '*see*' the selling as the insiders are desperate to hold the market at this level, selling into any remaining buying demand from the retail traders. This is the price action which creates the classic shooting star candle. It is our tug of war reflected in the price action of the candle. The associated volume is simply confirming there is a huge amount of volume here, which in turn is sending a clear signal this is the insiders selling into a very weak market. If this were not selling by the insiders the candle would have closed with a tall body. It has not and confirms this weakness.

From this we can deduce two things. First, we can expect the market to reverse in the short to medium term. Second, given the amount of selling activity the reversal is likely to be significant. This reflects Wyckoff's second law, the law of cause and effect. Here the cause is large (insider volumes over two or three candles) so we can expect to see a large effect as a result (a significant reversal). In this case, this is a very simple example which I have condensed, but in the real world this phase of price action could last for several candles or more. This is all explained in more detail in **A Complete Guide To Volume Price Analysis**, but the principles outlined here are the same.

At this point, if we had taken a long position in the market we would be considering closing this out and taking any profits off the table. Alternatively, if we were square the market we would now be paying attention, and looking for the opportunity to take a short position given we now have two very strong signals this market is very weak with the insiders also exiting fast.

Finally candle 6 arrives and once again it is a similar picture, confirming the weakness already signaled on candles 4 and 5. The price action is narrow with a deep upper wick. The associated volume is extremely high, slightly less than under our shooting star candle, but it is now telling us loud and clear the market is weak. Here we have three candles, 4, 5 and 6, where the price action has failed to make any meaningful advance higher. The high of candle 6 is only marginally above that of candle 5, which is slightly above candle 4. And yet these three candles are associated with huge volume bars. All three are anomalies. Price and volume are in disagreement. Had the price action followed through from candle 3 the market would have continued rising, and rising quickly. It has not. It has stalled at this price level, and given the associated volume we can see this weakness clearly on our chart. This is the power of volume price analysis. It brings the price action to life. It describes precisely what the insiders are doing, and when. In this case, they will have seen the initial weakness and so start the selling process. The question now is not *if*, but **when** will this market reverse.

Finally, a further tenet of our VPA methodology is the analysis of price in terms of support and resistance, and although we only have a very simple example here, the 'flattening' price action of the highs of candles 4, 5 and 6, coupled with the deep upper wicks to each, would be telling us the same story.

To take a further example only this time in a market that is falling. However, before we do, let me explain a concept new VPA traders often find difficult, and it is this. Intuitively we can all understand it takes effort for something to rise, primarily because we are all familiar with gravity. Throwing a ball in the air takes effort, and the amount of effort we apply is reflected in how far the ball travels - how high it travels. Gravity then brings it back down to earth.

In the trading world it is different. A market requires effort to rise, but it **also** needs effort to fall. If a market is falling fast the volumes will be high and rising, just as in a market which is rising fast. This is Wyckoff's second law applied to a falling market. In other words effort and result. Whether the market is rising or falling, effort and result will signal if volume and price are in agreement, or out of agreement. The rules are the same whether the market is rising or falling. Gravity plays no part.

More VPA in action

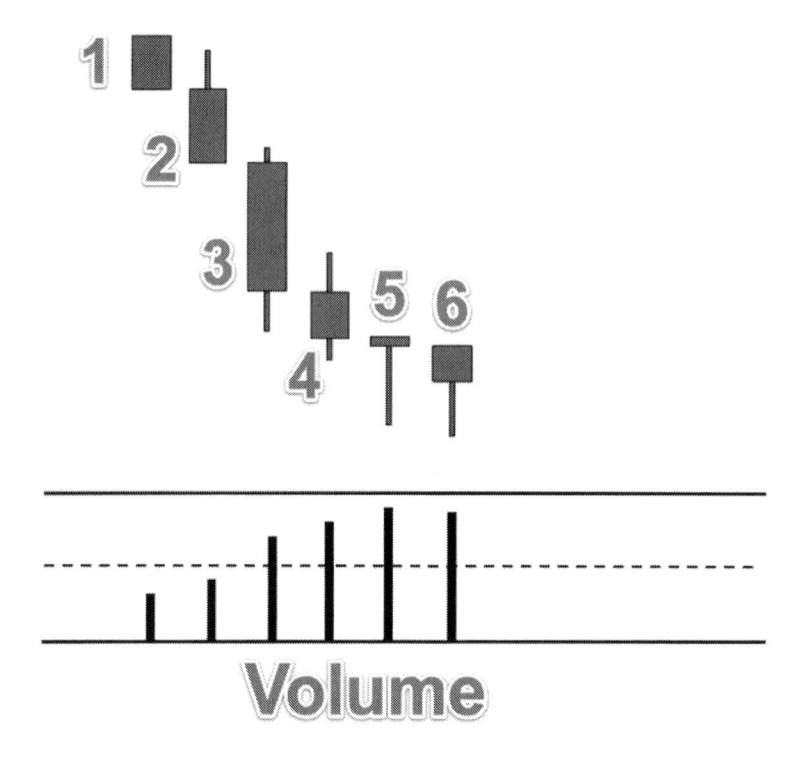

Fig 6.16 - VPA in action in a market moving lower

The process of analysis is exactly the same as in our previous example, and you can think of this as starting at the micro level, and then gradually moving to the macro level. It is rather like zooming out with a camera lens. We start focusing on one candle and one volume bar. We then move further out to focus on groups of candles to compare their respective volume and price action, before finally we look at the big picture. This will confirm if we are in an up trend, down trend or congestion phase. In other words we 'frame' the whole volume price relationship in the context of where we are in the trading journey for the market. As you will see shortly, we then bring in other techniques and tools to help us as part of the volume price methodology.

In Fig 6.16, once again candle 1 is in agreement with the volume, which is below average and as expected. There is no anomaly here. Candle 2 then closes with a slightly wider spread, and higher volume. Again all is in agreement. But now the market is starting to fall fast, and in candle 3 we close with a tall body to the candle. Volume is also high and confirming the price action. The selling is in full flow as the market plunges lower. Then in candle 4 we see our first anomaly. The price action and volume are no longer in agreement. Here we have a short body on the candle, but the volume is higher than on the previous bar. Selling pressure is starting to be absorbed as buyers come into the market at this level. The buyers are primarily the insiders as the volume is very high, and they are now buying as the retail traders sell. The retail traders are expecting a further move lower and do not wish to miss out on some 'easy profits'.

But how do we know the insiders are buying? If this had been primarily selling volume, the market would have closed with a very wide spread down candle, and certainly wider than candle 3. It has not. The falling price has been halted. Panic selling is now happily being absorbed by the insiders, and this is the first signal the current down trend is potentially coming to an end. Candle 5 gives us an even stronger signal and confirms candle 4.

Here we have ultra high volume associated with a hammer candle. Another of our 'premier' candles. The price action alone is telling us there is potential buying at this level. The volume is confirming this loud and clear, and also telling us the insiders are buying given the associated volume, which is extreme.

Candle 6 confirms this further with a further anomaly. A narrow body on the price action, but high volume. This is further buying by the insiders, as the retail traders continue selling on the expectation of a further move lower. The insiders however have other ideas.

The market here is starting to bottom out, but this may take some time, particularly if it has been a dramatic fall. As I always try to explain a market always has momentum, whether in an up trend or a down trend. The analogy I always use is that of an oil tanker. If the engines are stopped the oil tanker would continue for several miles under its own momentum. The market is the same. It will rarely reverse on one candle. What generally happens is the market trends strongly, and in this case downwards, and the insiders move in.

The insiders cannot hope to absorb all the selling pressure in one candle. It takes several attempts and at this stage the market is likely to consolidate and trade in a relatively narrow range. It's what I refer to as the 'mopping up' operation. It is much like mopping up water with a sponge. It takes two or three passes to dry any spill. The same applies at the top of an uptrend. The insiders are selling into waves of buying from the retail traders, and this up and down price action which then becomes a congestion phase, is simply the insiders mopping up the last of the buyers.

I hope in the above examples I have managed to convince you of the power of volume price analysis. It is a relatively simple concept developed over 100 years ago. It helped many of the iconic traders of the past to build their fortunes, using nothing more than the ticker tape, which displayed just two indicators. Price and volume. For us the glue that binds price and volume together is the candle, which then provides the graphical tool for our analysis.

In the context of binary options, timing is everything. And whilst we may see an initial signal of a reversal this may take time to develop fully. This is one of the many reasons why you need to have time on your side, and also consider longer term options. Timing a decision within a one hour timeframe is hard. Timing it within a few hours or daily is much easier.

To round off this introduction to volume price analysis, there are two other techniques which we apply to complement this approach. The first of these is in analyzing candle patterns, and the second is in considering support and resistance areas, all based around a multi timeframe approach.

Once again these are explained in greater detail in **A Complete Guide To Volume Price Analysis**.

Support and resistance is a pillar of technical analysis, and also a key element of volume price analysis. First, congestion phases of price action, which create these levels, are the areas in which trends are born and from where they develop. Second, using volume price analysis we can see these phases of price action building in real time through the prism of volume and price. And perhaps most importantly, once we see a breakout from these ranges, providing the volume is confirming the move, this presents excellent trading opportunities as a result.

From an historical perspective these regions provide targets at which price action is likely to find support or resistance, depending on the direction the market is approaching these levels. For example, suppose we are in an up trend. Ahead, we can see a deep area of price congestion, and at the same time our volume price analysis is signaling a possible reversal at this level. Clearly, we would be wise to take notice of this area of possible resistance and factor this in to our analysis. Equally, the same applies to a falling market. Here we may have already identified buying in the market, but if this is also given further weight by the presence of a potential region of price support this is then an additional powerful signal.

However, the irony of support and resistance is that it is in sharp contrast to VPA itself. Volume price analysis focuses on the 'leading' aspects of price and volume behaviour, giving us unique tools with which to analyse where the market is heading next. Support and resistance does this in a different way entirely, by focusing on what has gone before. The history of price behaviour, the 'lagging' aspects of price behaviour if you like.

Despite this paradox, it is the combination of the two which gives us a perspective on where the market is in terms of its overall journey. It tells us where the market might pause, breakout, or reverse, both now and in the future. These are all important markers for the entry, management and exit of trading positions.

To complete the VPA methodology we have candle patterns, another integral part of chart reading. Candle patterns are not specific to VPA, but simply a further analytical technique which is useful on its own, but takes on immense power when combined with VPA. Once again, these are based on the historic patterns created on our price charts. These include consolidation patterns such as rising and falling triangles, pennants and flags, and of course triple tops and triple bottoms. The key as always is volume. If these patterns are being created, and we see a breakout or move away combined with strong volume, this gives our analysis added weight, and we can take a position in the market with confidence.

And that in a nutshell is what VPA is all about. It will give you the confidence to take a position, based on sound logic and common sense. In addition, there is also one huge benefit that VPA bestows on you as a trader. Whenever we are analysing a chart in this way, it is preventing us from making an emotional decision. VPA stops us reacting emotionally once we have a position in the market. VPA forces the brain into analytical mode, and allows us to 'step back' from the market and make decisions based on logic and not emotion. This is a huge benefit which few traders ever appreciate, and yet it is one of the many strengths of this methodology and approach.

We will come back to this later in the book once we start to consider some examples and strategies.

Moreover, VPA is powerful when used on a simple chart, but when combined with multiple timeframes, it will take your trading to a new level.

Furthermore, in trading binary options, I believe this is the only approach that will produce consistent results for you and I hope you can appreciate why. With this primary methodology in place you can bolt on whatever secondary and tertiary indicators you wish. The difference is you are building your trading method on solid foundations, and not trying to trade using secondary indicators alone, which only work under some conditions and not others. Now you have a foundation methodology which not only works in all markets, but also in all timeframes and under all market conditions. In addition, it will also reveal those market conditions in all timeframes.

I hope this brief introduction has convinced you of the power of volume price analysis, or at least persuaded you to discover more for yourself. In the next chapter we are going to explore the world of volatility, a key element of every options market including binary options.

Chapter Seven

Volatility Explained

Volatility is a symptom that people have no idea of the underlying value

Jeremy Grantham (1938 -)

In the world of options trading there are two prime concepts which all traders have to embrace in order to succeed. The first of these is time. The second is volatility. No book on options, whether binary options or exchange traded options, would be complete without a chapter explaining volatility. It is time and volatility which together underpin the options instrument, and its associated reaction to the underlying market.

As we have already seen, time is a critical element in the options world. It is a wasting asset, and when considering any option is a prime factor in the decision making process. The wasting aspect of time can work both for us and against us. If the binary option is deep in the money then it's working for us. Alternatively, if a binary option is deep out of the money, then it is working against us, and the closer we move to the expiry of the option, the faster the time element erodes. Time then has two sides - good and not so good, and the same applies to volatility. There are times, as an options trader, where volatility is very welcome, but there are others where volatility is the last thing we want to see.

Before we explore what we mean by the word volatility, let me just plant this image in your mind, which I hope will help to provide a visual picture of the relationship between price, time and volatility. And the simplest analogy I can think of, is of a see-saw as shown in Fig 7.10.

Time, volatility & price

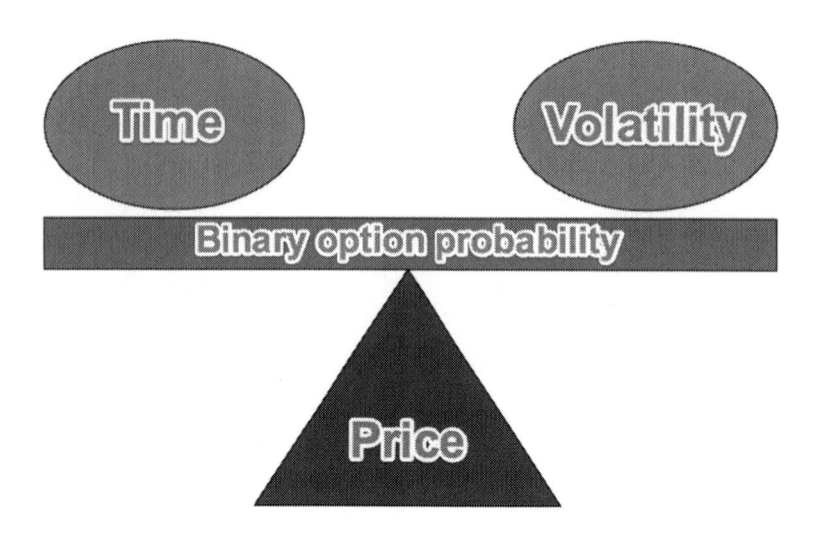

Fig 7.10 - Time, volatility and price for binary options

It is this simple triumvirate of time, volatility and price which lies at the heart of binary options and the associated probabilities which are then quoted on the order ticket. Of these, volatility is perhaps the most complex to understand, and least understood. However, my purpose here is not to delve deeply into the world of the Black Scholes options pricing model - a quick Google search will deliver all the information you could possibly want on the subject, and from a range of learned scholars. My objective in this chapter is to try to deliver something which is a little more practical, perhaps more straightforward, and which does not require a degree in higher level mathematics. In other words, an understanding of volatility in simple terms which can be applied easily, quickly and perhaps, more importantly, practically to help you in assessing risk when trading binary options. Binary options by definition are short term instruments, and whilst weekly vanilla options are a relatively new addition to the trading world, historically longer term timeframes have been the norm. And whilst some would disagree, volatility and risk in my opinion go hand in hand. We'll explore this in more detail throughout this chapter.

But let's start by trying to arrive at a simple definition of volatility, which is perhaps the most overused, misused and abused word in the trading world. And this is where the problems begin.

Volatility is one of those concepts and terms which is immensely difficult to pin down. It is a word which is used in many different fields and interpreted in many different ways. We talk of people being volatile, having an explosive temper - of chemicals being volatile, and of governments and countries being volatile, and perhaps herein lies the core principle of volatility. Volatility describes movements, actions or events which are considered to be sudden, and by implication, these actions and events are 'extreme' and so bring distance into the volatile equation. The two principles of volatility, purely from a common sense approach, would therefore suggest a sudden extreme movement could describe the word volatile. Not very scientific perhaps, but a workable description.

And here, it is important to state what volatile does not describe when applied to the trading lexicon, and that's direction. Volatility is a non directional measure. It says nothing about the direction of any price move either higher or lower, and in fact the market may simply move sideways in a whipsaw phase.

To summarize, volatility in a simple and common sense way, is simply a statement the market has seen sudden and extreme movements in price. It is bringing together the elements of time and price on our see-saw as shown in Fig. 7.10. As volatility increases, time and price are compressed and the easiest way to think of this is to consider a market, a stock index for example, such as the Dow Jones or the S&P 500. Suppose the Dow Jones moved an average of 100 points per day and over a week perhaps an average of 350 points higher or lower. Now imagine the index moved 350 points in one day. A week of price action has been compressed into a single day.

Time and price have been compressed and this, in a sense, is really what volatility is all about. It is the constant compression and expansion of time and price that leads to the constant changes in volatility in the market. You can think of this like an old fashioned bellows, sucking air in slowly, before driving it out fast to fan the flames of the fire.

The question now is how do we measure volatility in a more scientific or mathematical way, and more importantly, how can we then use this concept to help us succeed in trading options. This is where opinions on the approach to applying and interpreting volatility differ, and differ wildly, with two notable exceptions - and that is the interpretation and application of implied and historic volatility, which we'll look at shortly.

If the above 'definition' of volatility helps to give some context of the term, it is of little use without any practical application to the price chart, and this is where we step into the world of statistics and maths to help provide the framework of reference.

There are generally four principle mathematical concepts you will come across when considering the word volatility as it relates to trading, and these are:

- Standard deviation
- Variance
- Mean
- Average True Range

Each has their place in the trading lexicon and each has something to offer, although of the above, variance is perhaps the most complex and the most difficult to create visually. Let's take a look at these one by one, before moving to consider how to use them in a practical way on the price chart to forecast volatility, either high or low.

Standard Deviation, Variance & Mean

If we start with standard deviation this is one of the most widely used statistical measures of volatility, and is one that forms the basis of several trading indicators as well as the interpretation of volatility. You can think of standard deviation as the statistical distribution of prices. The spread of prices from what could be considered the norm or normal distribution. This raises one of the fundamental issues when considering volatility and statistics. Put simply it is this - does any market or instrument follow mathematical principles based on statistics? After all, if this were true, many of the mathematical models would have made their creators immensely wealthy, but the reality would suggest otherwise. I do not propose to put the case for alternatives as it is not appropriate in a book of this type, but merely highlight it so you are aware of the possible limitations.

Standard deviation is not perfect, but at least gives us a basis on which to measure and view volatility in a practical way. Indeed, volatility denoted in this way is often referred to as statistical volatility for that reason. The problem, of course is that whilst this methodology is perfectly acceptable from a mathematical perspective where data is stationary, in the financial markets this is far from the case as prices are fluid. The price of a stock or index will move as time passes, and to apply standard deviation in the context of static analysis of historic price action has little relevancy. Where it does become far more useful is in the application of indicators, and other methodologies where the context of time is applied.

If we begin by considering a data set in broad terms, any such set will tend to fall into the pattern of normal distribution, and what is generally referred to as the bell curve. All this means is most of the data set falls in a relatively narrow range with the extremes of data thinly populated. This is intuitive in many ways, and the most commonly used examples here are the height of people, tolerances of manufactured items, errors in measurements and exam results. If we take the height of people, instinctively we know there will be a few very short people, a few very tall people, but most will be of 'average' height. The result of such a survey would look something like Fig 7.11

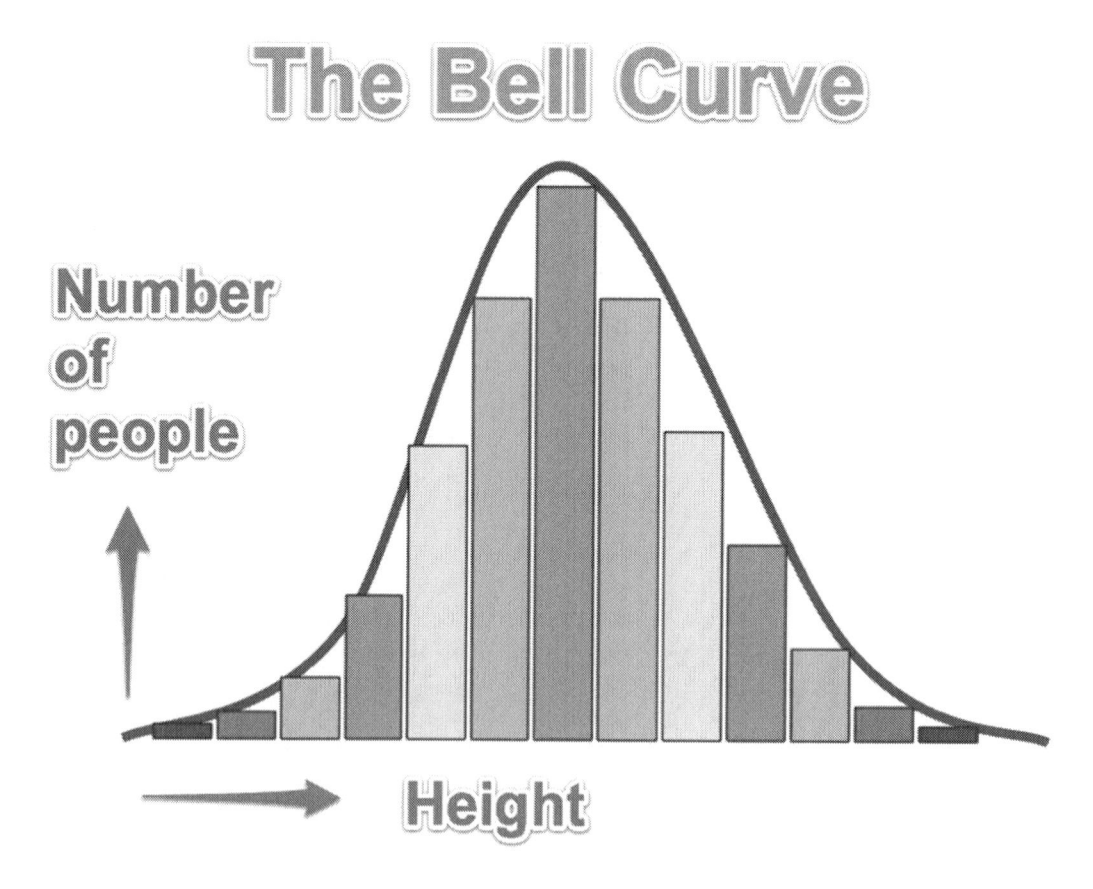

Fig 7.11 - The bell curve

This is the typical arrangement of data we would expect to see. On the horizontal axis is the height, rising from short to tall, whilst the vertical axis is the number of people sampled at each height. The majority of people are of average height and are centered in the middle, thereby creating the mean which is the peak of the bell curve. The distribution then falls away slowly to the extremes where we have those who are unusually short or unusually tall - very low numbers. This creates the classic bell shape, and what is called normal distribution. This implies a mean at the centre point, an even split of data, and symmetry about the mean. Whilst this is interesting graphically, it offers no measure of 'distribution' from the mean, and this is where standard deviation steps in to provide a solution and a yardstick by which to frame and measure volatility.

Let's take a very simple example as I don't want to get bogged down in the maths. I only want to outline the concepts of standard deviation, and how it is applied to provide a measure of volatility.

If we take the following seven numbers, an imaginary set of data, and then calculate the standard deviation, it would be as follows:

- 4, 6, 8, 2, 12, 10, 14 (count = 7)
- Sum = 56
- Mean = sum/count = 8
- Take each number, subtract the mean and square the result which gives the following:
- (4-8) x (4-8) = 16
- (6-8) x (6-8) = 4
- (8-8) x (8-8) = 0
- (2-8) x (2-8) = 36
- (12-8) x (12-8) = 16
- (10-8) x (10-8) = 4
- (14-8) x (14-8) = 36
- Then we sum all the differences squared from the above as follows :
- 16 + 4 + 0 + 36 + 16 + 4 + 36 = 112
- Divide this by the count = 112/7 = 16 - this is called the variance
- Finally take the square root of 16 = 4

In this example the standard deviation is 4. What does this tell us? It is saying if the mean of this set of numbers is 8, the range of one standard deviation will extend from 4 (4 below 8) up to 12 (4 above 8). You can think of standard deviation as a measure of how far the numbers in the data set are spread out from the mean. In other words what is 'normal' and what is 'abnormal'.

Within the normal distribution bell curve, typically one standard deviation will encompass 68% of all the values in the data set, whilst 2 standard deviations will encompass approximately 95%, with 3 standard deviations taking in 99.7% - almost every value in the data set. Fig 7.12 shows how standard deviation works when applied to the bell curve we saw earlier.

Standard deviation

Mean

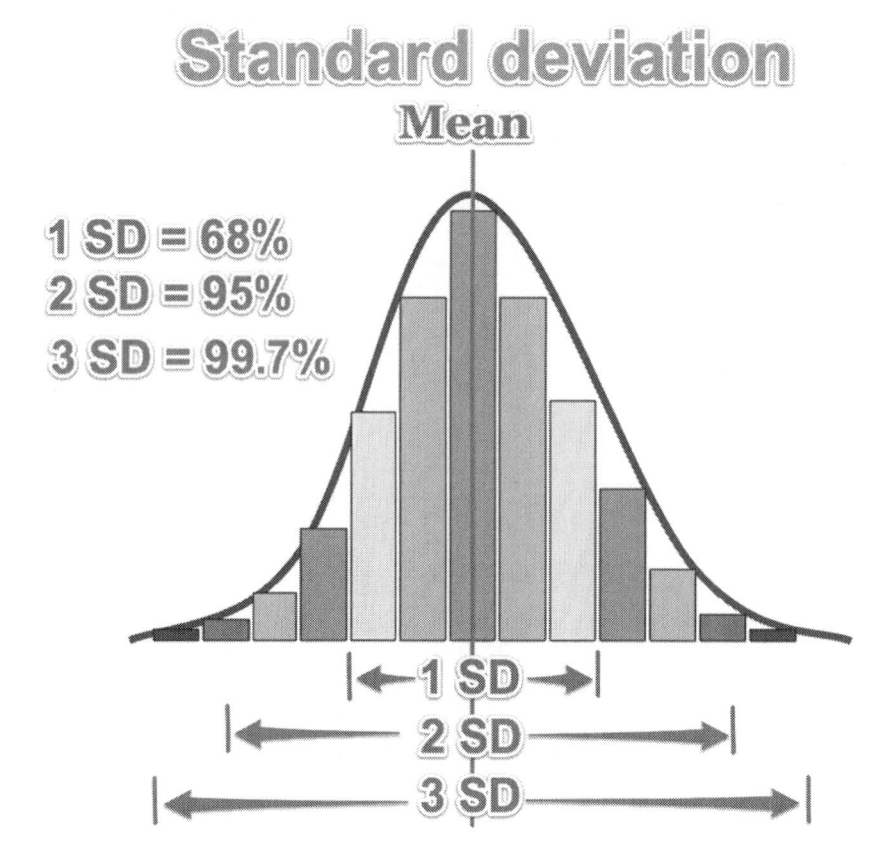

1 SD = 68%
2 SD = 95%
3 SD = 99.7%

Fig 7.12 - Standard deviation applied to the bell curve

As you can see from Fig 7.12, standard deviation now gives us a measure of what is normal or abnormal which can then be applied in various ways to give us a yardstick to judge whether a market or instrument is volatile, and if so the degree of this volatility.

Average True Range (ATR)

Average true range (ATR) is a further attempt to define and display volatility in a more meaningful way. It is very different from the standard deviation model, as ATR considers historical price action as the key event in forecasting future volatility. This was developed by J. Welles Wilder and started life as 'True Range' before a moving average was added to smooth out the calculation, and provide a more useful measure of volatility.

If we start with 'true range', this is calculated as follows, and is taken as the largest of three possible values. As you will see the approach considers not simply the current price bar, but also its relationship to the previous bar in terms of the spread of price action:

- The distance from the current high to current low
- The distance from the previous close to current high
- The distance from the previous close to current low

This is shown in Fig 7.13 and it is important to note that in calculating the second and third of these numbers, an absolute value is used. In other words no negative numbers, as the interpretation and measurement of volatility is non directional.

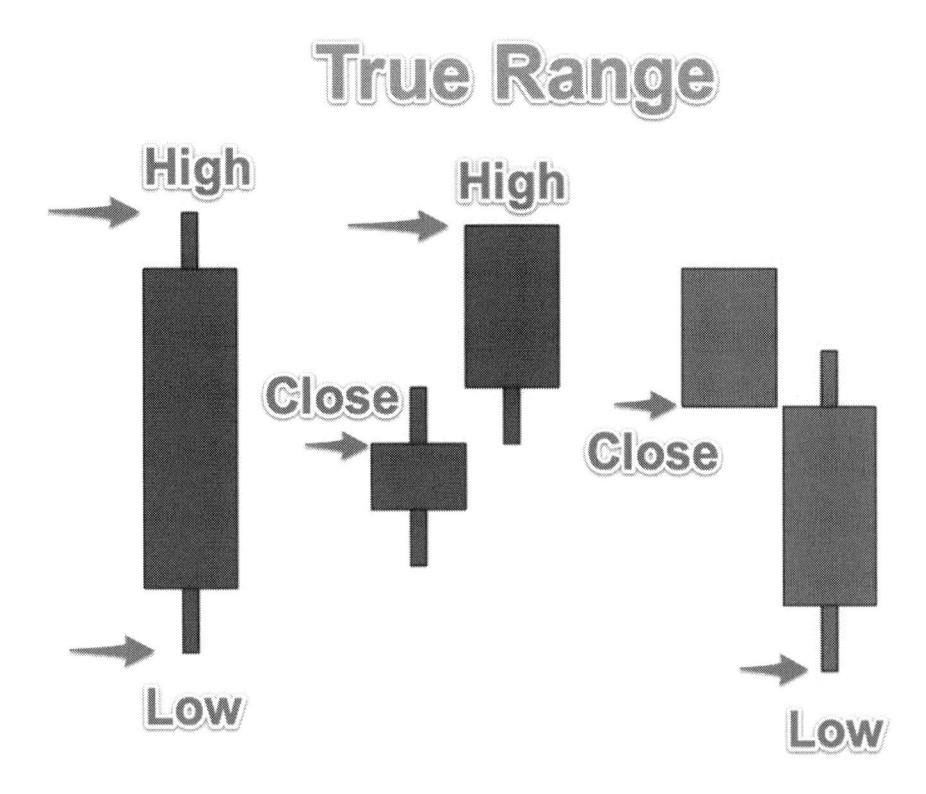

Fig 7.13 - True range calculations

In order to make this measure of volatility more meaningful, Wilder then introduced the 'average' over a given number of bars to produce the Average True Range or ATR. This is generally set at 14 periods as the 'norm' although values can be changed according to the timeframe under consideration.

There are many other models that have been developed to try to capture and display this ethereal term we refer to as volatility. Standard deviation and the ATR are just two, and two of the most commonly used by traders, but I must stress there are others. However, in my humble opinion it is these two models which have come closest, but as with every other measure these are premised on the belief markets follow mathematical principles, which clearly they do not. Therefore the best we can hope to come up with is a 'best fit' for measuring and interpreting volatility however we understand the term in the context of trading.

Every model is flawed in some way, and what we have to decide for ourselves, is which approach do we believe provides the closest approximation to market behavior. It is also important to understand that volatility, as a decision making tool, is not a standalone one. It is always used in conjunction with other tools, such as volume and a full array of analytical techniques. For option traders what it is attempting to signal is those periods of high, medium or low volatility, which are so critical in predicting the future behavior of the binary option, and the reason is very simple. It is to do with what is known as Delta.

Delta

In the world of vanilla options, Delta refers to how much an option price changes with that of the underlying market. Delta will vary over the life of the option, and will be influenced by the underlying market as well as the time to expiry for the option. Delta is expressed between -1 and +1 depending on whether we have a put or a call. In simple terms a Delta of + 0.5 indicates that for every $1 rise in the underlying price, the option price will rise by 50 cents. For put options the Delta would be negative.

However, the Delta in binary options is very different, and reflects the volatility associated with the binary instrument, and is what is referred to as exponential Delta. The relationship here is a non linear one. Imagine for a moment the binary option is very close to expiry, perhaps only seconds away and at the strike price. In this case, a 1 tick move or a 1 point or pip move would see the probability of the option swing from 100 to 0 and perhaps back to 100 again, literally in milliseconds. In other words huge volatility swings for tiny movements in price which confirms two things for us.

First, the volatility profile associated with a binary option is very different to any other instrument, and second, it is crucial you have the best tools and techniques to signal and forecast changes in the underlying markets. A binary option with a probability of 90 or above may look attractive, but if it is close to the strike price and close to expiry, exponential Delta will move this dramatically and suddenly. And if you have ever had the misfortune to suffer from clear air turbulence when flying, you will know the feeling. The plane literally appears to fall out of the sky. This is the effect exponential Delta has on binary options and on the probabilities being quoted, and it is why I have spent some time explaining the basics of this elusive measure we all call volatility.

Historic & Implied Volatility

Before we move to consider the practical applications of volatility to help us in our decision making, there are two other terms which help to 'frame' volatility and which underpin the options world. These are historic and implied volatility, and as you might expect, one is looking back at what has happened already (historic) and the other (implied) is looking forward. Both have their place, but the one most option traders focus on is implied volatility, since this is a measure of future volatility, and is therefore of much greater interest. Here again, I do not propose to delve too deeply into the maths, so let me give you some textbook definitions.

Historic volatility uses standard deviation to plot the volatility of an instrument, generally on a daily basis and annualized over a 12 month period. In other words, it is a graphical representation of the instrument based on how volatile it has been in the past. Standard deviation provides the benchmark for the calculations. You can think of historic volatility as the instrument's 'footprints in the sand' looking back.

Implied volatility is very different and is forward looking. As you will see when we begin to consider the volatility indices, these are all attempting to forecast the future. Implied volatility is based on, and derived from, the underlying options prices, which are of course changing constantly throughout the day and reflecting the ever changing views of market participants. This is why implied volatility is often the only focus for options traders. Suppose the market is waiting for a news announcement. Ahead of the news options traders will position themselves in anticipation of the release which will move the options' prices higher or lower. Following the news, these same option traders will either sell or buy depending on their view of the market, and any reaction to the release. All of this price volatility in the options market is reflected in the calculation of implied volatility for that instrument. To be precise, in defining implied volatility, it is in fact 'the expected future' volatility of the instrument as implied by the instrument's options price.

Given the formula for calculating implied volatility includes the instrument price, strike price, days to expiry, interest rates, and various other elements, you might be wondering which came first - the option price or implied volatility? And the answer is simply the market makers use the 'at the money' options as the benchmark and work out from there to calculate the implied volatility across the options chain.

However, I must stress, like all forecasting tools implied volatility can be wrong. It is only a tool and it is not foolproof. It is based on theoretical models, and theoretical models can and do get it wrong. So whilst it is important, and implied volatility can be used in conjunction with historic volatility to provide the 'characteristic' of the instrument, it is not there as a buy or sell signal. It is there to provide another piece of the jigsaw in your trading analysis - an important piece, but one which is not perfect.

So how do we interpret historic and implied volatility, and all the other applications of volatility we have discussed thus far? I will show you where to find all the information along with the volatility charts, which are generally freely available. There are one or two sites which offer more advanced charts as you develop your binary options skills. Historical and implied volatility analysis is only one aspect of volatility to consider - there are others which we will look at next, starting with some simple, quick and easy ways to use and interpret volatility in all timeframes and markets.

Getting Started

As I have mentioned before, volatility is a tricky and complex subject, and one on which there are a multitude of approaches and analytical techniques. The maths on many of these is complex, and only applicable if you are proposing to write about options theory.

My purpose here is to try to guide you to those practical applications which will help in your trading decisions. Some of these are very simple, others are more complex, but all I hope will help to provide you with that extra insight you need to trade binary options successfully.

And the starting point is to use one of the simplest volatility measures of all, namely the high/low price we touched on in the True Range calculations. This is one of the simplest measures of volatility, and the best place to start I believe, as we begin to add volatility to our decision making trading toolkit.

Whilst there are several places to find this information intraday, the best I have discovered to date is the one created and developed by OANDA. And the reason I like it is not simply because it offers a quick and easy comparison of the major currency pairs, it also offers the same tools for the exotic currencies as well as many of the popular commodities. Therefore an excellent place to start. So let's take a look and see how the analysis works in practice.

OANDA Currency Volatility Chart

The OANDA currency volatility chart is not only a good place to start, it's also free and updated throughout the trading session on the close of each timeframe. You can find it here:

http://fxtrade.oanda.co.uk/analysis/currency-volatility

The indicator updates on four different timeframes, the 15 minute, the hour, the day and the week, and shows both the extent and direction of price acton. On the right hand side of the chart is the range the instrument has travelled, from high to low in that timeframe. On the left hand side of the chart the equivalent price action is then displayed, either as a move higher or lower.

However, what is important here is not the direction of the price action, but the extent, and from this simple analysis we can draw some important conclusions. Indeed, you can think of this in much the same way as volume price analysis where we are looking for confirmation or anomaly between price and volume.

Here we are looking for confirmation or anomaly between range and price, and in addition which instruments are moving (volatile) and which are not. Whilst there is never any guarantee that historic price behavior anticipates future price action, what the indicator also shows is the relative nature of one instrument to another. This will then help to guide and shape your trading decisions, whether to get in, stay in or exit a position. As always, this is just the starting point. The next stop is the chart for further analysis. And you can think of this indicator as giving you a quick 'heads up' on the price/range relationship across several instruments and markets simultaneously.

And here is the 15 minute chart.

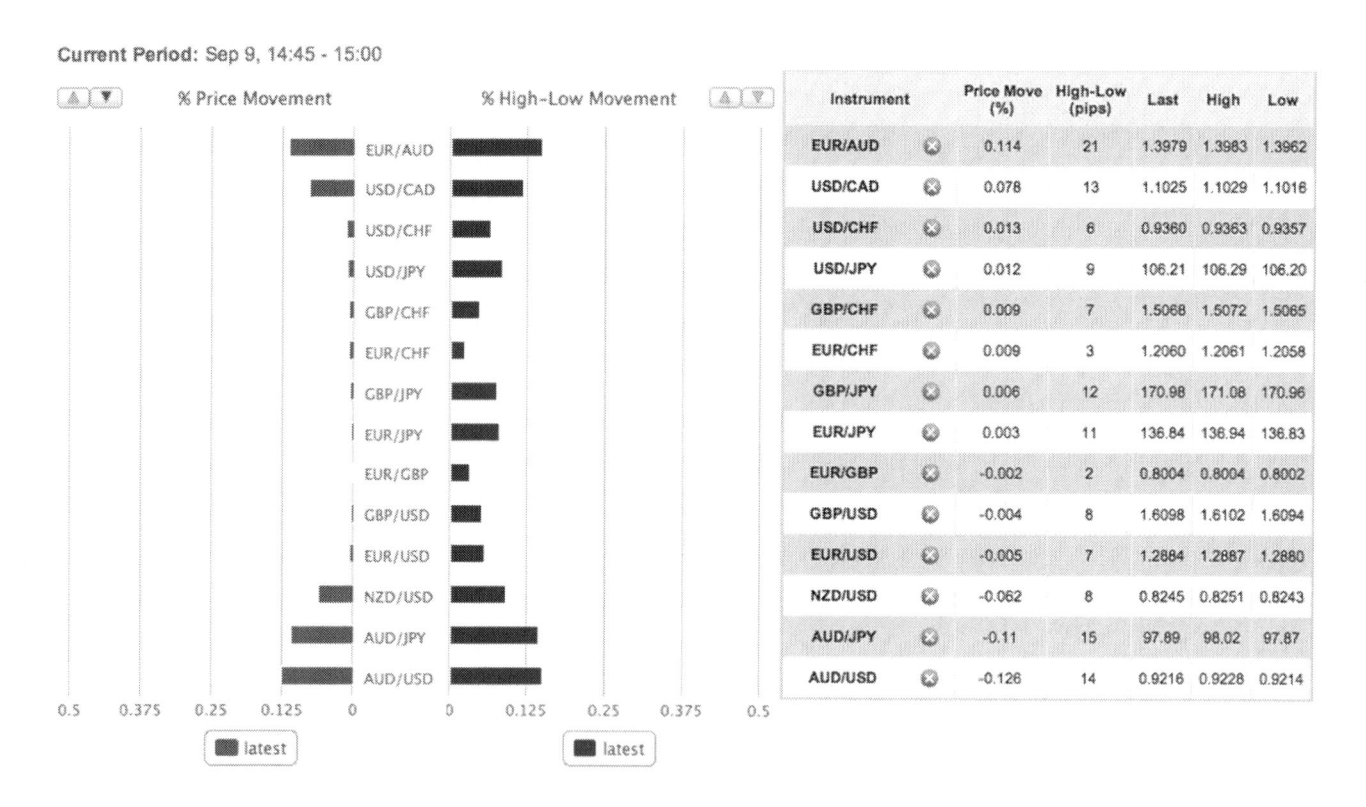

Instrument	Price Move (%)	High-Low (pips)	Last	High	Low
EUR/AUD	0.114	21	1.3979	1.3983	1.3962
USD/CAD	0.078	13	1.1025	1.1029	1.1016
USD/CHF	0.013	6	0.9360	0.9363	0.9357
USD/JPY	0.012	9	106.21	106.29	106.20
GBP/CHF	0.009	7	1.5068	1.5072	1.5065
EUR/CHF	0.009	3	1.2060	1.2061	1.2058
GBP/JPY	0.006	12	170.98	171.08	170.96
EUR/JPY	0.003	11	136.84	136.94	136.83
EUR/GBP	-0.002	2	0.8004	0.8004	0.8002
GBP/USD	-0.004	8	1.6098	1.6102	1.6094
EUR/USD	-0.005	7	1.2884	1.2887	1.2880
NZD/USD	-0.062	8	0.8245	0.8251	0.8243
AUD/JPY	-0.11	15	97.89	98.02	97.87
AUD/USD	-0.126	14	0.9216	0.9228	0.9214

Fig 7.14 - 15 minute chart - ©2014 OANDA Corporation. Used with permission. OANDA and the OANDA logo are trademarks and/or registered trademarks of OANDA Corporation.

If we start with the anomalies first. In the centre of the chart we can see the EUR/JPY and the GBP/JPY have both seen a relatively wide range in terms of the high/low movement, but the equivalent % price movement is very low. Here we might conclude the price has been in a whipsaw or congestion phase, and on the 15 minute chart this would be represented by a doji candle, signaling indecision and a lack of direction, with volatile price action. To a lesser extent the same could also be said of the GBP/USD and the EUR/USD where the high/low movement has not been confirmed with any move in the price.

Moving to the extremes of the indicator here we can see the Australian dollar in the AUD/USD, the AUD/JPY and the EUR/AUD has certainly been moving, with the high/low movement confirmed with an equally solid move in the price. Clearly the Australian dollar is a currency that is on the move with some momentum. Finally, two currency pairs most certainly not on the move are the EUR/GBP and the EUR/CHF. Here we have a low high/low range coupled with very low price movement.

But how can we use this information in our decision making process? And here let's start with the anomalies first. For the EUR/JPY and the GBP/JPY this is clearly signaling currency pairs that are volatile, but not moving at the moment in this timeframe. This could be as the result of a news or data release, but may simply be a short term reaction. It may be this represents a possible turning point, or pause in a longer term trend. If we have no position in the market it may be a signal to stay out. Alternatively if we are looking for a volatility based trading position, or if we have already taken a position, it may be good news or not so good news. Possibly good news if the probabilities are in our favor (although this could change if the pause is only temporary), and possibly bad news if they are not. However, the indicator is sending us some clear signals of indecision coupled with volatility which require further analysis of the chart.

The Australian dollar on the other hand is certainly moving against several currencies, with strong price movement coupled with a good price range. The currency here may be trending, or it may be reacting to news. But one thing is clear, the AUD pairs have not been in congestion in the last 15 minutes. Good news if you are looking to enter a position where volatility or trend is required.

Finally to the last of the group, the EUR/GBP and the EUR/CHF, these are certainly not pairs you would be considering if volatility was required.

However, if you were already in the market with a position in either of these pairs, and the probabilities were heavily in your favor close to expiry, this lack of volatility would be welcome and give you the confidence to continue to hold until expiry. Conversely, if you were looking for volatility to move the probabilities in your favor, the prospects for any recovery would be slim.

The same principles apply to the other timeframes. And moving to the hourly chart also takes the analysis into applying multiple timeframes. This helps to contextualize the relationships between the various timeframes.

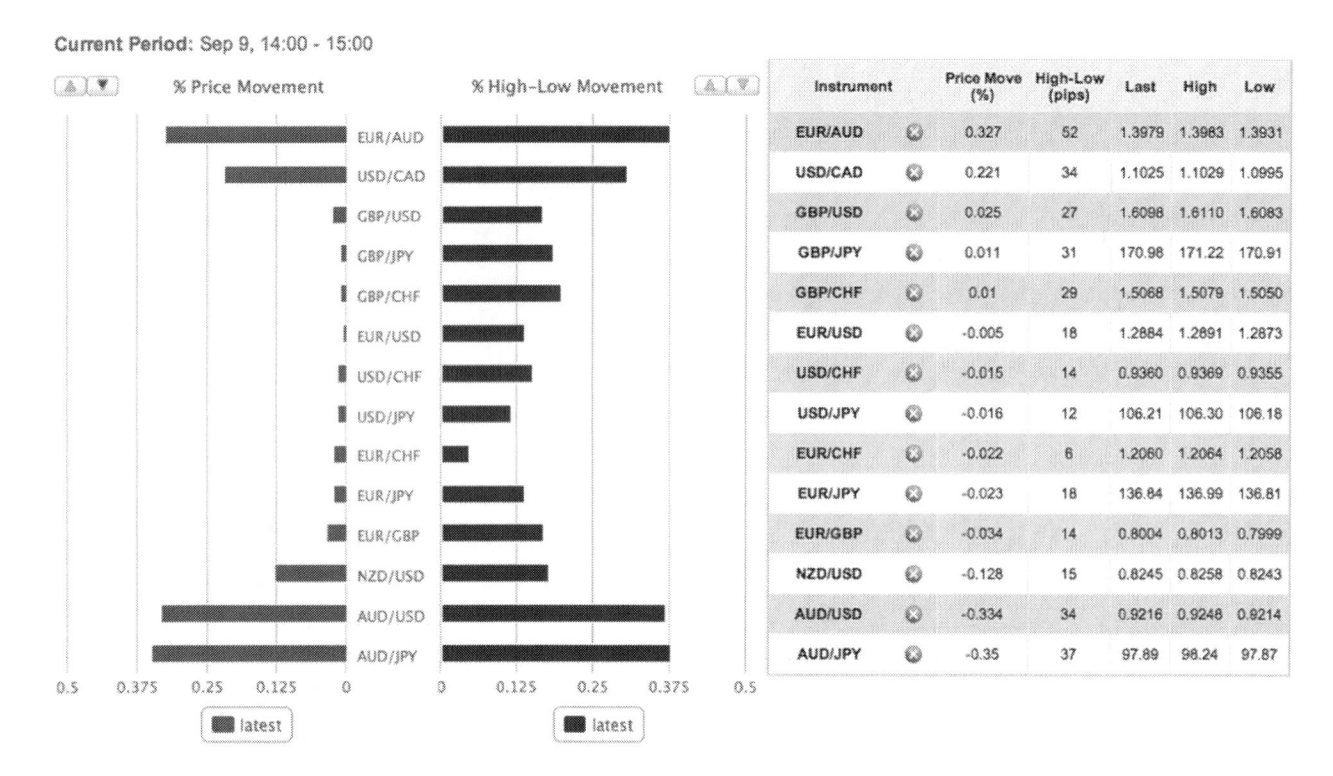

Fig 7.15 - hourly chart - ©2014 OANDA Corporation. Used with permission. OANDA and the OANDA logo are trademarks and/or registered trademarks of OANDA Corporation.

If we start in the same order as before with the anomalies, the picture here is slightly different. In this timeframe it is the British pound which has seen some big swings in terms of the range, but this has not been matched with big moves in the price action. Clearly the price has been whipsawing in the last hour for pairs such as the GBP/JPY, the GBP/CHF and the EUR/GBP, with others such as the USD/CHF, EUR/USD and USD/JPY showing similar behavior. Moving to the extremes, the Australian dollar is once again the currency which is moving strongly, and confirming the picture on the 15 minute chart with the AUD/JPY, the AUD/USD and the EUR/AUD all signaling solid price movement. The EUR/CHF continues to remain waterlogged in this timeframe with a low range and small price movement.

As always with any analysis, this is highly dependent on your time horizon and on your perspective. It is also dependent on the context of whether you are considering entering or exiting a position, or perhaps looking for confirmation. Confirmation to hold an existing position may be signaled either by a lack of volatility or as a result of volatility. It all depends on the probability of the option position and the time to expiry. Volatility may give you the confidence to enter a new position, it may also trigger a decision to exit, as indeed may a lack of volatility.

Volatility is non directional and all we are trying to do here, in a very simple way, is to view the historic price behavior over four distinct timeframes to describe the instrument and the range/price relationship in a clear and quick way. The indicator provides a perspective against which further analysis can be carried out on the chart. For completeness let's consider the last two timeframes, namely the daily and the weekly charts.

Current Period: Sep 8, 15:10 - Sep 9, 15:10

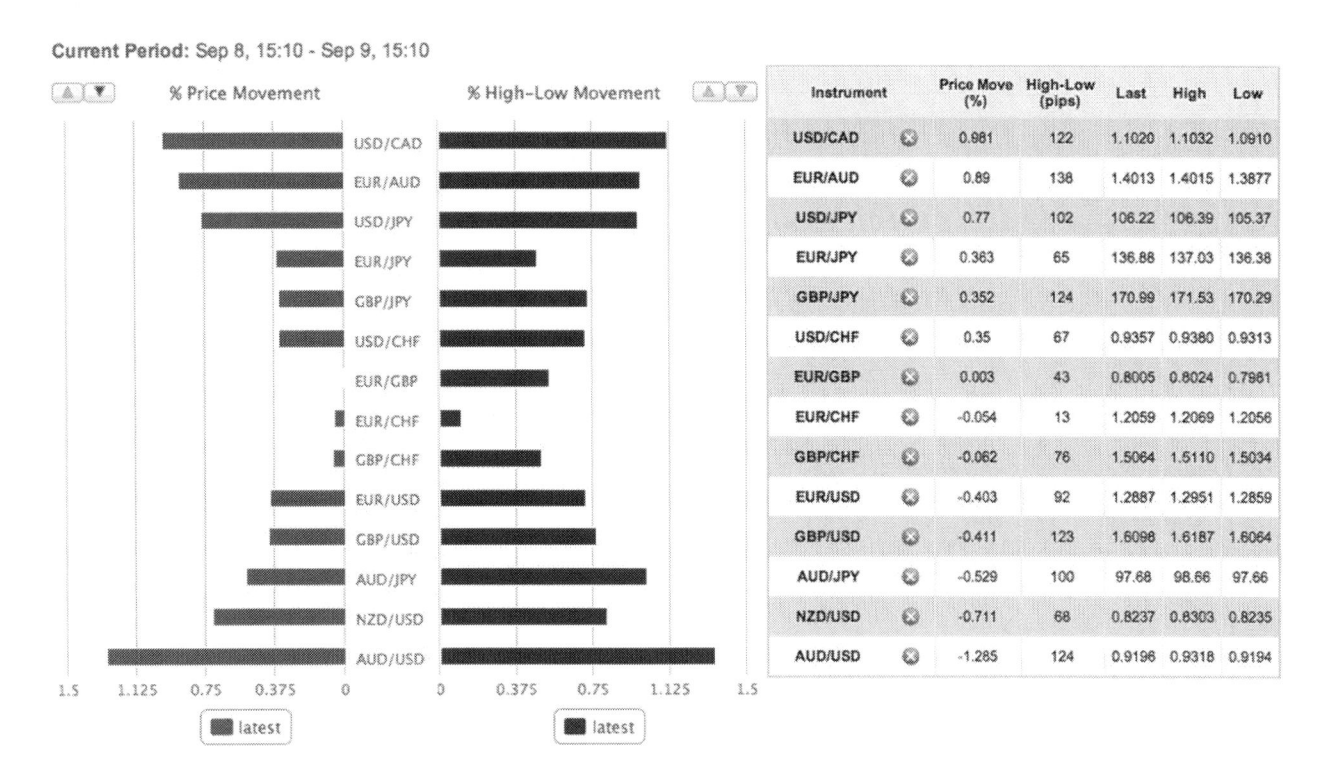

Instrument	Price Move (%)	High-Low (pips)	Last	High	Low
USD/CAD	0.981	122	1.1020	1.1032	1.0910
EUR/AUD	0.89	138	1.4013	1.4015	1.3877
USD/JPY	0.77	102	106.22	106.39	105.37
EUR/JPY	0.363	65	136.88	137.03	136.38
GBP/JPY	0.352	124	170.99	171.53	170.29
USD/CHF	0.35	67	0.9357	0.9380	0.9313
EUR/GBP	0.003	43	0.8005	0.8024	0.7981
EUR/CHF	-0.054	13	1.2059	1.2069	1.2056
GBP/CHF	-0.062	76	1.5064	1.5110	1.5034
EUR/USD	-0.403	92	1.2887	1.2951	1.2859
GBP/USD	-0.411	123	1.6098	1.6187	1.6064
AUD/JPY	-0.529	100	97.68	98.66	97.66
NZD/USD	-0.711	68	0.8237	0.8303	0.8235
AUD/USD	-1.285	124	0.9196	0.9318	0.9194

Fig 7.16 - Daily chart - ©2014 OANDA Corporation. Used with permission. OANDA and the OANDA logo are trademarks and/or registered trademarks of OANDA Corporation.

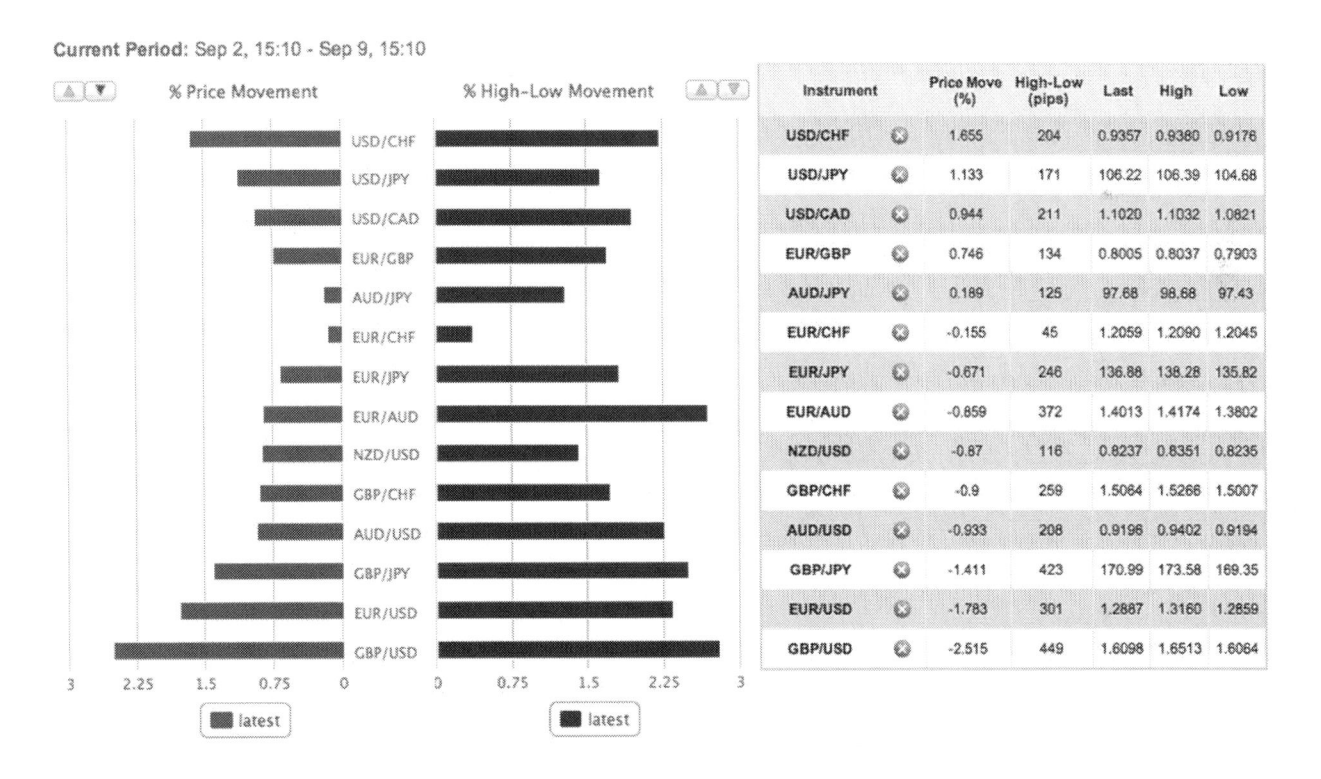

Current Period: Sep 2, 15:10 - Sep 9, 15:10

Instrument	Price Move (%)	High-Low (pips)	Last	High	Low
USD/CHF	1.655	204	0.9357	0.9380	0.9176
USD/JPY	1.133	171	106.22	106.39	104.68
USD/CAD	0.944	211	1.1020	1.1032	1.0821
EUR/GBP	0.746	134	0.8005	0.8037	0.7903
AUD/JPY	0.189	125	97.68	98.68	97.43
EUR/CHF	-0.155	45	1.2059	1.2090	1.2045
EUR/JPY	-0.671	246	136.88	138.28	135.82
EUR/AUD	-0.859	372	1.4013	1.4174	1.3802
NZD/USD	-0.87	116	0.8237	0.8351	0.8235
GBP/CHF	-0.9	259	1.5064	1.5266	1.5007
AUD/USD	-0.933	208	0.9196	0.9402	0.9194
GBP/JPY	-1.411	423	170.99	173.58	169.35
EUR/USD	-1.783	301	1.2887	1.3160	1.2859
GBP/USD	-2.515	449	1.6098	1.6513	1.6064

Fig 7.17 - Weekly chart - ©2014 OANDA Corporation. Used with permission. OANDA and the OANDA logo are trademarks and/or registered trademarks of OANDA Corporation.

For a lack of volatility it is the EUR/CHF which grabs the attention, showing the smallest range/price relationship by some way. At the extremes, it is the major currency pairs which dominate in both timeframes, suggesting US dollar strength is driving the markets here.

Volatility Indicators

Using a volatility chart such as the one developed by OANDA, is a quick way to provide a 'heads up' on those instruments which are moving and those which are not, along with any associated anomalies. This in turn tells us where we need to focus our attention, whether we are looking for high, medium or low volatility opportunities, either helping us to get in, to stay in, or indeed to exit a position.

The next logical step is to consider 'on chart' volatility. In other words, directly on the trading chart in real time, and one of the easiest ways to do this is by using a volatility trading indicator. This can then provide an analysis of the instrument's volatility directly.

Whilst there are several of these available, the two we are going to look at in detail here, are Bollinger bands and Starc bands. The first was developed by John Bollinger and his indicator incorporates standard deviation as the primary methodology. By contrast Starc bands were developed by Manning Stoller and they adopt the ATR approach. Whilst both display bands on the chart, many traders wrongly assume they are similar - they are not, and this was one of the reasons I introduced the two concepts of standard deviation and average true range at the beginning of this chapter. I did this in order to explain these two indicators in more detail.

There are several other volatility indicators, which I'm sure have their own advocates and you may have already discovered these for yourself. My own opinion is simply that Bollinger bands and Starc bands are a good place to start as the basis for any volatility analysis. You should find both of these indicators on most good charting packages. Using an indicator to analyze volatility directly on the chart has several inherent benefits.

First, the analysis applies directly to your chart, and hence your trading timeframe. Second, no matter what the timeframe of the binary option, the timeframe of the analysis can be closely matched. Third, any analysis can be applied from 1 minute to 1 month and everything in between. Fourth, it's fast with no other charts required. Fifth, it can be applied across multiple timeframes for additional analysis. Finally it's fast and easy to change instrument and spot other trading opportunities quickly. So let's start with Bollinger bands.

Bollinger Bands

Bollinger bands were developed by John Bollinger as an easy way to display price action in the context of its relationship to the mean. If you recall from the normal distribution chart, here we saw the mean at the peak of the bell curve, with one, two or three standard deviations then applied.

Typically, 2 standard deviations will encompass 95% of price action, and this in essence is what is displayed on the screen using Bollinger bands. Three lines are displayed on the chart, the one in the centre is a simple moving average, usually defaulted to 20 periods, with the two lines on either side denoting 2 standard deviations above and below the mean. In other words, moving standard deviations which then track the price action candle by candle. This is shown in Fig 7.18

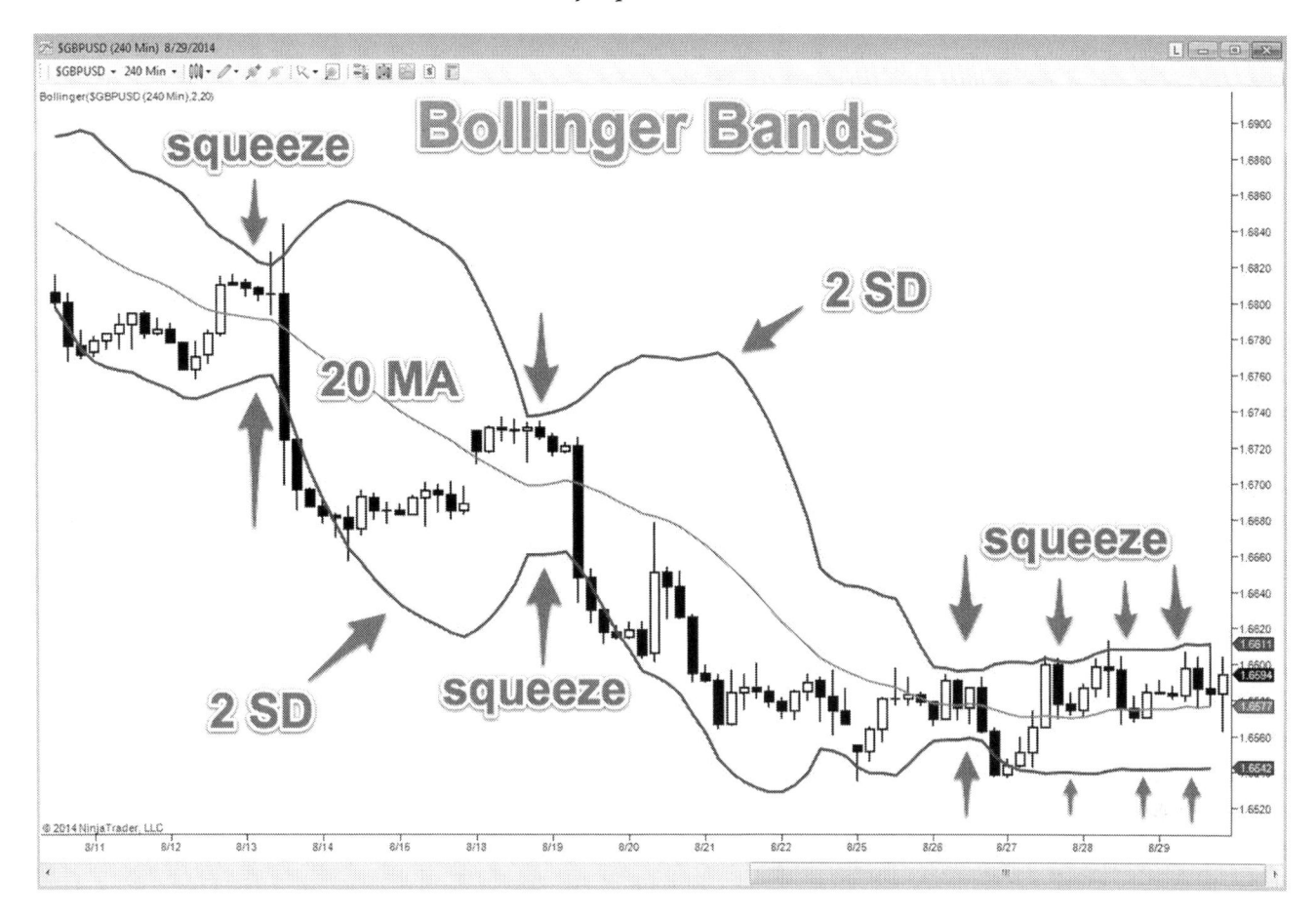

Fig 7.18 - Bollinger bands - chart courtesy of NinjaTrader.com

The example here is from the NinjaTrader platform, and as you can see we have three bands on the chart. The upper band and the lower band represent the two standard deviations 2 SD, whilst the middle band is the 20 period simple moving average (20 MA), the mean in other words.

One of the most important aspects of using Bollinger bands to interpret volatility is what I call the 'squeeze' regions, and as you can see we have three such areas on this chart. This is where the upper and lower Bollinger bands have started to revert back to the mean. Volatility is declining and the price action is entering a congestion phase of relatively low volatility, with the bands then 'squeezing' together to form these classical patterns. In squeeze phases, volatility has drained away from the market, which may be good news if the probabilities are in your favor, but not such good news if the probabilities are against you. But if you are not in the market, it may also present other trading opportunities using some of the more exotic binary option contracts which we will be looking at later in the book.

But the key point is this. The squeeze is a simple and clear signal volatility is ebbing away, and one that will be confirmed on the OANDA volatility indicator. Once the squeeze starts, we know consolidation will follow, as we await the breakout and a widening of the bands as volatility increases once again. And this is key because you can consider the squeeze in two ways.

First, volatility has drained away for the time being. Second, and perhaps less obvious, once the squeeze is in place, you know at some point the market will break out, with an increase in volatility as a result. This will be signaled by the bands widening once more as volatility increases, and in terms of anticipating the breakout, other techniques such as volume price analysis, support and resistance, candles and candle patterns will all then come into play. You can think of the outer Bollinger bands as the lungs of the market, helping it to breathe. They rise and fall in the same way, first filled with air, which is then expelled as the constant rise and fall of market volatility ebbs and flows across all the timeframes.

However, I cannot stress too strongly Bollinger bands are **not** trading signals, **nor** are they trend indicators. In my opinion, for what it is worth, they are a volatility indicator and nothing more. The bands are describing volatility directly on your chart, and in all timeframes. As volatility increases so the bands will move apart, and as volatility subsides they will move together to form the classical squeeze pattern. It is a visual picture of how far the price action has moved away from the mean, and once there you can be sure of one thing - the price action will revert back to the mean in due course, with the bands narrowing once more. It is just a question of time, and timing is of course everything when trading all types of options. The answer to the question of 'when', will be answered in other ways, and not by using Bollinger bands.

The 'when' is often referred to as the volatility breakout, and is a classic example of the power of combining two techniques to provide the complete picture. Bollinger bands on their own simply reveal volatility, no more no less, but combine them with volume price analysis - and voila - the complete picture is revealed. If volatility is low and the squeeze is on, but then the bands start to widen, it's time to study the chart to consider the volume associated with any move higher or lower. This analysis coupled with an analysis of the price action, support and resistance, candles and candle patterns, and using multiple timeframes will then confirm if the move is valid. If so, it may be time to take a position in the market if you are looking for one where volatility is required.

You may also view a squeeze period as an opportunity to consider options where the probability is at an extreme. Alternatively you may simply decide it is time to stay out. Either way having a view of volatility, whether high or low, rising or falling, will give you that vital element so critical when trading options.

Finally before moving on, let's consider an example on the 5 minute chart for gold based on the GC futures contract.

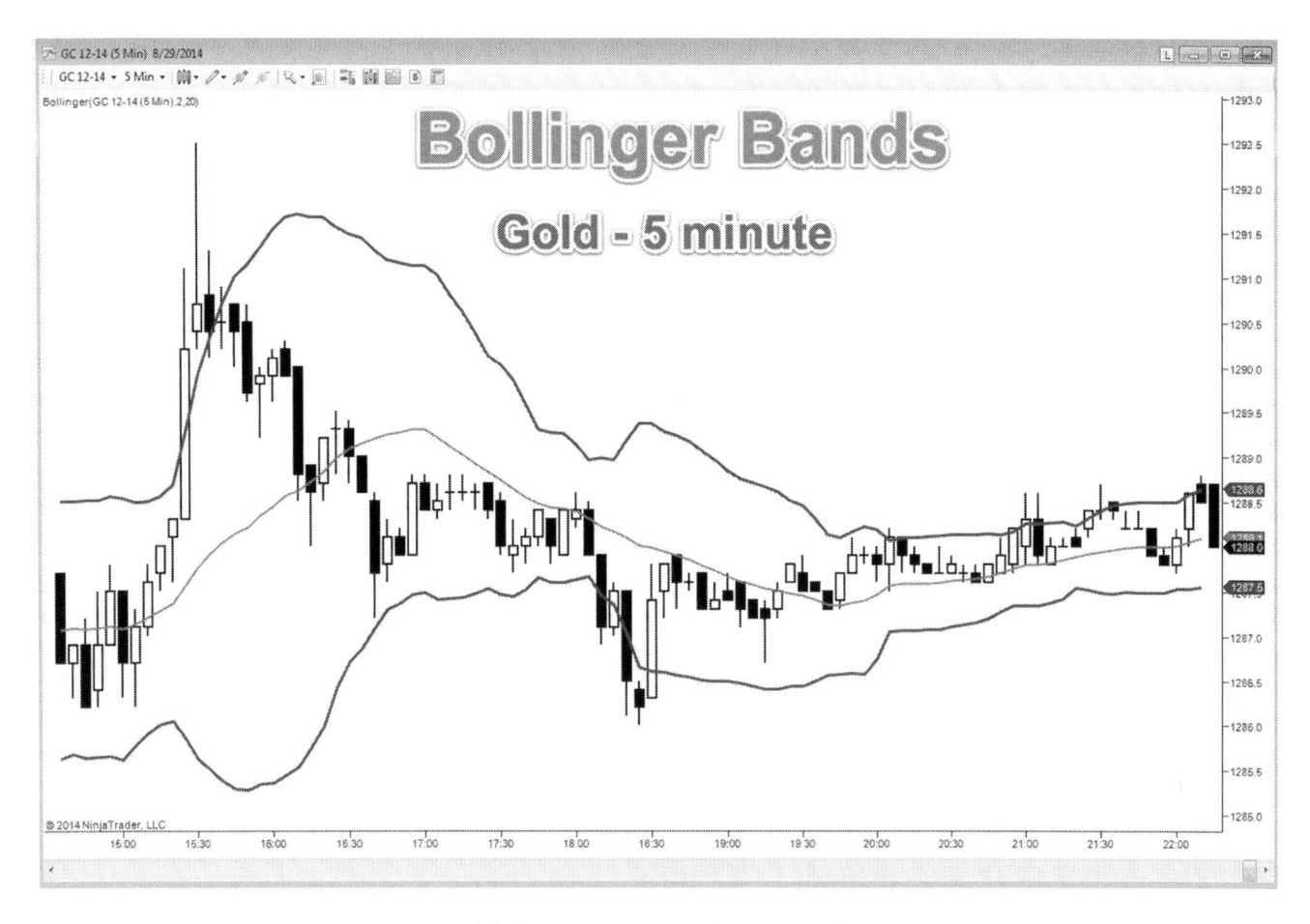

Fig 7.19 - Bollinger bands on 5 min gold chart, courtesy of NinjaTrader.com

Once again we can see a rapid expansion in volatility to the left of the chart, before the bands begin to narrow, getting ever tighter as the market moves to the close of the session. And this highlights a further aspect of volatility when viewed through the prism of a Bollinger band which is this. The bands will also provide a perspective on historic volatility, one that is based on price, and the likely distance any move the instrument might make from the mean. On the right hand side of the chart the market is moving ever further into consolidation, with the price of gold trading in a tight range. To the left we have the yardstick of two standard deviations with which to judge any breakout, when it arrives. This, of course, is pertinent to this timeframe, but nevertheless when considering historic volatility on longer term charts, this provides a further benchmark with which to gauge and judge price action and volatility in a purely objective way. And it is even more powerful when applied to multiple timeframes.

Starc Bands

Moving to the second of our volatility indicators, namely Starc bands, whilst these appear similar when applied to the chart, their calculation is very different to that of Bollinger bands. Bollinger bands use standard deviation, whilst Starc bands use average true range. This results in some interesting differences when applied to the same chart.

The calculation for the Starc bands themselves is a little more complicated, but as with Bollinger bands this is all done automatically within the indicator. The formula for the upper and lower bands are as follows:

- Upper Starc band = (6 - period SMA) + (ATR)*2
- Lower Starc band = (6 - period SMA) - (ATR)*2

In simple terms, both the upper and lower band step back six periods from the simple moving average period, which is generally either 14 or 20. For simplicity and comparison with Bollinger bands, I have set this to 20 in the following examples.

And here we have an example using the Emini ES futures contract on a daily chart.

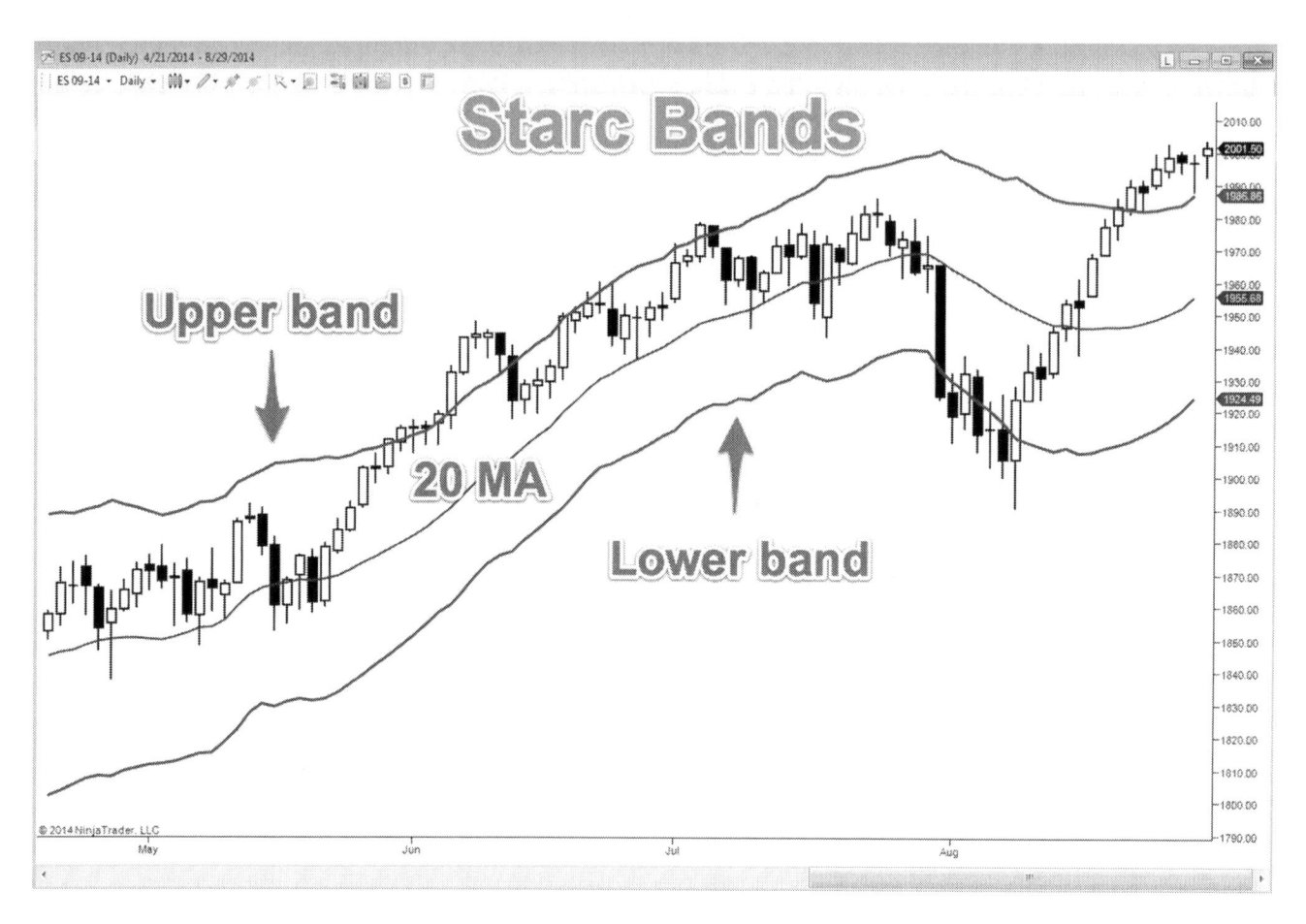

Fig 7.20 - Starc bands on Emini ES daily chart - courtesy of NinjaTrader.com

At first glance this looks very similar to Bollinger bands. We have three lines, one upper band, one lower band and the 20 period simple moving average in the centre. However, look more closely at Fig 7.20 - where are the squeeze zones? These appear to have been smoothed out in the calculation, and to confirm this, take a look at Fig 7.21 which is the same chart, but this time replaced with Bollinger bands.

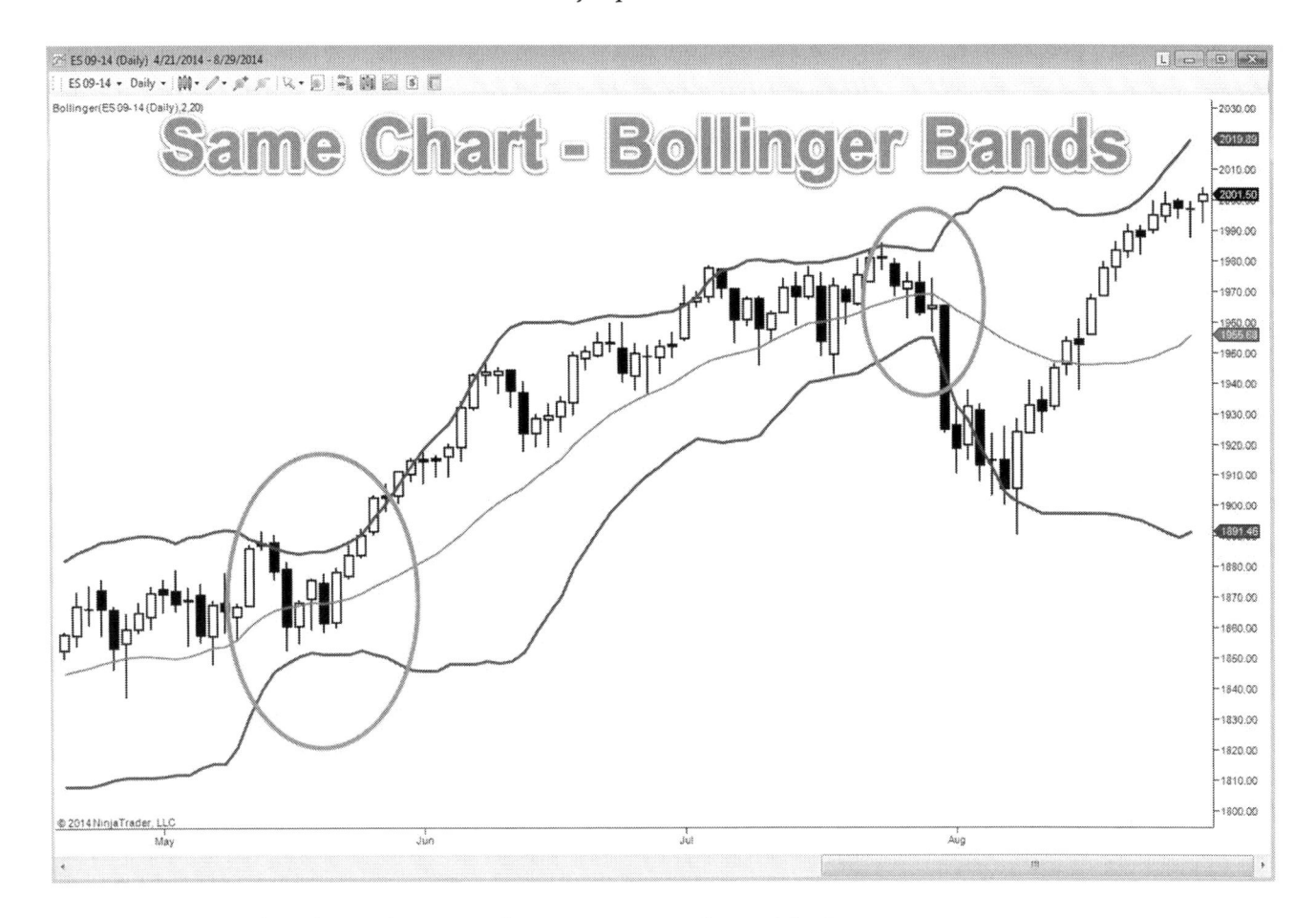

Fig 7.21 - Bollinger bands on the same chart - courtesy of NinjaTrader.com

As you can see, the distinct squeeze zones of the Bollinger bands are now back, with that descriptive rise and fall as the volatility ebbs and flows. The Starc bands, on the other hand, are smoother and lack these distinctive variations, from which several questions follow. Such as, why, which indicator is the right one to use, and is there a place for both?

And to answer the last question first, I believe there is a place for both. Whilst both indicators are measuring risk, the information they display is very different.

Volatility and risk go hand in hand. One cannot exist without the other, and this is how to consider these two indicators. Bollinger bands are more suited to describing volatility, whilst Starc bands are more suited to describing risk. But what does this mean?

If we start with standard deviation, the basis for Bollinger bands, standard deviation is a measure of how disperse prices are from the mean. You can think of this like plucking a guitar string - first it is pulled, then released, and the string subsequently vibrates several times before returning to rest in the same position it started.

Starc bands however, take a different approach. In using average true range, they are considering the range rather than the dispersal of price action. You can think of this in terms of target shooting and the analysis of the target hits. In one case you would be considering the grouping, the spread if you like, and whether the target hits were closely grouped or widely spread, whilst the second approach would be to consider the range of spread, the extremes if you like. A simple analogy perhaps, but this in essence is the difference between an approach to volatility using standard deviation and one using range. Bollinger bands use the closing price for calculation, whereas Starc bands use the average of the range.

There is no right or wrong way to apply these indicators, just the best way for you. Moreover, all indicators except volume and price are lagged in some way. Indicators are there to help us fill in some of the blanks of trading, of which volatility is one of the most difficult to pin down. Bollinger bands and Starc bands are not entry or exit indicators, but are there to provide us with a better understand of volatility, and to describe it for us simply, clearly and in a meaningful way.

But which do we use and how? And here I can only try to offer you some guidance. Starc bands were originally developed for trading commodities using slower time frame charts.

Volatility and risk go hand in hand and this is perhaps the best way to think of these two indicators. Starc bands are essentially attempting to define the risk associated with the market volatility. In other words, the bands themselves are more important here, as they are trying to define risk extremes, overbought or oversold and as such, potential points at which the market may reverse.

Some traders attempt to use Bollinger bands in this way, but in my opinion this is flawed given the underlying mathematics of the indicator. Starc bands on the other hand are trying to signal just that, with the two outer bands defining risk.

As price reaches these bands, the risk of a reversal is increased. In addition, and given the underlying calculations, Starc bands take a more 'considered' view of price action. A longer term view, a more 'in depth' view of market volatility.

Bollinger bands focus more closely on the 'near term' aspects of volatility using standard deviation, which is why we see the squeeze so clearly defined when using this indicator, and not when using Starc bands.

My suggestions are therefore as follows, but as always these are only my own observations based on my knowledge of the market. I would certainly **not** suggest you apply both to the same chart. Not only will this confuse you, but it will also give you too much information to process.

Use Bollinger bands for intraday trading, particularly for currency pairs, indices and certain commodities. These are markets where volatility can move from extremes before reverting to mean very quickly.

Economic news is unrelenting and has a particular impact on the twenty four hour foreign exchange market. Here you will see constant movement from consolidation to trend and back again in all timeframes.

Indices can be extremely volatile, and with the futures markets now also trading twenty four hours a day on Globex and other electronic markets, these too are subject to the constant stream of economic releases.

However, bear in mind it is at the open of the physical when volatility and volumes really explode, with the Emini ES (the future for the S&P 500) one of the most volatile of all the popular indices. The same applies to the others such as the Emini NQ and the Emini YM.

With regard to commodities, I would suggest using Bollinger bands for those commodities such as gold, silver, natural gas and oil which can be extremely volatile during the open of the physical session. Also for bonds if these are available.

In terms of timeframes for Bollinger bands, I would suggest they are applied to faster charts, for both tick and time. I will be covering tick charts in more detail shortly as this is another excellent way to consider and view volatility. For time based charts, this will depend on the binary option being traded, but anything from 5 to 15 minute through to hourly charts, and beyond, will work well.

Use Starc bands for a more considered view of the price action, and on longer term charts, perhaps from four hour through to the daily and the weekly timeframes. This provides the 'overview' of volatility through the prism of a longer term perspective. Naturally Starc bands can be applied to any market, but in particular for stocks and commodities, and for a longer term view on indices.

I hope the above has given you some food for thought, and convinced you how these two indicators can co-exist in your trading toolkit. No indicator will deliver buy or sell signals. All they can hope to achieve is to fill in the gaps of our knowledge, and provide meaningful information to help in our trading decisions. These are just two which I have covered in detail. There are others, but in my opinion these are tried and tested, and if used in the ways outlined above, will help to give you the complete volatility picture on your chart, whatever instrument or market you are trading.

There are many other ways to consider volatility, and now I want to move into more complex areas, and consider volatility indices of which there are many.

Volatility Indices

As I have already stated, volatility is an ethereal subject. It is one which is constantly in the spotlight as traders try to expose its hidden secrets. Over the decades there have been many attempts to make sense of the term, and to convert the concept into meaningful charts, and leading the way has been the CME (Chicago Mercantile Exchange), and more recently the CBOE (Chicago Board Options Exchange).

Each exchange has produced an increasingly diverse range of products to help traders make sense of the volatility conundrum. Volatility indices is where the world of vanilla options and binary options meet, albeit on nodding terms only.

The principle behind all volatility indices is very simple. Their purpose is to present the market's expectation of implied volatility. In other words, to provide a forecast of where volatility is heading in the future. Historic volatility is all well and good, but it is just that - historic. It certainly has a place when considered in conjunction with implied volatility, but for traders, it's all about the future. This is what a volatility index is attempting to do - to forecast where volatility is heading for that instrument and in that timeframe. For a 30 day index, it is forecasting implied volatility in the next 30 days. For a 9 day index, it is the next 9 days.

The basis for all these calculations are vanilla options, both calls and puts, which is why I said this is where binary and vanilla options meet.

Speak to any options trader, whether electronic or from the pit, and the one aspect they all focus on is implied volatility. As with everything in trading, forecasting the future is very difficult, and implied volatility can be just as tricky. But at least it's a place to start and can provide the framework for trading both binary options as well as more conventional instruments.

As we go through the indices, I will try to highlight some of the underlying methodologies, without too much reference to the maths, as I believe understanding how to use them and where to find them is much more important. Moreover, you do not need a futures brokerage account to discover this information for yourself. Most is freely available, but of course with a futures account and feed, you will be able to see live intraday prices - whilst the free versions are generally delayed (although not greatly).

The guiding principle for all volatility indices is relatively straightforward. Each analyzes the underlying put and call options to gauge whether speculators, traders and investors are either bullish, bearish or neutral, and to gauge the extent of this sentiment. At the simplest level, call options are generally bought when sentiment is bullish, and put options when sentiment is bearish. It is the analysis and interpretation of the underlying options for an instrument or market which are described graphically in the form of an index. The chart describes the market's expectation for the future (implied volatility), based on what is happening in the buying and selling of options in the present.

VIX

The VIX is the granddaddy and an index you may have already come across. It was originally introduced by the CBOE in 1993 as an attempt to measure the volatility associated with US stock markets. The index quickly became the benchmark for forecasting volatility over a 30 day period, and it is often referred to (myself included) as the 'fear index'. The initial index calculated implied volatility based on at the money options for the S&P 100. This underlying methodology was replaced in 2003, along with two major changes. First, the S&P 500 was used as the benchmark, and second the analysis included options with a range of strike prices, duly weighted and covering both near and next term expiry. Until this change in the underlying methodology, the VIX had been considered somewhat abstract and lacking in any real meaning for traders. The index was interesting from an academic perspective, but not much use for trading. The changes in 2003 provided the basis for the product to be launched as a futures instrument in 2004, followed by VIX options in 2006.

However, there are a couple of points I have to make clear. First, whilst the VIX is forecasting implied volatility over the next thirty days, the timeframe for analysis is not limited to 30 days. As a futures contract in its own right, prices are quoted intraday just as for any other market or instrument. So just as for any other index (whether cash or a future) the VIX will rise and fall throughout the day. The index can therefore be considered on any timeframe from tick to hours and from daily to weekly. Intraday scalping traders in the futures and options markets will have a workspace devoted entirely to the VIX.

This workspace provides a complete picture of changes in volatility on a second by second basis, as the underlying options are bought and sold to reflect changes in sentiment, and hence implied volatility.

This is an important point. Many traders fail to appreciate that volatility indices can be used as an intraday tool in just the same way as any other. Whatever binary option timeframe you are trading, volatility indices are directly relevant. Do not fall into the trap of thinking they are purely for longer term traders and speculators. I can assure you they are not.

My second point concerning the VIX is perhaps even more fundamental (if you will excuse the pun), and relates to the directional aspect of volatility indices.

Volatility is a non directional concept. However, over the years much has been written about the close correlation between the VIX and equity markets, which when you think about it is no great surprise. This is the reason it has been christened the fear index. As option buyers panic, they buy puts as protection in a falling market, either as a hedge or to take direct advantage of bearish sentiment because a put will increase in value as the market falls.

Likewise, when markets are bullish, or perceived as bullish by options traders and investors, call buying dominates. It is therefore no surprise there is a direct correlation between the VIX and equity markets, since the VIX is derived from the S&P 500 options themselves.

If fear is in the ascendancy then the VIX will rise, and if complacency (or lack of fear) is the prevailing sentiment, the VIX will fall. As the S&P 500 (and other indices) rise, the VIX will fall and if indices are falling the VIX will rise. This would suggest that volatility indices are directional. They are not. It just so happens the VIX, which is the most well known and oldest volatility index, does indeed have a directional bias, but only because of the unique nature of the options base from which the VIX itself is derived.

I will restate once again. Volatility as a concept is non directional. However, for certain indices, such as the VIX and others we will look at shortly, there is a directional bias, but *only* as a result of the underlying options. To put this into simple terms, the VIX is not so much about the probability the market will rise or fall, but more a measure of fear that it will.

To summarize this for you in terms of trading binary options for indices. Volatility is a non directional concept, but when associated with certain volatility indices, these will often correlate to a market through the relationship with the underlying options. Do not fall into the trap of believing that all volatility indices behave in this way - they do not. It is certainly true for index indices there is a relatively close inverse correlation, but for others this is most certainly not the case. Finally, even though an index may be forecasting volatility over a 30 day period, this can be used on an intraday basis over minutes or hours as intraday volatility ebbs and flows in the market.

The demand for tradable volatility indices is growing all the time, with the market expanding, both in terms of the markets offered, as well as the type of index available. Every major exchange will generally offer some type of volatility index for their principle markets. However, for the purposes of simplicity, I have focused here on the volatility indices from one exchange, namely those offered by the Chicago Board of Options Exchange (CBOE).

CBOE Volatility Indices

If we were to scroll back ten years, all we would have found at the CBOE would have been the VIX. Now you can find volatility indices for all the benchmark equity markets, commodities, currencies and even individual stocks. In addition, with the advent of weekly options, we are increasingly beginning to see 'weekly' based volatility indices, bringing timeframes more in line with the binary options world.

Given the number of volatility indices available, I have decided to focus on just one or two, as the broad principles of interpretation are the same. I am going to use the CBOE ticker notation for each and you can find the current list here:

http://www.cboe.com/micro/IndexSites.aspx

- GVZ - Gold ETF volatility index
- VXN - NASDAQ - 100 volatility index
- EVZ - EuroCurrency ETP volatility index
- VXST - Short term volatility index

Whilst the first three are based on a 30 day implied volatility forecast, the last of these, the VXST is one of the new generation, short term volatility indices, and is based on 9 days.

And I want to take a brief look at each in turn, and the information they reveal, and how they can help us make some informed trading decisions based on the forecast volatility.

GVZ Gold ETF Volatility Index

The GVZ volatility index charts implied volatility for gold over the next 30 days, and uses the same underlying methodology as for the VIX. However, in this case the index uses options on the SPDR Gold Trust ETF (GLD), one of the most heavily traded ETF funds, which is backed by the physical asset. The CBOE presents the index using six timeframes as follows, so whether you are trading intraday or even longer term, you will find all the information you need:

- Intraday
- One week
- Three month
- Six month
- One year
- Five year

However, implied volatility is only a forecast of future volatility - there are no guarantees the market will behave in the way it is forecast. Nevertheless, it is an excellent starting point, and by using multiple timeframes this will also help to give a complete picture of where the current forecast is in relation to the past.

For example, trading a weekly binary option, whilst the weekly volatility may be high, in the context of the 3 month volatility it could be low. It is all relative, and as with volume analysis, the key is to reference what is high, medium or low across the various timeframes. Equally, on an intraday basis, volatility may be high, but in the context of the week, may be low. All this will help to 'frame' the volatility and help to determine the trading decision, whether for entry or exit, or for trading strategies based on volatility, or the lack of volatility.

Before looking at some examples for the GVZ, I would like to reiterate the point I made earlier about correlations. As you begin to study this index in detail and any associated moves with the underlying GLD ETF, you will quickly realize there is no relationship that can be considered reliable in the context of correlation. As volatility rises, so the price of gold may also rise, and vice versa. But this is *not* the VIX. Do not fall into the trap of believing that an inverse relationship exists - it does not. The volatility index for gold is non directional. As volatility increases the price of gold may move sharply higher or lower. It will not forecast direction. What it will do, is to provide that key piece of the jigsaw - a view on the current and future volatility, framed against the past.

Whilst I have shown all six timeframes here for gold, in the other examples I only propose to highlight one or two to keep the number of schematics to a manageable number.

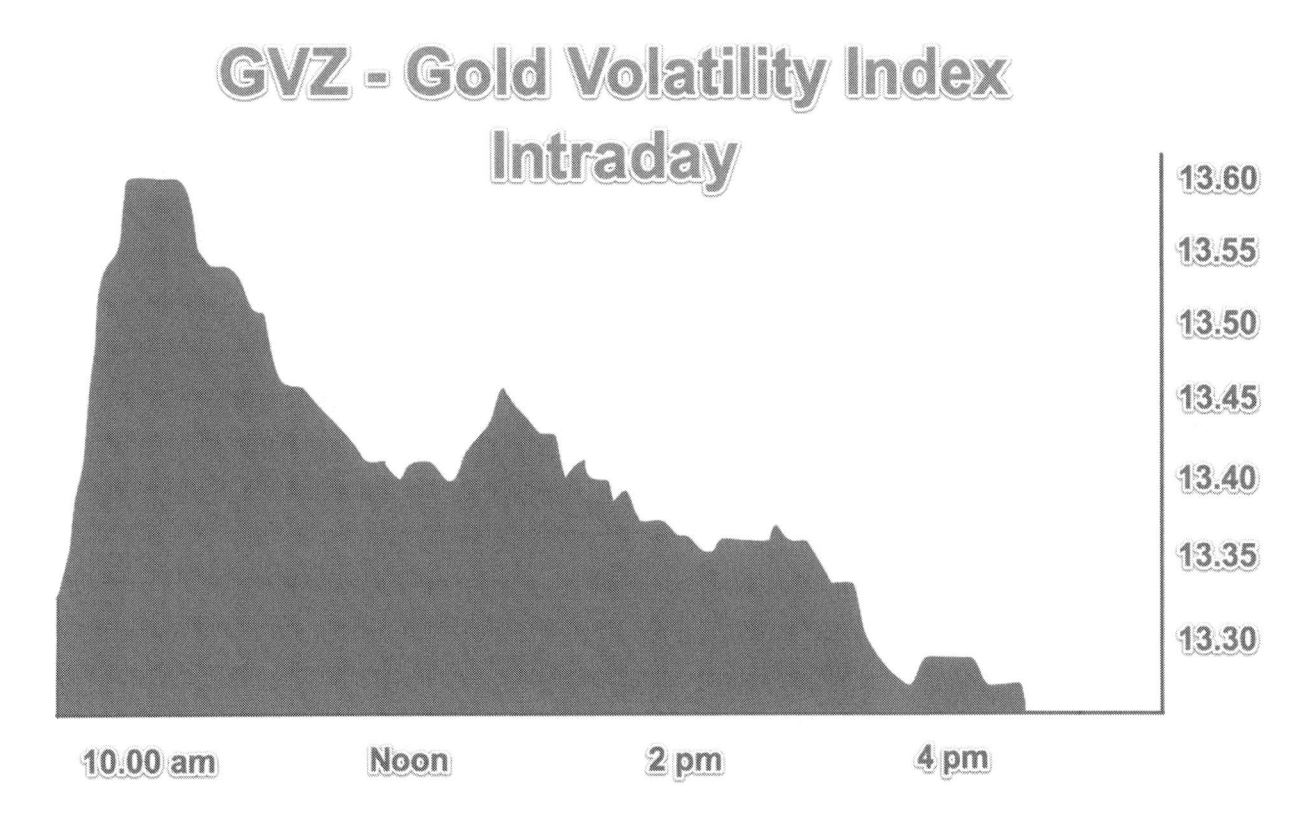

Fig 7.22 - GVZ intraday schematic

The intraday schematic is typical of what we might expect to see as trading moves from the electronic into the physical trading session. Gold futures will have been trading overnight on Globex, but as always the main activity in the commodity is when the physical exchange opens with the futures leading the way. This leads to a surge in volatility at the open, and in this case the index moved from 13.35 to 13.61, before sliding lower throughout the remainder of the trading session as the initial volatility drained away, no doubt associated with the price of gold trading in a relatively narrow range.

Note this says nothing about the direction, simply that the price action was volatile at the open for a relatively short period, peaked, and then declined steadily for the remainder of the day. So two points to note here.

First, this gives us an intraday view of volatility as the session unfolds, and second it also lays down a marker of the expected range which can then be 'framed' against the volatility of the slower timeframes. This is not to say volatility will always be in this range. It will vary depending on market conditions. However, as you begin to consider these on a regular basis, you will quickly build a picture of what is high medium or low within each timeframe. In this case, as the volatility declined past 12 pm and onwards, a 'low volatility' strategy may have been appropriate for entry, and for an existing position, perhaps giving the confidence to hold. This assumes there are no major news releases, or shocks to spook the market.

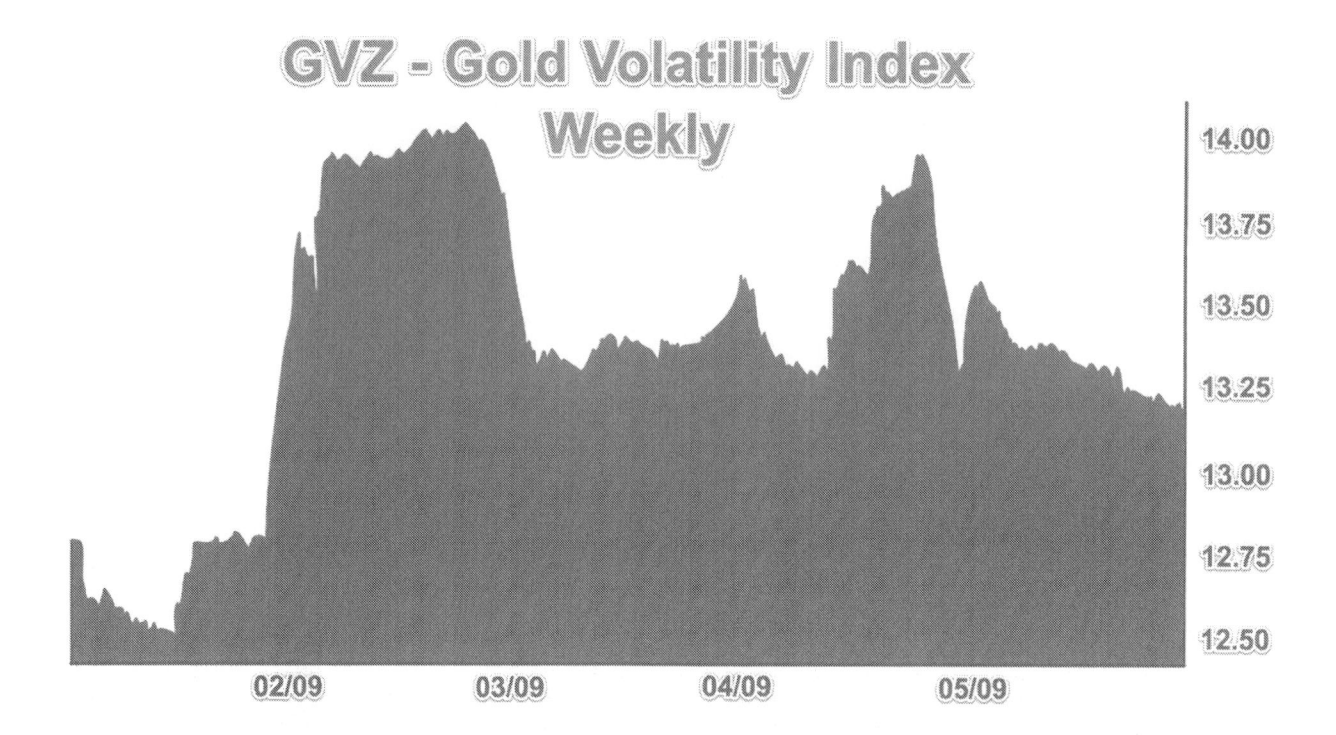

Fig 7.23 - GVZ weekly schematic

Moving to the weekly schematic. The week began quietly with the index trading between 12.60 and 12.85, spiking higher on Tuesday in a more volatile trading session, before sliding lower during the remainder of the week, with a temporary spike on Thursday.

This schematic highlights one of the principle characteristics of implied volatility, which is a tendency to mean reversion. A spike in volatility which sends the index sharply higher is equally likely to see this volatility ebb away, with the index declining as a result. This is the effect of mean reversion, and as I outlined earlier is like the plucked string on a guitar. Once plucked, the string vibrates before returning to mean. It is the same here, with the mean based on this schematic somewhere in the 13.25 to 13.50 region. This is not to say it will always be in this range. Gold prices can be extremely volatile, and the index may move considerably higher or lower. Whilst in theory an index can go to zero, in practice this is unlikely, and as always it is a question of judgement. As the index moves to the extremes, either high or low, at some point, the index will revert back to the mean in that timeframe.

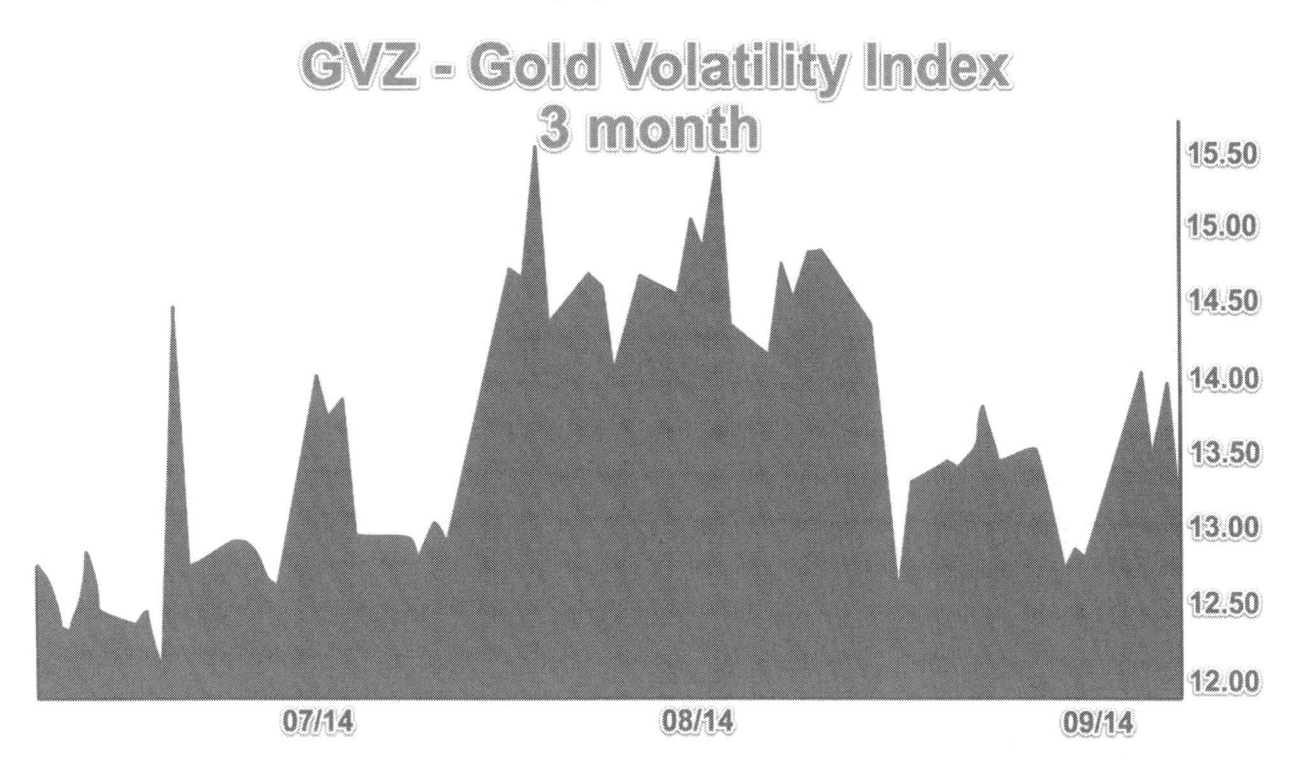

Fig 7.24 - GVZ 3 month schematic

The principles outlined above apply to all the other schematics. On the three month schematic, periodic spikes in volatility have pushed the index to a peak of 15.50 and a low of 12.15, with a return to the mean in the 13.25 to 13.75 region.

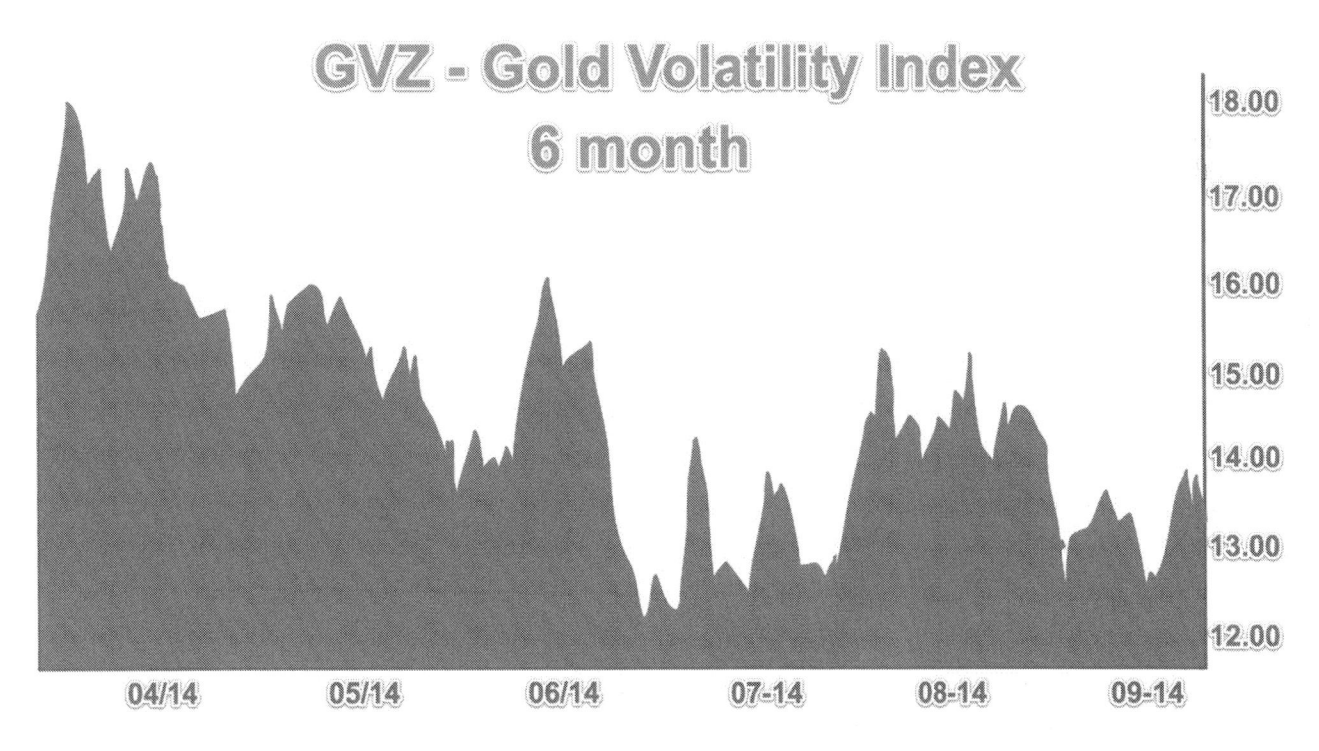

Fig 7.25 - GVZ 6 month schematic

The six month schematic, provides some additional perspective, pushing the extreme to over 18.00 earlier in the year. The interesting feature here is the slow and steady decline of volatility with the index trading in a relatively narrow range.

Fig 7.26 - GVZ 1 year schematic

The yearly schematic mirrors this trend, with the index peaking at over 26, before declining steadily towards the current price below 14.00. Once again, this is a characteristic of volatility. Moves higher in the index will be sudden and sharp, whilst moves lower are likely to be far more controlled and steady. Again, think of the guitar string - the first action is sudden, the subsequent vibrations are more controlled and extend over a period of time before gradually dying away.

GVZ - Gold Volatility Index 5 year

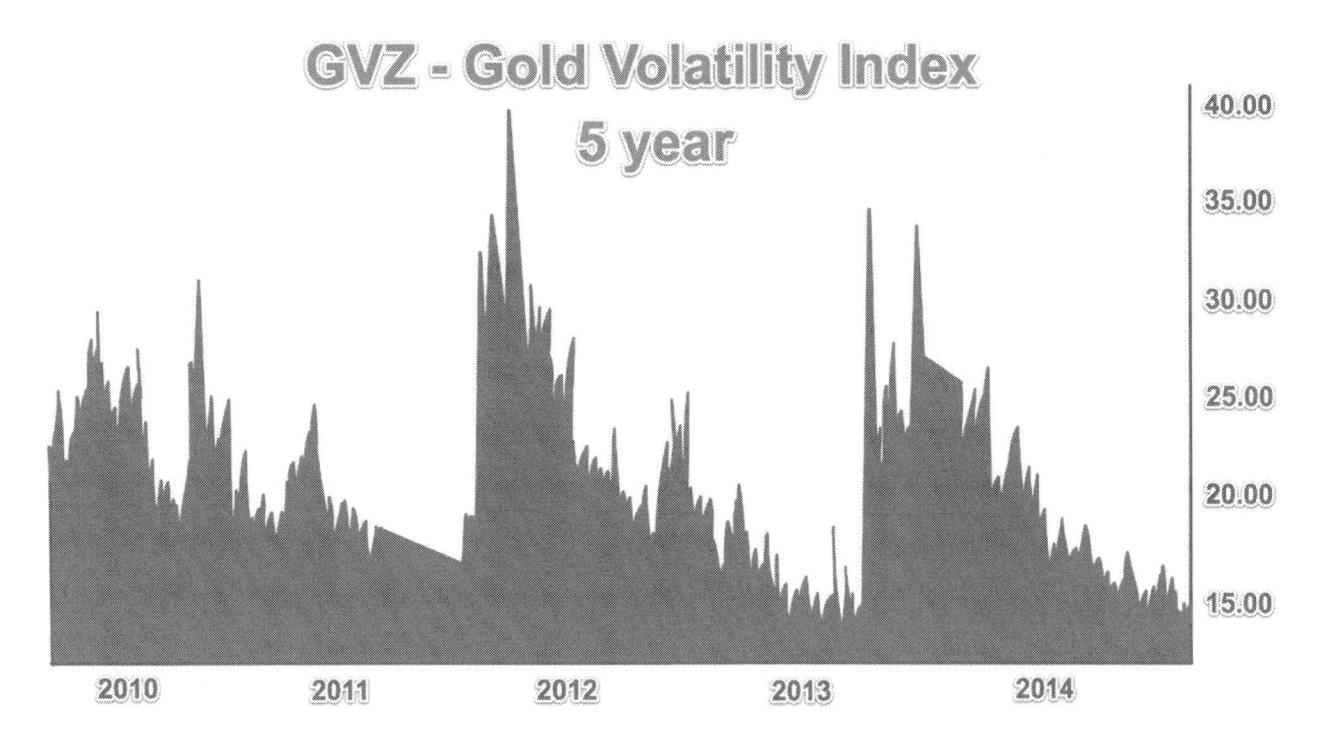

Fig 7.27 - GVZ 5 year schematic

And finally to the five year schematic which defines the extremes, and given the current period of low volatility might suggest we are due for a further spike. This really sets the scene for the index. Now the intraday volatility, weekly and slower timeframe schematics can be seen in the context of the 5 year timeframe where we have a period of declining to low volatility since the start of the year.

As with all volatility indices, it is the underlying asset and the associated options which will ultimately be reflected in the index. Gold can be extremely volatile, given the number of diverse factors which can drive prices higher or lower. Gold still remains the ultimate safe haven asset, with either market or global shocks sending investors running for cover. Next, with commodities priced in US dollars, any reaction in the dollar may also be reflected in gold. Gold also reacts to changes in perceived inflation, often triggered by interest rate announcements or decisions or even comments suggesting an increase.

Furthermore, any shock global event can create extreme volatility, with a flight to safety as a result. Whilst a volatility index will not forecast such events, it does help to contextualize implied volatility and the 'sea state' of the market. Are we heading into a force 10 storm, becalmed in the Doldrums, or happily sailing along in a nice steady force 3 or 4 wind? The last of these is the 'mean', the norm if you like, and just like the weather, calm normal conditions are punctuated with extremes from time to time for short periods, before reverting back to the mean.

I now want to consider one or two other markets, but with only two schematics from each.

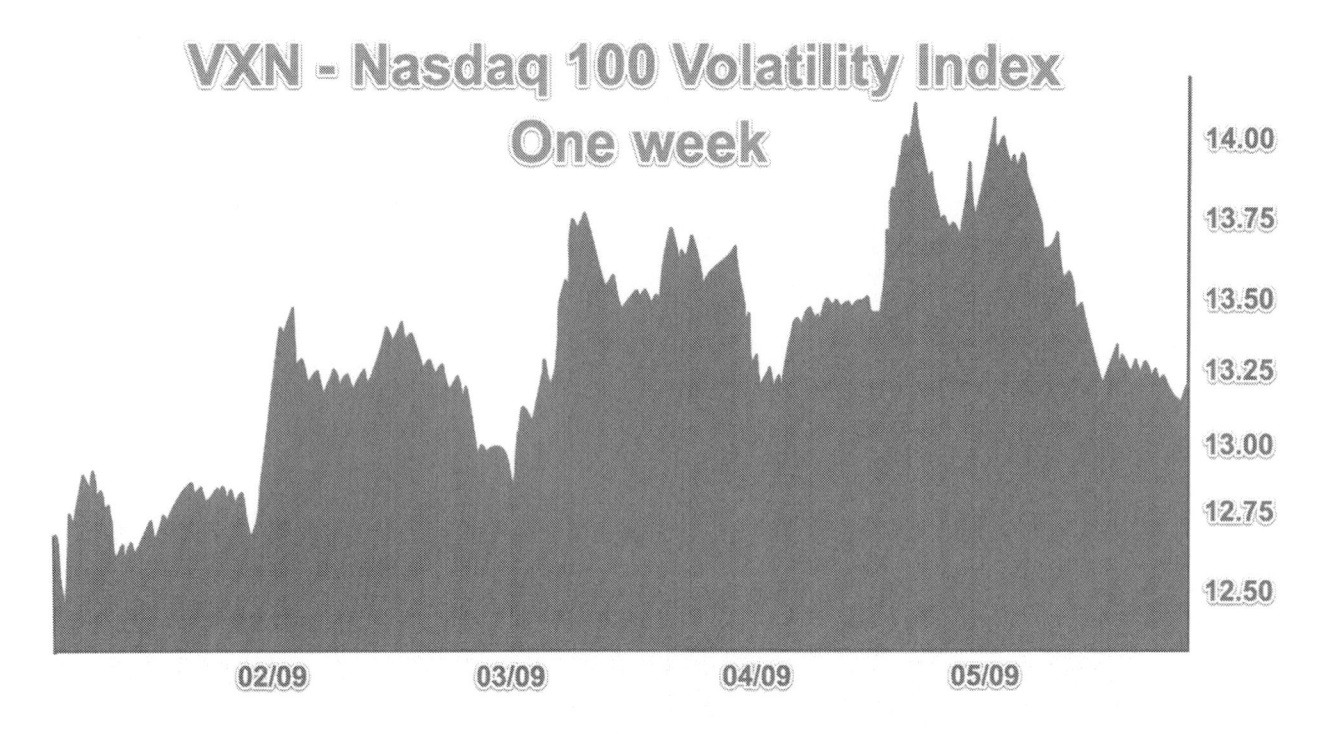

Fig 7.28 - VXN 1 week schematic

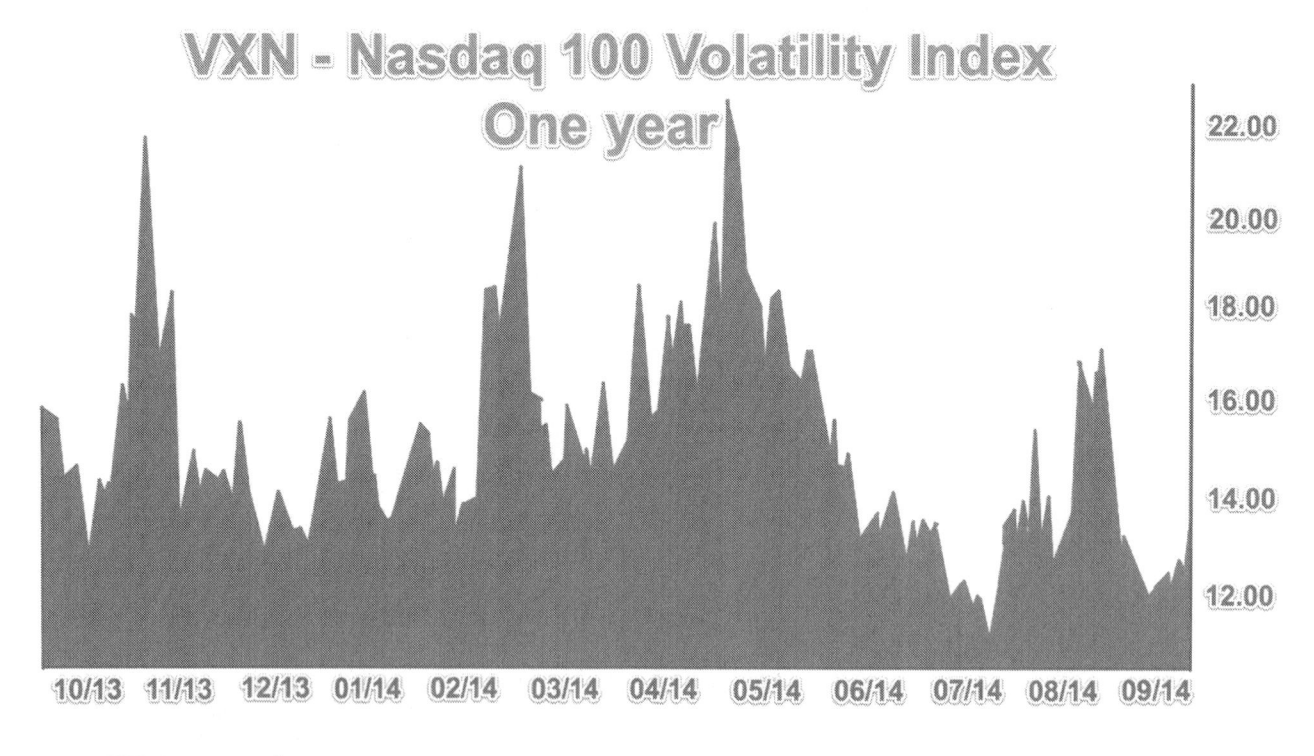

Fig 7.29 - VXN 1 year schematic

The VXN is the volatility index for the Nasdaq 100, and here we are back to an index based on index options. As a result, the VXN does have a directional aspect with the underlying Nasdaq 100, in much the same way as the VIX with the S&P 500. In other words, a directional aspect to the volatility index, with an inverse correlation once again. As we can see from the two schematics, volatility was rising slowly day by day throughout the week, and this was no surprise given the yearly schematic where volatility was touching the lows of 12 and just above. With a peak at over 22, and a low of 11.50, the index is reverting back to the mean.

The next index is a relatively new addition and is for the euro, and reflects volatility on the most liquid of currency pairs the USD/EUR.

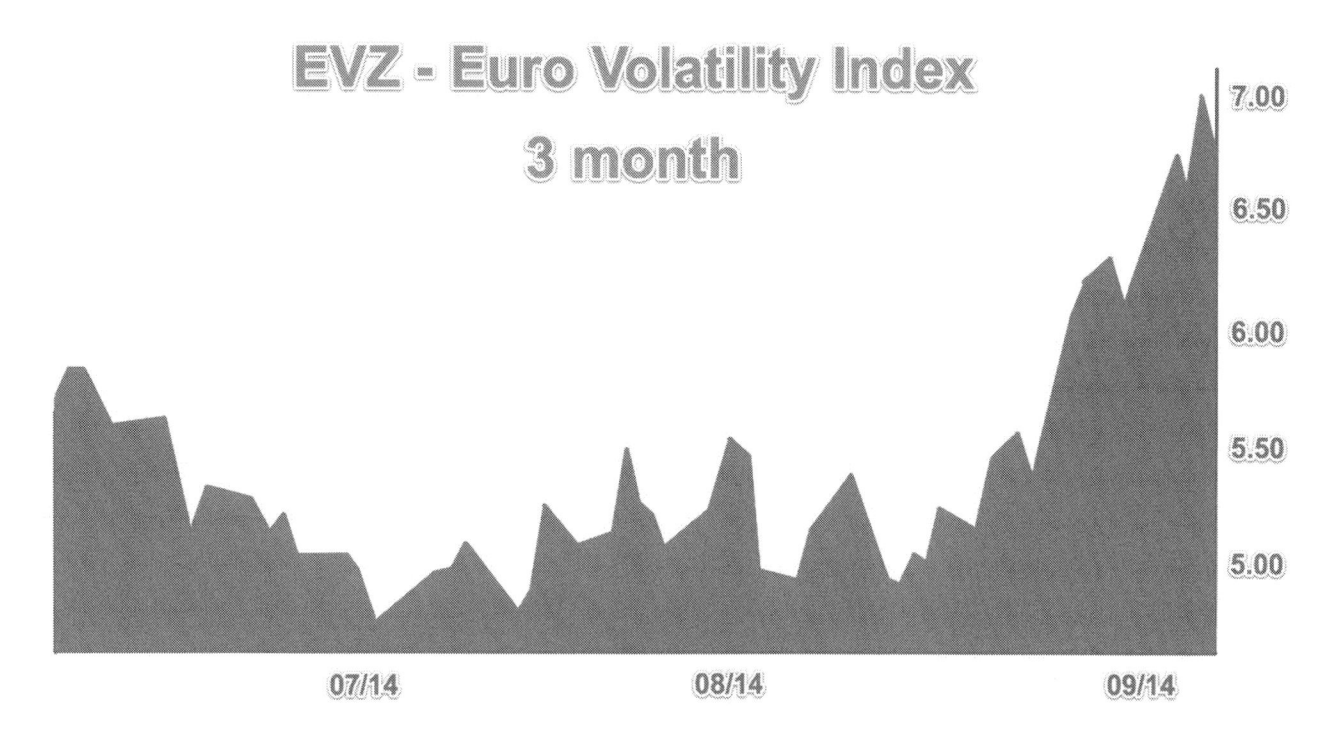

Fig 7.30 - EVZ 3 month schematic

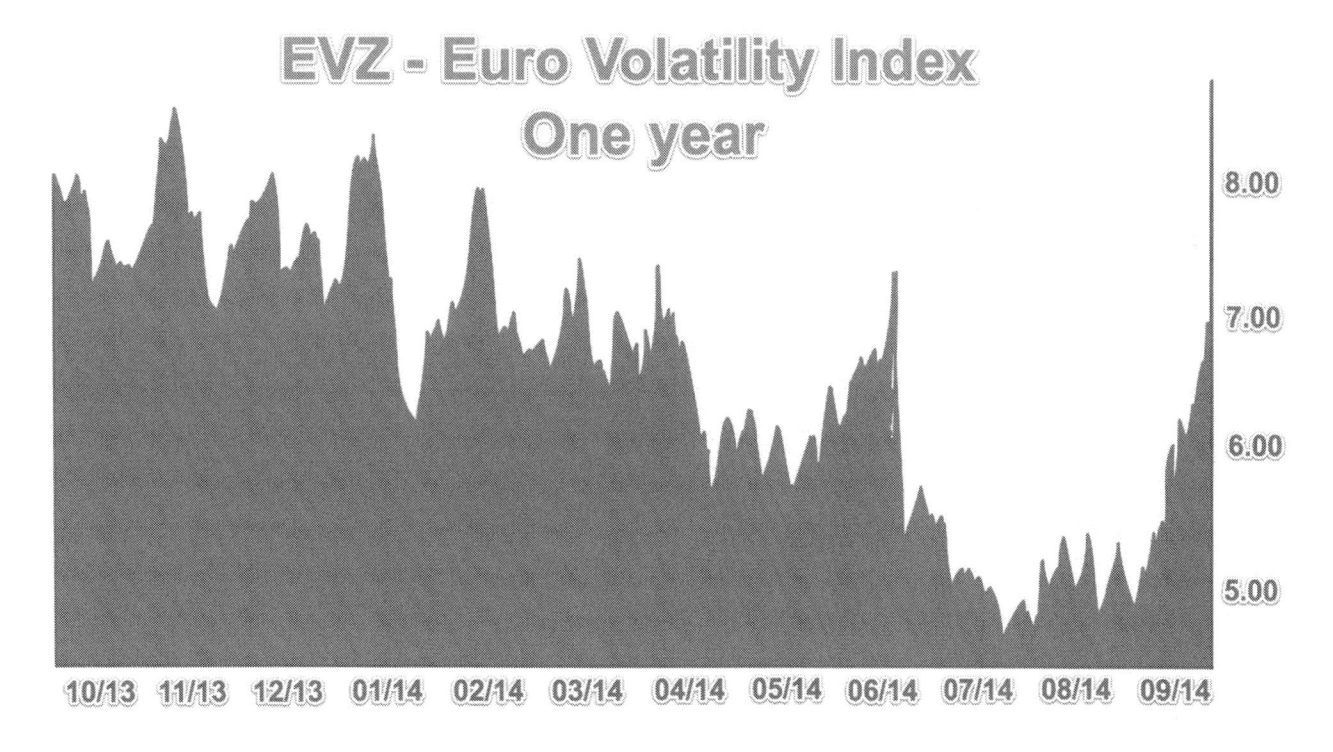

Fig 7.31 - EVZ 1 year schematic

The EVZ volatility index uses the same approach as the GVZ, and utilizes options on the CurrencyShares Euro Trust (FXE) to calculate and forecast implied volatility for the next 30 days. As such, there is no directional bias to the index. The three month schematic is certainly interesting and given the very low volatility for the pair over the last two months, it was no surprise to see volatility increasing, moving the index off the ultra low levels of 4.70 and up towards 7.00, and bringing a close to the long slow decline of the yearly chart.

Now to the last of our examples, the short term VXST which provides a short term view of the VIX over 9 days. This is based on SPX weekly options, and just like its more illustrious parent, has an inverse directional relationship to the S&P 500.

As you might expect, the 9 day index is more volatile than the 30 day equivalent - volatility on volatility if you like and is a valuable tool as it offers a 'zoomed in' view of volatility for the most heavily traded index across all instruments.

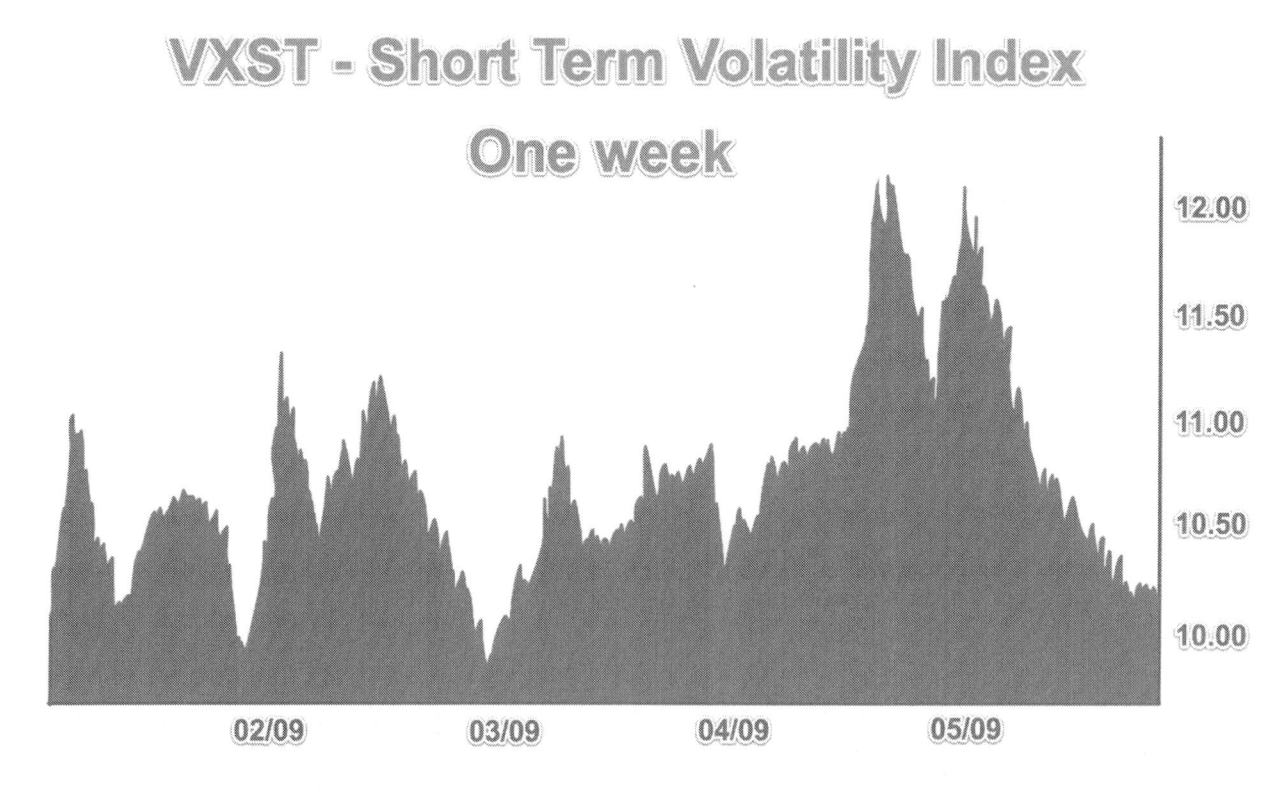

Fig 7.32 - VXST 1 week schematic

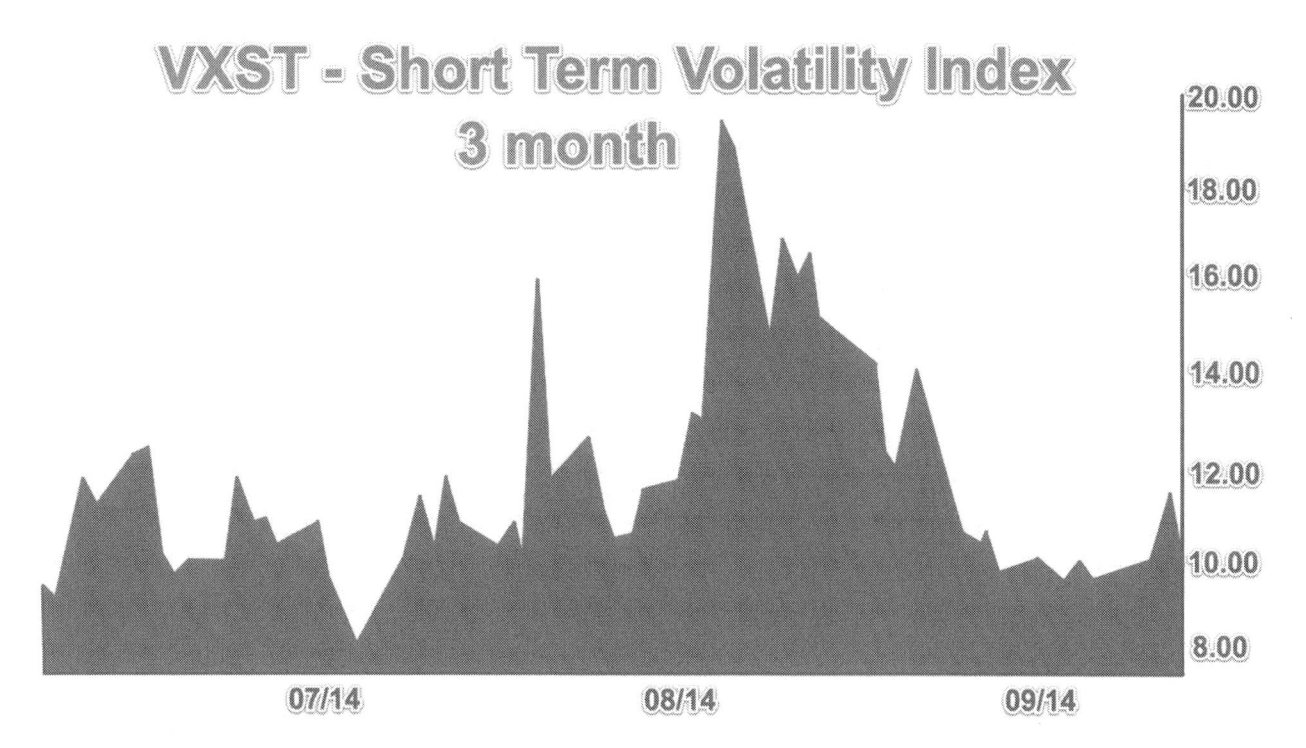

Fig 7.33 - VXST 3 month schematic

Again, the same principles apply to the above schematics. The weekly reflects 5 days of activity at both ends of the volatility spectrum with moves into single figures below 10 being reversed by intraday spikes higher to over 12.00 before reverting back to the mean at the end of the week. The three month schematic puts this into context, with a volatility spike higher to just below 20 and which can now be seen ebbing away as the index returns to a relatively low level.

These then are the volatility indices as schematics. There are many more for other popular markets, such as the Russell, the DJIA, crude oil and Treasury notes, and the list is growing all the time.

Regardless of the timeframe you are trading, volatility is one of the key factors you simply have to take into account, when trading any option, whether binary or vanilla. So please do take the time to study, understand and include this vital piece of the jigsaw in your trading decision. It is not perfect, but it is the best we have.

Let me also highlight another resource at the CBOE which is the IV Index. Again this is a free resource, and in this case can be used to provide a snapshot chart to which we can apply both historic and implied volatility. This offers us a perspective on the relationship between the two. Historic is backward looking and implied is forward looking, and over time the two will tend to revert to the mean. In other words, if the two are diverging, we can reasonably expect the two to converge in due course. If implied volatility is significantly above the historic, we can expect it to return to the historic mean by falling. Equally, if the implied volatility is significantly below the historic, then we can expect it to return to the historic mean by rising.

You can find all of this information in the Tools menu under Volatility Optimizer. Simply click on the link for the IV Index. On the right hand side of the page you will find a volatility chart. Enter your instrument in the Symbol finder, and the appropriate chart will then be displayed.

Before we leave the CBOE site, the exchange also offers two binary instruments. These are the BVZ and the BSZ. The first is a binary option on the SPX, and the second is a binary option on the VIX, which perhaps suggests we may see more on exchange binary instruments as the market develops. Whilst these binary options do have some similarities to those from Nadex, there are several important differences. First, you will not be able to trade these directly with the exchange, only through a regulated options brokerage account. Second, they are quoted in option chain format with puts and calls in the same way as for vanilla options. This means you can buy and sell both puts and calls. When selling, you receive income in the same way as an options writer in vanilla options. The difference here is that any downside risk is limited to $100 as a maximum per contract. Third and last, these options are only quoted currently with monthly expiries.

In terms of the binary quote itself, this is from 0 to 100 in 1 cent increments, so each binary option contract is cash settled to $100 or $0, and you can close the option at any time before expiry. The options chains for the BSZ are quoted in five point strike price intervals, whilst the BVZ quotes in one point strike intervals.

The above binary options have much in common with vanilla options, and as your experience trading binary options grows, are well worth a longer look.

Before we conclude this chapter on volatility, let me introduce one further aspect of price behavior which I believe is a less mathematical way of interpreting volatility, and is based on a type of chart we use for trading. This is the tick chart, as opposed to the more conventional time based chart. Here we are removing the time aspect from our chart, which you may think is ironic given the focus we have placed on time.

Imagine for a moment you are standing at the edge of an open outcry pit - the sort of pit that was once commonplace and filled with traders, all wearing brightly colored jackets. It is minutes to the open of the exchange and the tension is building. All is quiet. The bell rings, the market explodes, and the pit is enveloped in a cacophony of noise. Testosterone fueled traders yell and scream orders as fear and greed drive prices. As the crescendo rises so does volatility, and equally as it falls, so the pit calms.

A market in full cry is a sight to behold, and is a visual expression of volatility. If the pit is quiet with little activity, you can be assured the market is also quiet. If the pit is roaring, the market is in full cry and prices will be moving fast. And just as standing outside a football stadium will give you some idea of the score simply from the noise of the crowd, so standing watching the pit will give you a view of whether there is activity or volatility.

As trading pits have declined in favor of electronic trading, so traders have had to find other ways to 'sense' this activity, and one such is to us a tick based chart. A tick chart is the closest we can ever come electronically, to replicating the pit on our desktop. Let me explain.

A tick is simply a trade, and each time an order is placed it registers as a tick, irrespective of size. A 100 tick chart will therefore display the price action over 100 trades or ticks. And at this point, you might say... so what. The 'so what' is this. A tick chart is devoid of time in the sense that each tick bar or candle forms in a time dictated by the speed of the market. If the market is moving slowly each bar or candle might take minutes to form, but if the market is moving fast, each bar or candle may form in seconds or even micro seconds. In other words, a tick chart displays speed and momentum directly. If a market is moving fast, the tick bars will be delivered quickly. If the market is moving slowly, the tick bars will be delivered slowly.

This is something you will never see on a time based chart. Time charts simply reflect the price action, and are governed by the setting on the chart. Tick charts reflect the price action and are governed by the market. That's the difference. In trading any market using a tick based chart you are literally 'seeing' the market volatility reflected in the tick activity. For evidence, you only need to watch an index such as the S&P 500 prior to the open in the futures market. Ahead of the open, the tick count may be a few hundred per minute, but as the market opens this will rise to a few thousand as the physical exchange takes over from the electronic and the number of traders and trades increases exponentially. If you remember back to our first example for the GVZ volatility index, this is a graphic example of the surge in activity, and consequent volatility at the open.

To summarize. In this chapter, I have tried to explain the concept of volatility, as well as provide practical applications to help you when trading binary options. Volatility lies at the heart of all options trading, and whilst there is no perfect or simple solution, I hope the resources mentioned will give you some ideas to help in assessing each trading decision from the standpoint of volatility.

It is a huge subject in itself, and the market for these instruments is growing all the time. The CBOE is just one example, but there are many others, and not just in the futures market. There are many now available as ETFs in their own right. The general principles outlined here are broadly the same, as we search for ever more accurate and reliable ways to forecast future volatility. An almost impossible task perhaps, but one that will no doubt continue to captivate and bewitch those of us trying to harness its elusive power.

Chapter Eight

Binary Option Products

Risk comes from not knowing what you are doing

Warren Buffett (1930 -)

The binary options market is nothing if not fast moving. Even during the course of writing this book, brokers have come and gone, new products have been launched whilst others have been withdrawn. Moreover the cost of attracting new clients is rising inexorably, and with most binary option clients having a shorter survival rate than those in the more mature forex market, customer retention remains the number one issue for most binary brokers. In addition, in such a hugely competitive market, and with most binary brokers offering white label solutions, the products on offer are generally 'me too'. That said, in the last few months binary options on the weather are likely to launch soon adding another dimension to the binary world.

Whilst products form the core of the client offering, increasingly social trading is now seen as the way forward, mirroring moves in the forex world, along with client education and better charting packages for greater transparency.

In such a fast moving market it is also no surprise to see forex brokers launch their own products to take advantage of the lucrative opportunities presented by this market.

Therefore, in order to follow the structure of the book, let me break binary products up into the two primary groups, namely those offered by off exchange brokers, and those offered by on exchange brokers. However, I must stress these will no doubt change and develop quickly, with new ones being added and less popular ones being withdrawn.

Off Exchange Binary Option Products

Call Up/ Put Down

The simplest of all binary options is the up/down proposition. Here the decision is simple. All you are being asked to judge is whether the market will end high or lower by the time the option expires. These options go under several different names, and you may come across them as any of the following:

- Rise/Fall
- Above/Below
- High/Low
- Call/Put

If you are right the option closes in the money. If you are wrong at expiry, the option closes out of the money. This type of product is the bread and butter for all off exchange binary options brokers. It is the basis for pure betting on expiry times from seconds to minutes. Longer term timeframes will be offered such as hours, and with these you may have the opportunity to close out early, either to take a profit or to reduce a loss.

One Touch

As its name suggests, this option is designed to trigger if a certain price is hit during the life of the option. The price to be touched may be above or below the current price.

If the price specified is touched before expiry, the option expires instantly in the money. If the price specified is not touched then the option expires out of the money. A one touch option requires you to correctly forecast both direction and volatility since the one touch price is likely to be some distance from the current market price.

Forecasting price direction within a time frame is difficult enough, adding volatility to the prediction makes it almost impossible. This is why the one touch option is often marketed and promoted as one offering extraordinary returns, up to 500% and even more and the only thing to say here is if an offer sounds to good to be true, then it generally is. What you will typically discover with this product is the target for the one touch is a significant distance from the underlying market, and when any price move is converted into its equivalent percentage move, then the reality of the option is revealed.

This is the reason returns are so high. The probabilities are most definitely not in your favor. These types of options are usually sold as single units with a cash amount, and generally the target is fixed as is the expiry with no facility to close out early.

No Touch

The no touch option is the opposite of the one touch option. In this case the option will expire in the money if the price specified is not touched before expiry. If it is, the option expires worthless. There are some key differences between the one touch and the no touch options which are worth remembering.

With a one touch option, the further the strike price is from the market, the greater the potential return. In other words, the probability of the event happening decreases the further away the price is set, and therefore the higher return if it does. Here again you will find very high potential returns being quoted of 500% or more.

The opposite is true for a no touch option. The further away the price is set, the probability of the event not happening increases and the return falls. Or put another way, the closer the trigger to the underlying market, the higher the return.

Furthermore, volatility is required for a one touch option to succeed, whilst a benign market with no volatility is required for a no touch option to succeed.

Ladder

The ladder option is a relatively new addition to the products now on offer from most binary brokers. Two or three years ago this option was unknown, but is now being taken up as a standard product offering. This approach is one familiar to vanilla options traders, and is generally referred to as the bull call ladder (or long call ladder), an extension of another strategy known as the bull call spread. This is something we will look at in more detail later in the book.

The ladder is created by combining three call options, on the expectation of low volatility in the underlying market but with a bullish tone. The opposite is a bear call ladder, or short call ladder, and is one where volatility is required. There is one significant difference between a binary ladder and a vanilla options ladder namely the risk profile.

Risk and reward in a binary option are capped. In a vanilla option they are not, and whilst they may have similar names, the risk and reward profiles are very different. Nevertheless, the binary world has adopted this term to describe a binary equivalent product, which in essence is a ladder of three strike prices with different expiries.

Whilst the principle of the product may be common from one broker to another, the structure of the product offering may vary dramatically. This is a new product which is still evolving, and one which is also complex. Its longer term success will depend on whether it is embraced by the market as offering a solid methodology, or is viewed as simply another way for the brokers to stack the odds in their favor.

The ladder trade is structured in the way you would expect. A ladder of strike prices with different expiry times. Those strike prices closest to the current market offer the lowest returns, whilst those farthest away offer higher returns. The theory is that as the market 'steps up the ladder', the payouts are triggered accordingly as each strike price is achieved. You might be wondering why anyone would want to add a further level of complexity. After all, the proposition here is not only judging the direction of the market, the extent of any trend, but also the time this trend will take to develop. It should come as no surprise this is considered a more advanced product.

The reason it has attracted growing interest from binary traders is that some brokers allow them to create their own ladder. In other words to set the expiry times and the price steps, which are normally three strike prices, although some brokers offer five. The option expires in or out of the money depending on whether all or some of the strike prices have been met. If none are met then the option expires out of the money.

Tunnel

The tunnel, like the up/down product is another well established product offering, and is generally available from most binary brokers. Some brokers refer to it as the tunnel, others call it the boundary option or range option, and the concept is very straightforward. The binary is defined with a price above and below, and for the option to expire in the money, the price has to stay within the tunnel or range.

You can think of this as a congestion phase on a chart, with a support line below and a resistance line above. The analysis here is to find a market that is likely to remain rangebound, in a congestion phase for the duration of the option. If the price remains in the tunnel until expiry, it expires in the money. If the tunnel is broken, either above or below, the option expires out of the money.

Some brokers do offer variations of this product, sometimes referred to as the 'in/out' option, and these are generally as follows:

- Ends in the tunnel/Ends out of the tunnel
- Ends in the tunnel/Moves outside the tunnel

The first is a variation of the standard product. Here you can select the option either ending in the tunnel or outside the tunnel, a choice between a lack of volatility (ends in the tunnel) and volatility (ends out of the tunnel).

In the second variation, here the option remains within the tunnel until expiry, or moves outside at any time to expire in the money.

Hi/Lo

No not a misspelling. This is a variation of the up/down proposition, and of a tunnel option outlined above. Here the trigger is in forecasting a target range of a high and low price. A close above or below expires in the money, with a close between ending out of the money.

Target

As the name suggests this is a target that has to be hit, and so combines both direction and range. The target range is specified, either up or down, and if the target price is achieved the option closes in the money. If not, it closes out of the money.

Pairs

Once again the clue is in the name, and whilst this product is less widely available, and generally only from a specialist binary broker, this approach is gaining in popularity. Pairs trading, like the ladder, has been developed from the vanilla options world.

The proposition is based on forecasting the behavior of two assets, relative to one another. You can think of this product as being market neutral. What you are trying to do here is to assess the relative performance or how the two assets will behave relative to one another, irrespective of the market conditions.

At present the most popular market for pairs is stocks. In this instance the option is presented as a choice between two stocks and their relative performance over time. Once the option is purchased, the two stocks are reset to zero and their relative percentage performance is then measured from the start of the option through to expiry. What you will also find with this type of option is the expiry periods are likely to be much longer, and more in line with an investment approach, aligned to the underlying assets. For example, you could consider the performance of Apple against Microsoft, or Facebook against Google.

At present two variations are offered as follows:

- Fixed
- Floating

With the fixed approach, the pairs are reset as outlined above, and reset to zero. In the floating approach, the two assets are not reset, but left to float with their relative performance differences intact from the start of the life of the option. This gives you increased opportunities in terms of the relative performance over time, but one downside of this approach is the expiry times will generally be much shorter - relatively speaking.

As with everything in the binary options world, this is another product which is starting to incorporate other assets. It has also been taken up by the primary platforms and you will find examples at Binary.com, and is gradually becoming more widely available via the multitude of white label binary brokers. Instruments such as gold against silver, gold against oil, index pairs and stocks are now increasingly available. The choice here is growing fast, and like many of the products outlined above will continue to evolve and change as the market matures.

On Exchange Binary Option Products

Moving to option products offered on the exchanges, the choice here is currently as follows. In terms of exchange traded binary options, there are several available, namely those offered by the CBOE, Nadex and the NYSE.

In the future other exchanges will come on stream, and waiting in the wings is Cantor Fitzgerald who received authorization both for clearing and for market making by the CFTC. This will allow Cantor to begin offering binary options in due course, but at time of writing there is no date set for the launch of this exchange.

If we start with the binary options offered by the CBOE (Chicago Board Options Exchange) there are currently two options available, the BSZ and the BVZ. The first is based on the S&P 500 index, and the second on the CBOE volatility index. As always with any exchange traded product the role of the exchange is to match buyers and sellers and create an orderly, fair and transparent market. To trade these options offered by the CBOE, you will need a specialist futures and options broker as unlike Nadex, you cannot trade direct with the exchange.

BSZ

In many ways the BSZ binary option is a hybrid as it bridges the gap between the world of exotic and vanilla options. The key points are as follows with the underlying market being the S&P 500:

- At expiry the option either pays $100 or $0
- Prices quoted are the probability of reaching or exceeding the strike price at expiry
- Options are quoted as Calls or Puts
- Strike prices are quoted in a conventional option chain and with a 5 point interval
- Three consecutive near term contract months will be listed
- These are European style binary options which can only be exercised on the last business day prior to expiration

- Bids and offers are expressed as 0.01 to 1.00 with a minimum tick of $1 (0.01) and a contract multiplier of 100
- The option can be closed at any time prior to expiry by reversing the opening position
- Last trading day for the BSZ is Thursday before the third Friday of the expiration month
- Expiry is the Saturday following the third Friday of the expiration month
- These binary options can be bought or sold to open, just as for regular vanilla options
- A margin account will be required for writing options

As you can see from the above, this form of binary option is really a bridge between vanilla and exotic options. For example, the ability to buy or sell to open is very different from the off exchange approach. Here a sell order to open results in a credit in terms of the 'premium', but also requires margin to cover the balance of any open positions in your account, which is of course limited by the capped risk. This is very different from writing vanilla options where risk can be unlimited - something we will explore shortly.

BVZ

The BVZ binary is similar to the BSZ, and is based on the VIX, so here you are trading volatility directly, by taking a view on the VIX which is the underlying asset in this case. The key points for this option are as follows:

- At expiry the option either pays $100 or $0
- Prices quoted are the probability of reaching or exceeding the strike price at expiry
- Options are quoted as Calls or Puts
- Strike prices are quoted in a conventional option chain and with a 1 point interval
- Three consecutive near term contract months will be listed
- These are European style binary options which can only be exercised on the last business day prior to expiration
- Bids and offers are expressed as 0.01 to 1.00 with a minimum tick of $1 (0.01) and a contract multiplier of 100
- The option can be closed at any time prior to expiry by reversing the opening position
- Last trading day for the BVZ is Tuesday before the expiration date of each month
- Expiry is the Wednesday which is 30 days prior to the third Friday of the following month
- These binary options can be bought or sold to open, just as for regular vanilla options
- A margin account will be required for writing options

Once again to trade these binary options you will need a margin account and specialist broker.

The next group of binary options is more extensive and are offered by the New York Stock Exchange (NYSE). However, they are not referred to as binary options, but as binary return derivatives and classified on the exchange as ByRDs. There are approximately 70 of these currently available primarily covering individual stocks, ETFs and funds. The instrument is quoted as one of two types:

- Finish High ByRDs
- Finish Low ByrDs

You can think of these as calls and puts. The Finish High is a call and the Finish Low is a put. The broad principles of these are the same as for those offered by the CBOE, and the key points are as follows:

- At expiry the option either pays $100 or $0
- Prices quoted are the probability of reaching or exceeding the strike price at expiry
- Options are quoted as Finish High or Finish Low
- Strike prices are quoted in a conventional option chain and with various intervals according to the underlying asset
- Three consecutive near term contract months will be listed
- These are European style binary options which can only be exercised on the last business day prior to expiration
- Bids and offers are expressed as 0.01 to 1.00 with a minimum tick of $1 (0.01) and a contract multiplier of 100
- The option can be closed at any time prior to expiry by reversing the opening position
- These binary options can be bought or sold to open, just as for regular vanilla options
- A margin account will be required for writing options

In contrast to the binary options offered by the CBOE, the list available for ByRDs is more extensive. Here are just a few of the more popular ones:

- American Express
- Amazon
- Apple
- Citigroup
- Caterpillar
- Facebook
- SPDR Gold shares
- IBM
- ishares Russell 200
- Microsoft
- SDPR S&P 500 ETF
- AT & T
- United States Oil Fund

One of the principle differences you will discover with the options from the NYSE, is these are now following the trend of shorter term timescales for options, reflecting moves in the vanilla options world, so you will find weekly ByRDs options available.

Finally we come to the binary options offered by Nadex and IG, and here they fall into two distinct product groups. The first is the familiar binary option, and the second is the bull spread option.

Binary Option

As we have already looked at this product in great detail I do not propose to dwell on it here, but simply add it in for completeness.

There is one big difference with Nadex as an exchange. Here you can trade direct with the exchange, something which is not available with the others listed here which all require a specialist broker. In addition many of the Nadex products are also available through IG index.

Bull Spread

The bull spread is a variant of the binary option, and one we will look at in more detail when considering some binary trading strategies later in the book.

For now let's look at what this instrument does and how it differs from the binary option product itself.

You can think of the bull spread as a simplified version of the bull spread strategy available in the world of vanilla options, where the structure of the trade is created by buying and selling calls with different strike prices. With Nadex the hard work has been done for you, with the same risk profile created through a single instrument. And here it is important to note the settlement is against the underlying spot market price, and not 0 or 100. Whilst the risk and reward profile is fixed, it is fixed in a different way using the spot market to create the floor and ceiling of the instrument.

The spread referred to is the difference between the floor and the ceiling of the instrument which then defines the upper and lower levels of risk. As with the binary option product, this is an instrument which has defined and limited risk, and defined and limited profit. An example of how this is quoted is as follows:

- GBP/USD - 1.6400 to 1.6550 at 4:00 pm
- The spot market is currently trading at 1.6450

The spread here is 150 pips and defines the floor and ceiling of risk. In other words, these are capped, so even if the market moved outside this range at expiry, your profit and loss would be capped and defined by these levels. As you would expect, you can buy or sell the contract, depending on whether you think the market is moving higher or lower in this timeframe and before the expiry of 4.00 pm.

Let's assume we are indeed bullish and buy at 1.6450, this sets the floor and ceiling of profit and risk as follows:

- Maximum profit - 1.6550 - 1.6450 = 100 pips
- Maximum loss - 1.6450 - 1.6400 = 50 pips

This defines the maximum profit and loss on the position, whatever happens to the underlying spot market, and even if there were a volatile move and the spot rate fell to 1.6300, or moved to 1.6600, the maximum profit and loss profile would remain the same.

In this example, if the market did indeed move higher by expiry, but remained below the ceiling of the spread, your profit would simply be the difference between the open and closing price of your order ticket. Equally if the market moved lower, but remained above the floor, any loss would simply be the difference between the open and closing prices of the order ticket.

However, it is important to note even if the underlying market does move outside the spread, this does not trigger a close of the option. The bull spread option only closes at expiry, but you can close it yourself by reversing the opening order. A buy order is reversed with a sell order, and vice versa. Again you can trade in multiple contracts and also remove partial contracts during the life of the option.

The bull spread is an extremely versatile variant of a binary option and removes the complexities of creating this strategy through multiple option legs in the vanilla world. As you will see when we look at binary option trading strategies, this unique product lends itself to many different uses, but all are defined with the same limited risk and limited profit profile.

In summary, just as in the off exchange binary world, the on exchange products now available are beginning to increase to offer broader market opportunities. Those I have highlighted in this chapter are the primary ones available today, but the list is growing all the time, both in terms of the products themselves, and also the markets.

The binary spread with Nadex is a classic example, as this is now available not just for forex, but also for commodities and indices as well as across a variety of timeframes from hours, to days weeks and months. And if you prefer to trade options through your futures broker, these too are increasingly available. So some interesting times ahead as this market develops and matures.

Chapter Nine

Vanilla vs Binary Options

One of the funny things about the stock market is that every time one person buys, another sells, and both think they are astute

William Feather (1889 - 1981)

Whilst this book is primarily about binary options, I do not feel it would be complete without including an introduction to vanilla options for several reasons.

First, and perhaps most importantly, I believe binary options provide a stepping stone into the world of vanilla options. Second, much of the terminology used in vanilla options is increasingly filtering its way into the binary option lexicon. Third, binary options, and in particular binary spreads, are now starting to mirror option trading strategies from the vanilla world, and therefore an understanding of the risk and reward profiles of the two, helps to explain where these worlds meet.

One such example is the bull spread from Nadex, which we will cover both in this chapter, and also in the next. This is one of the many examples of a 'hybrid' option, which is now drawing together aspects of both the binary and vanilla options worlds. This creates an instrument which combines power with simplicity and flexibility. The bull spread is particularly interesting, despite the fact as with other on exchange options it has a limited risk and limited reward profile, but when combined with other markets offers an elegant and sophisticated approach to managing risk.

I believe binary options, even with all the marketing hype, do offer a stepping stone into the world of vanilla options. Options are fascinating, complex and highly versatile instruments, which have often had a bad press. Whilst it is undoubtedly true they can be high risk, they also offer equally low risk strategies, and provided these differences are clearly understood, options are yet another valuable trading tool to have in your toolkit. And in writing this chapter I hope to achieve two things.

First, highlight the differences in risk profiles between binary and vanilla options. And secondly in doing so, to open your eyes to the future potential vanilla options can offer you as a trader, as your knowledge and experience grows. This chapter will not tell you all you need to know about vanilla options. What I hope to achieve is give you a flavor of how the two compare, the advantages and the disadvantages of each, and in doing so give you a complete picture of the options world from the binary and vanilla perspective.

Vanilla Options

If we begin with the word option, this really does describe the origin and purpose of this instrument. It gives someone the '*option*' to do something, but they do not have to exercise this option (choice).

If you are the holder of an option on something, the choice is yours as to whether you decide to exercise this right which is yours as the option holder. As an option holder (buyer), you have paid a premium and bought the right to exercise this option.

If you have bought an option, someone else has sold an option, and thinking logically, if you have a right to exercise the option, someone on the other side (the counter-party), has the obligation to deliver on the option.

This in a nutshell, is what the options market is about. On the one hand you have an option buyer, and on the other you have the option seller. The option buyer has rights, the option seller has obligations.

And herein lies the most fundamental aspect of any vanilla option, in that it is a contract between two parties, a buyer and a seller, and just like any other contract between two parties, one has rights and the other has obligations. For example, a contract between a client and their builder. The client has the right to expect a completed house to the specification agreed, the builder has an obligation to deliver on time and to budget.

For a vanilla option, the contract specifies in very precise terms the amount of the underlying asset, the expiry date, the strike price and the type of delivery of the underlying asset. In other words, a vanilla option is standardized, and can therefore be listed and traded on more than one exchange. They are referred to as fungible.

Vanilla options are quoted as calls and puts, with calls rising in value as the underlying asset increases, and puts rising in value as the underlying asset falls. When you buy an option you pay what is called a premium, and when you sell an option you receive this premium. The value of the premium changes minute by minute, and day by day depending on the movements in the underlying asset.

As an options trader or investor, you can be either a buyer or a seller of an option. However, each has very different contractual obligations and risk profile, depending on whether you are a buyer (holder) or seller (writer). These are as follows:

- *Call buyer (holder)* - you have the right, but not the obligation to buy the underlying asset at expiry at the strike price
- *Call seller (writer)* - you have an obligation to deliver the underlying asset at the strike price if assigned
- *Put buyer (holder)* - you have the right, but not the obligation to sell the underlying asset at expiry at the strike price
- *Put seller (writer)* - you have an obligation to take delivery of the underlying asset at the strike price if assigned

What does this actually mean? It means buyers (holders) have rights, and sellers (writers) have obligations.

At a very basic level, buying an option, whether a call or a put, is low risk, whilst selling an option, whether a put or a call is high risk. And this encapsulates one of the primary differences between vanilla options and binary options which is the risk profile of each instrument.

When you buy a call or a put to open a position, your maximum risk is the cost of the option, no more and no less - the premium in other words. In essence what you are doing is buying an option which gives you the right to do something in the future, ***if you wish.*** You have no contractual obligation to do anything.

When you sell a call or a put, the situation is very different. Here you receive a premium - your reward if you like - for taking the additional risk of writing (selling) the option. You retain this premium whatever happens thereafter. However, as a seller you now have an obligation to deliver (or take delivery of) the underlying asset, should the holder (buyer) of the option decide to exercise their right as the option holder.

Here is an example. If we take a US stock option, where the underlying contract quantity is 100, the relationship between the option buyer and seller is very straightforward. If a call buyer has the right to buy the underlying stock specified in the contract, the call seller has the obligation to deliver the stock at the agreed price.

Similarly, if a put buyer has the right to sell the stock, the put seller has the obligation to take delivery. It's a 'push me pull you' relationship. These rights and obligations then define the risk profile for each, which is very different from the binary option.

Each option is classified according to class and series, with associated options chains. An option chain simply displays all the strike prices available, the calls and puts and the latest prices.

To summarize:

- An options buyer (holder) purchases a contract to open or close a position
- An options seller (writer) sells a contract to open or close a position

The option is specified in standard terms so it can be traded across exchanges. These are as follows:

- Every option has a specific contract size associated with the option. In the case of a stock option, in the US markets this is 100 shares, or 10 shares for a mini option
- Every option has an expiry month (or other period) and last trading day
- Every option has a strike price
- Every option specifies how the underlying asset is to be delivered, whether physical or cash settled
- There are two styles of options, American and European. European options can only be exercised on the day of expiry, whilst American options can be exercised at any time
- Options are specified in option chains by series and class

Unlike the binary option which has a simple fixed risk, fixed reward profile, the vanilla option offers combinations of profiles mixing limited and unlimited risk and reward depending on whether you are an option buyer (holder) or option seller (writer). This is one of the many advantages of a vanilla option, namely the number of strategies, both simple and complex which are not available using a binary option. Finally, vanilla options can only be bought or sold through an authorized brokerage account, and there will be commissions to pay on each transaction. In addition the margin requirements will vary according to the strategies adopted.

The risk profiles as a buyer and seller of vanilla options are also very different.

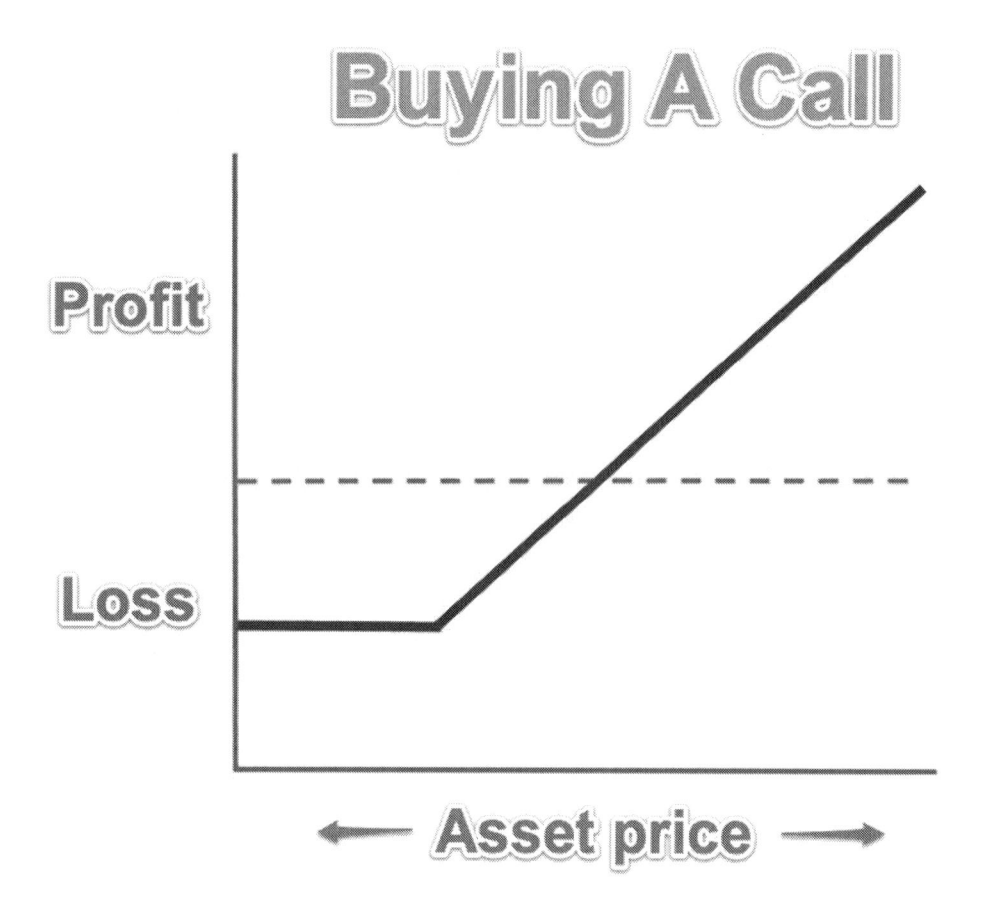

Fig 9.10 - Buying (holding) a call risk profile

The risk associated with buying, or holding a call option is limited to the cost of the premium. As we can see from Fig 9.10, the break-even point is denoted by the dotted line, with the risk and reward profile defined by the solid line. The vertical axis is the profit and loss on the option position, whilst the horizontal axis is the price of the underlying asset. Assume this is a stock option with 100 shares as the contract.

Here we have purchased a call option, and as the share price rises, so will the value of the option, moving through the break-even point from loss (the premium paid for the option) and into profit. As the share price continues to rise, so does the value of the option, ever higher until expiry. There is no limit to the profit potential from the option, it is uncapped. The risk however, is limited to the premium paid for the option, and can never be any more. Even if the underlying share price collapsed, the option would expire worthless, with any loss capped to the premium paid, plus any broker commission.

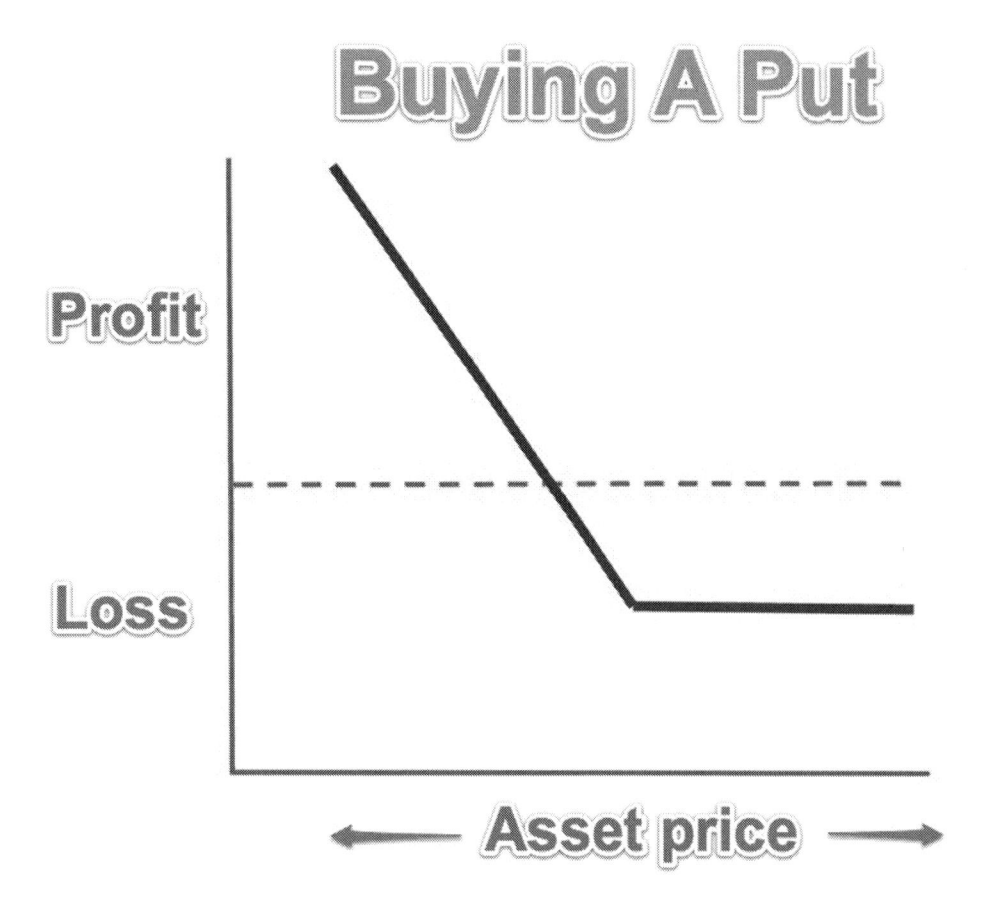

Fig 9.11 - Buying (holding) a put risk profile

The risk and reward profile for buying or holding a put is the same as for buying and holding a call option, but in reverse. A put increases in value as the underlying asset falls, so once again, the risk on the option is limited to the premium paid - no more and no less. If the stock price rises the maximum loss is the premium paid.

If the stock price falls and moves through the strike price and beyond, the value of the option will continue to rise with unlimited profit potential until expiry. One could argue, since a stock price can in theory only go to zero, the profit potential here is in fact limited.

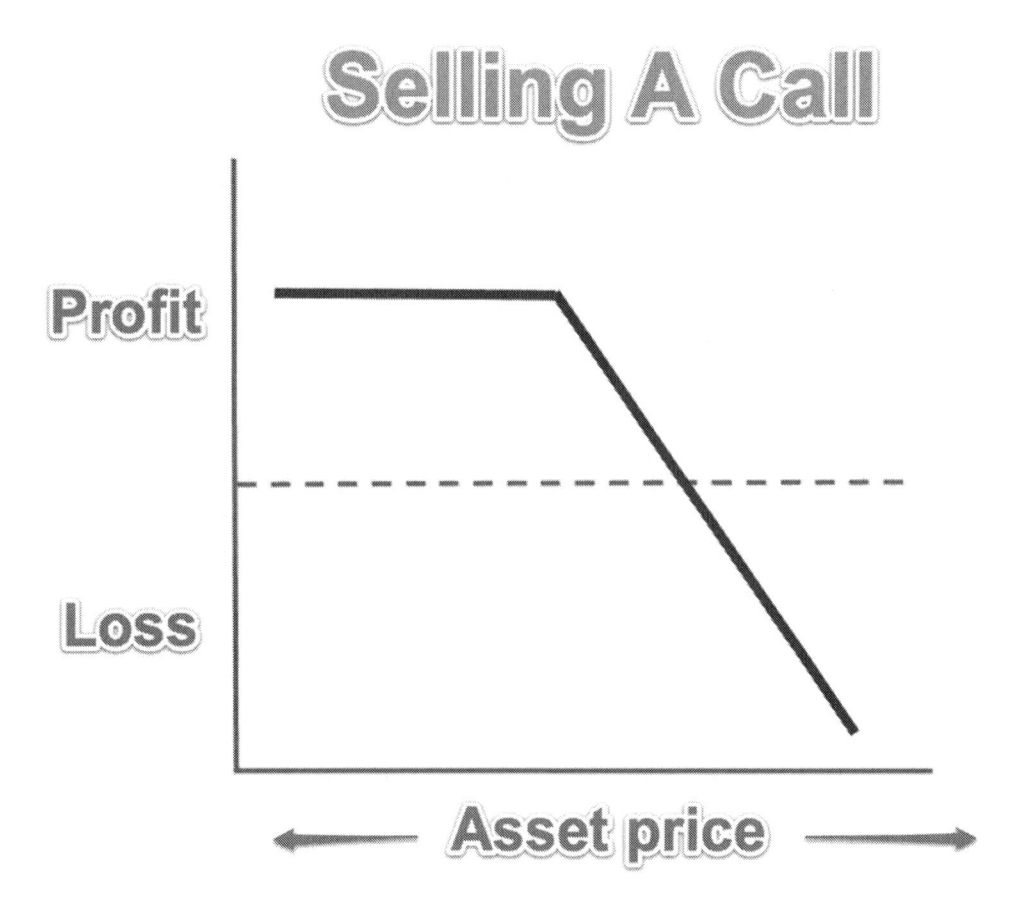

Fig 9.12 - Selling a call risk profile

Now we move to the other side of the fence and become an option seller or writer. In doing so it completely changes the risk and reward profile, and we move from the low risk proposition of buying puts and calls, to the high risk strategies associated with selling calls and puts.

In Fig 9.12, the option seller has sold or written a call, and for taking this risk is rewarded with the premium, which is the fixed element of profit. However, if the underlying share price rises through the strike price and higher, the loss on the option continues to build and is unlimited. Writing or selling calls, is the exact opposite of buying or holding a call. As the seller of the call option you have limited profit (the premium received) but unlimited risk potential. The counter-party who has bought your call has limited risk (they have paid you a premium) and unlimited profit potential. As the call seller this is often referred to as selling naked, as this is precisely what it is. You have not 'covered' your position by holding the underlying asset, which is why it is considered to be very high risk, because the risk is not capped.

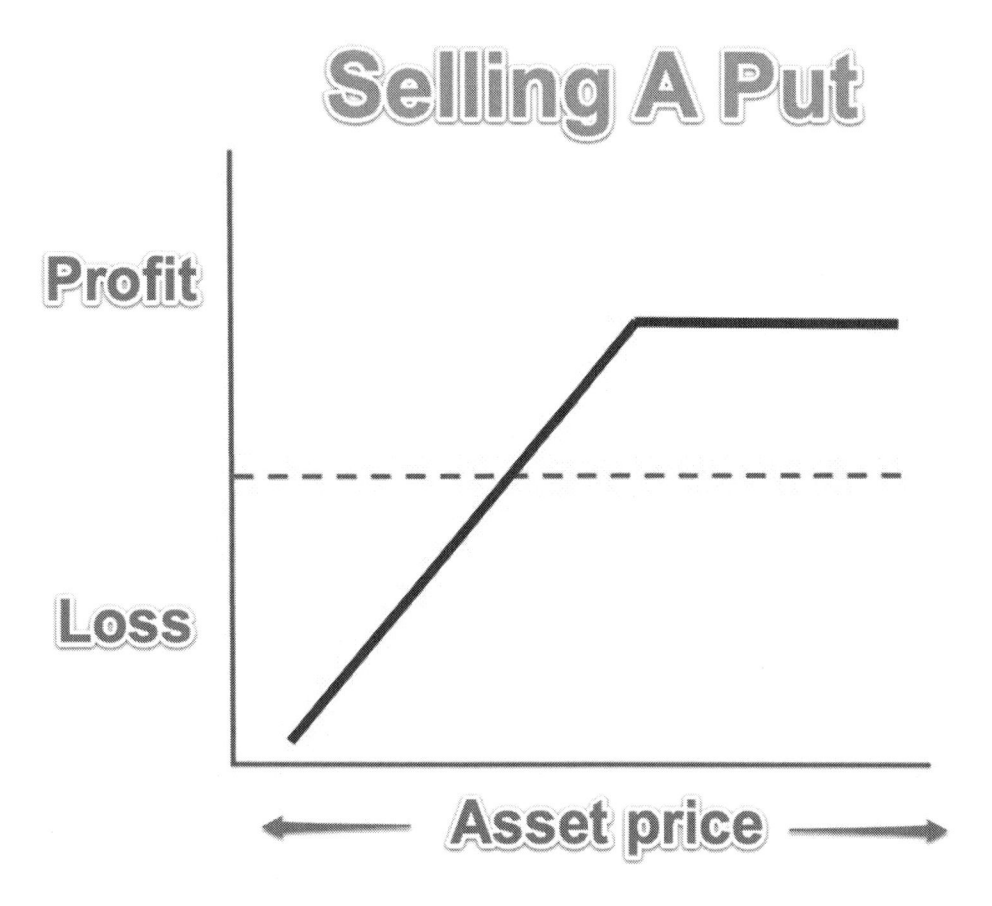

Fig 9.13 - Selling a put risk profile

Finally, we come to the risk and reward profile for selling a put. Once again as with selling a call, the seller receives the option premium which they keep for taking the risk for selling the put.

However, as with selling or writing a call, the risk of loss is unlimited. Here if the underlying share price begins to fall, and to fall fast as most markets do, any loss is uncapped. In theory if the stock price fell to zero, the loss would be staggering. Stocks can and do go to zero - one only has to remember Enron, Lehman Brothers and many more.

This is one reason why selling options in this way is referred to as 'naked selling' as you are in effect 'naked'. There are ways to protect the downside risk, including holding the underlying asset, and one very popular strategy for stock options is called covered call writing. This is a particular favorite of mine and a topic for another book. In simple terms, covered call writing is when you hold the underlying asset. In the case of a call option, if you were selling this as a call writer, you would hold the underlying asset, in other words 100 of the shares, as protection. The worst that happens here, is you have to sell your shares to the buyer. But you always keep the premium. You can think of this as earning rent on a property you own.

I hope from this brief introduction to vanilla options, you can appreciate two things. First, the immense flexibility these complex instruments can offer, and second the very different risk profile they provide compared to binary options. Much has been written about binary options, and indeed much of the focus and the marketing message centre on management of risk, namely the fact a binary option has a capped risk which is always known and defined.

However, as we have just seen the same is true for a vanilla option **provided** you are a holder or buyer. It is in the profit potential returns that the two diverge. With the binary option any profit is capped. With a vanilla option, profit is uncapped. There are many strategies for trading vanilla options, but the simplest of all is buying or holding, which then opens the prospect of unlimited profit potential, should the underlying asset move in the right direction, and before expiry.

All I am saying here is this. Understand the risk and reward profile of the binary option in the context of the vanilla option. As a vanilla options trader, there would be times when you would create a capped risk and reward profile, and other times when you would not, and this would depend on your analysis of market conditions. Vanilla options give you this flexibility - binary options do not. And it is is always something to bear in mind whenever you are trading these instruments.

Moreover, as I wrote earlier in the book, a capped risk and reward profile flies in the face of perceived wisdom for longer term trading success. This is generally premised on frequent small losses outweighed by larger but less frequent profits. It's simply something to think about.

What perhaps the above discussion also leads onto, is the question of how to use binary options in a more creative way, and to move away from this very simple model. This is something we are going to look at shortly, but trading binary options as a simple up/down proposition is unlikely to lead to longer term profitability, since the risk/reward profile is not working for you. Being more creative by constructing more sophisticated strategies is the answer, and in doing so turns the binary option into a more effective and elegant instrument in your trading toolkit.

Convergence Of Binary & Vanilla Options

Before moving on to consider the Nadex bull spread option in more detail, perhaps at this point it is appropriate to recap on the risk reward profiles we have considered in the book thus far.

If we start with off exchange options instruments, here the risk and reward profile is capped, with returns typically ranging between 70% to 100%, but for certain products such as one touch and no touch options, these can be dramatically higher. When we move to the on exchange world of binary options, whilst the model is still one where risk and reward are capped, the flexibility of the instrument allows us to define our own returns and manage them more directly. This facet of flexible returns is one of the key features offered by an on exchange binary option, and only available as a result of the instrument's unique design.

In the world of vanilla options, the risk and reward profile changes once again, and will also depend on whether we are a buyer or seller. For option buyers, the risk is always limited to the premium paid with an associated unlimited profit. For option sellers, the profit is always limited to the premium received with an associated unlimited risk.

You may be forgiven for thinking that option buying would seem to make perfect sense from a risk and reward perspective. But you would be wrong. It is in fact option sellers who have the probabilities and the maths on their side, and not option buyers. There are many reasons for this, but time and in particular the wasting aspect of time is one of the biggest factors. There are others, and in a book such as this it would take too long to explain all the research and facts surrounding this apparent paradox. But take in on trust, this is the case with somewhere between 75% to 85% of vanilla options expiring worthless.

As a result vanilla options traders have developed a huge range of sophisticated and complex strategies in order to blend together the buying and selling of puts and calls to take advantage of a variety of market conditions. One such is the spread strategy, and what is perhaps both curious and apparently paradoxical is that once again we are returning to the fixed risk and fixed reward profile. However, as with the on exchange binary option which offers increased flexibility in defining and managing the returns, here it is in the application of the option when used in conjunction with the underlying market, that its true power is revealed.

The Nadex bull spread pulls together the unique aspects of a binary option, and then combines these with this tried and tested strategy borrowed from the vanilla options world. This in turn creates an elegant, yet simple and powerful instrument, which when combined with the underlying market offers the best of both in one simple instrument.

Bull Spread - Vanilla vs Nadex

The construction of a spread position is one many vanilla option traders adopt. There are too many to consider here. However, what they have in common is the risk to reward profile, where the profit and the loss are capped. As with buying calls or puts, this is considered to be a relatively conservative approach since risk is capped, which is the quid pro quo for relinquishing unlimited profits.

The vertical option spread is created using vanilla options, and involves buying and selling a call option, of the same expiry, but with different strike prices. As a general rule, the bull vertical call spread is created by buying the option with the low strike price and selling the option with the high strike price - (a bear vertical spread takes the opposite approach). These are the two legs of the option strategy which then create the following risk profile. There are, of course debits and credits here, as part of the buying and selling of the options, but for our purposes I am simply interested in explaining the risk reward profile and how this relates to the Nadex bull spread equivalent.

Bull Call Spread

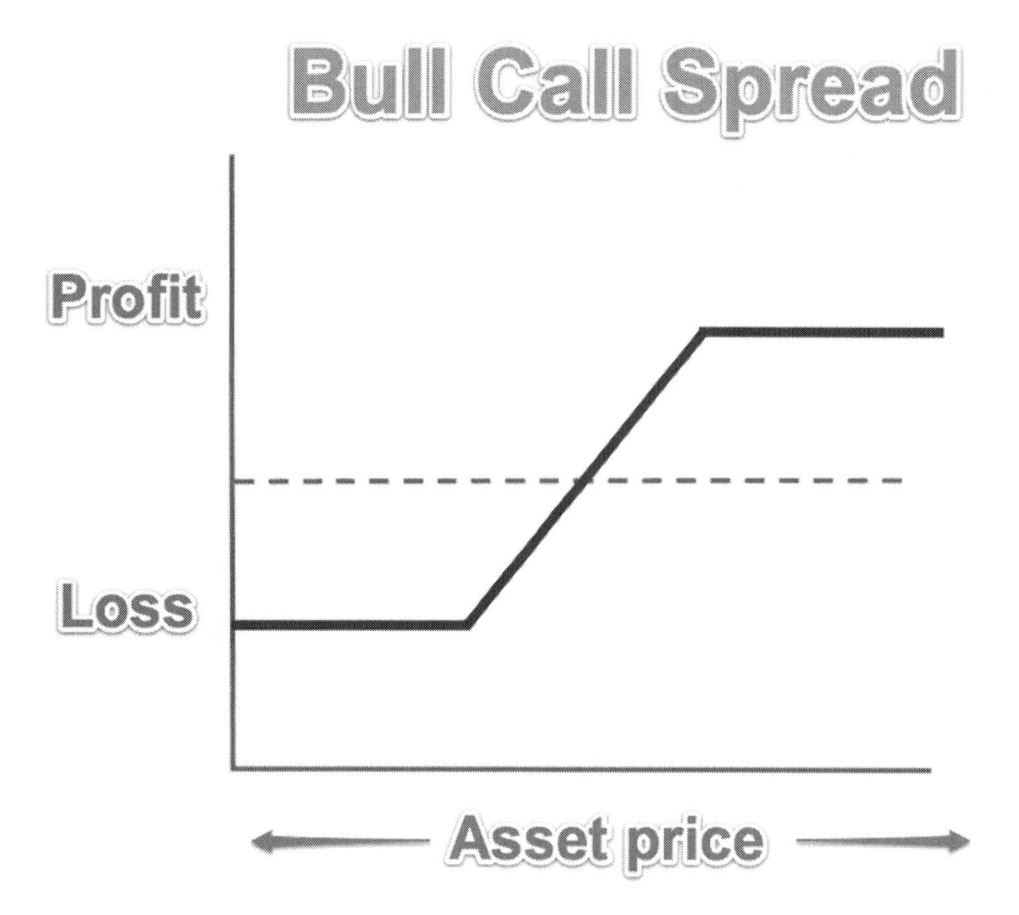

Fig 9.14 - Vertical bull call spread

The risk reward profile is as shown in Fig 9.14, and is the same whether you are trading a vanilla option bull call strategy or the Nadex equivalent bull spread. The strike price of each call defines the upper and lower boundaries of profit or loss, which are both capped. If the underlying asset moves sharply higher during the life of the strategy, your profit is limited as you have given up this potential return in favor of taking a reduced risk. Your risk/reward profile is capped and defined by the spread between the two strike prices of the call along with any net debit or credit on the two legs of the options. On the Nadex equivalent there are no debits or credits to worry about as there are no premiums to collect or pay on this instrument. It is simply the risk and reward profile that is common to both.

The bull spread is just one simple example of how binary options and vanilla options are moving ever closer in terms of their risk and reward profiles. The two worlds do have many other common characteristics in terms of time, expiry, volatility and probability, and I hope in exploring and explaining these concepts it has at least opened your eyes to where binary options stop, and vanilla options start.

In the next chapter we're going to look at the practical application of binary options in a variety of trading strategies.

Chapter Ten

Preparing To Trade Binary Options

An investment in knowledge pays the best interest

Benjamin Franklin (1706 - 1790)

I trust by now, you feel you have a deeper understanding of what constitutes a binary option, and perhaps what does not, and of the potential these instruments offer. Their potential is only limited by your imagination. The range of products available is diverse, and ultimately the choice of what you consider to be a binary option will be yours. In this book I have given you my own opinion, but it is just that, my opinion, because as always there are two sides to every debate. No doubt many readers will disagree with my ideas and suggestions and you may be one. All I have tried to do throughout is to probe deeper into the world of binary options, and the possibilities they offer. To offer a balanced view and to argue my case.

My own preference is the on exchange binary option which is more flexible and powerful, whilst the off exchange is less so. However, both on exchange and off exchange are perfectly valid trading instruments. Nevertheless, it is not for me to judge. Off exchange products are everywhere and it would be churlish of me not to include them in this chapter. They are a perfectly legitimate trading instrument when used in the correct way, but there is a problem.

Far too many off exchange products are promoted as a simple yes/no decision, with no other thought process involved. The flip of a coin, the roll of a dice or the draw of the card. I am also conscious on exchange products are not for everyone, or simply may not be available. The exchange traded products of the CBOE and the NYSE require specialist accounts and deeper funding. The binary options from Nadex and IG index, may not be available in all jurisdictions. Off exchange products are much more widely available, and my task in this chapter is to provide as much information as I can about the pre-trading decision process.

Whatever the instrument, the steps involved are identical and embrace a three dimensional method. Whether you are trading off exchange or on exchange options, the starting point is to consider these three elements, namely the technical, the fundamental and the relational. If you want to treat binaries as gambling, then this is your choice.

If you have read any of my other books, you will know I have my own trading methodology developed over 20 years. It's based on volume price analysis. It works in all timeframes and in all markets. It is what I believe in and use in my own trading and investing. All I am saying here is, whatever approach you adopt, analysis comes first, opening positions second.

If I can start by saying the following ideas and strategies are more appropriate for 'longer term' timeframes, and by longer term I mean those binaries which are a minimum of 15 minutes. Whilst this is an arbitrary number, it does draw a line in the sand. My view, rightly or wrongly, is it almost impossible to forecast market direction with any degree of confidence on timeframes below this. Those binaries operating on seconds and minutes, are simply betting. They can be great fun, but not for sustained and consistent profits. You may even feel 15 minutes is perhaps too short, and I would tend to agree, but we have to start somewhere.

In taking a position using a binary option, whether on exchange or off exchange, there are some core principles which apply, and which will help to frame the context of any trading position.

First, and perhaps foremost, is the knowledge that no market ever trades in isolation. We can all look at a chart as the price action unfolds, but every market is linked to every other, and it is the constant changes in sentiment from one to another, which ultimately drives money flow. When you stop and think about this logically, it makes perfect sense. The financial markets are about one thing and one thing only. Risk and return. Higher returns require higher risk, lower returns lower risk, and it is this constant oscillation between risk on and risk off, which is reflected in every market second by second and day by day. The VIX we looked at earlier in the book is perhaps the classic example, as fear and greed ebb and flow on the index, but this principle applies to all markets, of which the forex market sits at the heart.

The foreign exchange market is unique in many ways, not least in the variety and range of risk which is displayed by all the currencies and their associated pairs. Understand the characteristics of a currency, and you begin to understand its relationship to related markets, which in turn will help give you a deeper understanding of the market. It will help you understand why a market is behaving in the way it is, and in turn how to look for signals and clues in related markets. The clues are there, you just have to find them. Far too many traders spend their time transfixed on one chart studying the price action intently. Using a single chart, and this myopic approach, is limiting to say the least.

Every price move in one market has a consequent reaction in another. It's common sense, since selling one asset class and moving to another, will be reflected in the associated price action. You can think of the principle markets as a Venn diagram as shown in Fig 10.10.

Market Relationships

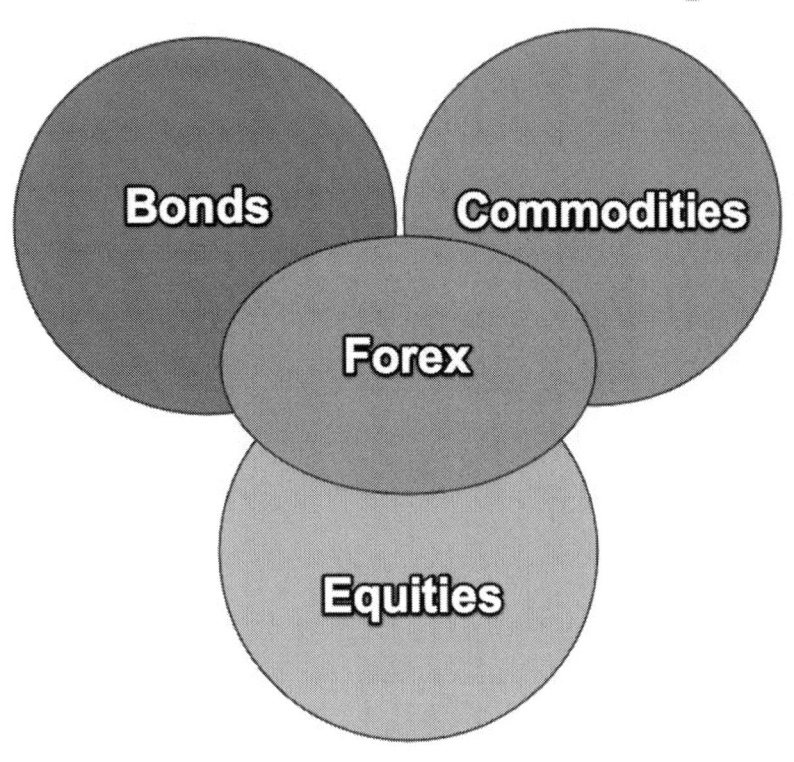

Fig 10.10 - The inter relationship of markets

As you can see, the forex market sits at the centre. It is the gateway for the massive flows of money, which are constantly seeking out higher returns when risk appetite is high, and lower returns when risk appetite is low. Each market, except for forex, has a personality, a risk profile if you like. The relationship between markets and what they reveal is a big subject, and one that I have covered in detail in **A Three Dimensional Approach To Forex Trading** which you can find on Amazon.

My purpose here is to give you an overview of what I believe will provide a top down approach, from the macro to the micro, from the global to the local. In other words, assessing the current mood of the market, and then seeing how this is reflected on the charts. What I will also provide, are the signposts and signals I think you should check either daily or intraday, and more importantly where to find this information quickly and easily.

If we start with bonds, these are generally considered to be low risk, and one of the safe haven resorts when risk appetite is low. This is reflected in bond prices and bond yields, and the benchmark here is the US bond market. The US Treasuries market is the largest in the world, and indeed is larger than the foreign exchange market by some distance. Bonds are loans and reflect the cost of money, and are considered in one of two ways. The bond price or the bond yield, and this relationship is an inverse one.

As bond prices rise, bond yields fall, and as bond yields rise, bond prices fall. The reason the yield is so important is it reflects the flow of money, as indeed do bond prices. In terms of the yield, if the yield is rising, bond prices are falling, in other words, the flow of money is away from bonds and into another market. In this case, we can assume risk appetite is rising, as investors and speculators are prepared to take on more risk for higher returns in other markets. Equally, if we see the yield is falling, then bond prices are rising, with the money flowing in, as investors and speculators look for a safe haven, low risk environment.

The easiest way to think of bonds is in terms of a house and the rental return. Imagine you are a landlord and buying a house to rent. The property costs $100,000 and the annual rent is $12,000, the yield would be 12%. If the property rises in value to $120,000 so the yield falls to 10%. You would be delighted with the capital gain in the value of your property. Equally, if house prices fall and your property is now worth $80,000, the yield rises to 15%. Good news for yield, not so good for your longer term investment.

This principle underpins the bond market, and you can see this in action throughout the trading day. It is not a relationship which is only appropriate to longer term investing and speculating. The bond yield changes second by second and you can see this on a chart. I'll explain where and how shortly. The benchmark bond to watch is the US Treasury 10 year note.

Next, is the commodity market and a popular one for binary options traders. Commodities are generally considered as risk assets, although this is an over simplification of their role. Commodities, other than gold, are typically governed by two primary drivers. The US dollar, and the supply demand curve. In terms of the first, I'm going to cover this shortly when we move to look at the forex market in more detail. With regard to the second, the supply and demand relationship is influenced by many different factors, which could loosely be summed up under the word 'news'. For soft commodities the news may be the weather, which can affect the harvest and yield, changes in legislation, or health trends. Conflicts and trade embargoes also play their part here. For oil and the energy sector in general, news and geopolitical events are likely to influence this market heavily. Furthermore, any slowdown in economic growth, particularly in China, is likely to be reflected in a fall in commodity prices, including base commodities. Oil has its own pricing control mechanism with OPEC which manages the supply from its member countries.

Moving to metals, silver and gold are both considered as precious metals, but silver is in fact classified as an industrial metal, given its wide use in industry. In the last few years, with gold prices rising, silver has filled the gap with many investors buying the metal as the price of gold moved ever higher.

Gold is a complex commodity, which is neither consumed nor used, but simply stockpiled and moved from one holder to another. It is the ultimate safe haven when markets are in turmoil, and is also a hedge against inflation. As with all commodities it has a strong relationship with the US dollar.

Naturally like any other market, each commodity will be quoted on a chart, in the cash, spot, or the futures equivalent. For market sentiment for commodities, the starting point is the Thomson Reuters Jeffries CRB or TR/J CRB for short. The index is constructed from 19 of the primary commodities. Again, do not think of this as a long term investors index - it is not. The index updates in realtime throughout the trading session and provides an instant broad view of the market on one simple chart.

Moving to equities, and the market perhaps we all understand intuitively. Equities are generally considered as high risk, and when investors and speculators are taking on more risk, equity markets will rise. This relationship between fear and greed is reflected in the VIX which we looked at in detail earlier in the book. As equity markets rise the VIX falls and vice versa, so when you are trading an index, this is an excellent inverse index to watch, particularly if you are trading the US markets. As this is a risk market, money flow in will be reflected in money flow out, often from bonds, which in turn will then be displayed in the yield. Markets move on money flow and if you know where to look, whether intraday or longer term, the clues are there.

For equity markets, the charts are straightforward. We have the benchmark indices which are the most widely reported. These represent the so called 'cash markets' where real money changes hands for real investments - shares. In general, global equity markets will tend to move in the same direction, but not always.

Local markets will have local forces, and the starting point for gauging market sentiment is to focus on the major global indices. Furthermore, it is important to remember an index is not necessarily representative of the economy of the country. The FTSE 100 for the UK, only represents 100 companies, most of whom generate their income from overseas - hardly representative of the UK or its economy. The Dow Jones Industrial Average in the US is even less representative with just 30 companies.

Nonetheless these are often the two indices focused on by the media as a short hand to report stock market price action. The reason is very simple. It's quick and easy and most people have heard of them, but from an inside perspective they are anything but representative.

Which indices to focus on will depend on where you are in the world. Each stock exchange will have a physical open and close, and whilst the cash market may be closed the electronic futures market will still be trading globally - it's a 24 hour market. This is where I began my own trading career, trading index futures and in a way you can think of the cash markets in a similar way. Somewhere in the world throughout a 24 hour period, a major stock exchange will be open, and even if they are closed the price action on the day will reveal market sentiment.

Below are all the global stock exchanges and their local opening times for the cash markets:

- NYSE -New York Stock Exchange 9.30 - 16.00
- TSE - Tokyo Stock Exchange - 9.00 - 11.00 & 12.30 - 15.00
- LSE - London Stock Exchange - 08.00 - 16.30
- HKE - Hong Kong Stock Exchange - 09.30 - 16.00
- NSE - National Stock Exchange of India - 09.00 - 15.30
- ASX - Australian Securities Exchange - 10.00 - 16.00
- FWB - Frankfurt Stock Exchange - Deutsch Borse - 09.00 - 20.00
- RTS - Russian Trading System - 09.30 - 19.00
- JSE - Johannesburg Stock Exchange - 09.00 - 17.00
- DIFX - NASDAQ Dubai - 09.00 - 14.00

During any twenty four hour period there will often be several exchanges open simultaneously, and not only the index you may be tracking or trading. Each will provide a view on sentiment, directly or indirectly.

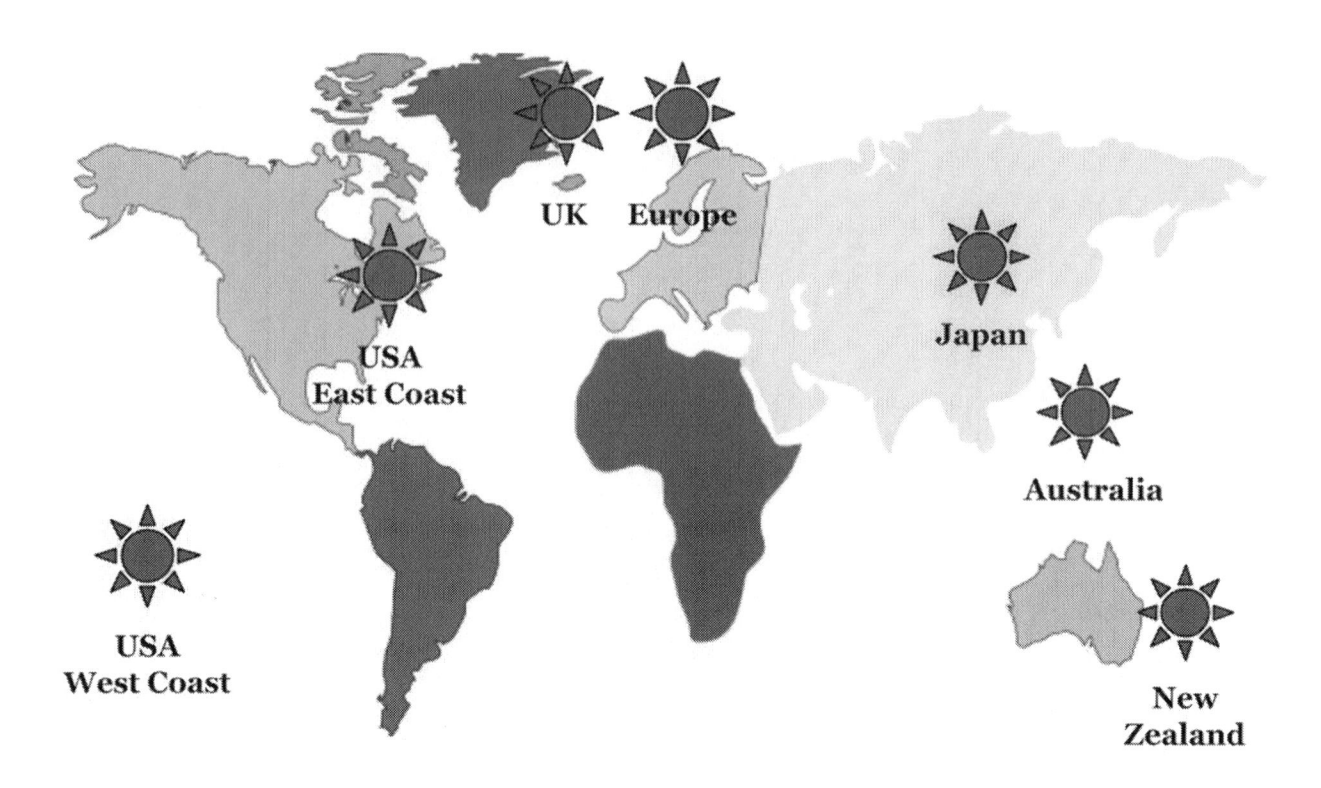

Fig 10.11 - The twenty four hour cycle of the cash markets

As you can see from Fig 10.11, the markets follow one another around the clock, beginning with New Zealand and Australia, before moving to Japan, through to Europe and London, and then on to the US markets before repeating the cycle.

There are many overlaps, with each picking up the tone from the previous. To give an example. Sentiment in the Far East and Asia will be dominated by Chinese economic news, and if the news is good, this is likely to be reflected in the principle indices along with commodity prices. This sentiment is then likely to ripple through into UK and US cash markets with the index futures leading the way.

Whilst many binary options traders are aware of the forex market trading 24 hours a day, few ever think of the equities markets in these terms, and yet this is even more fundamental to long term success using these instruments. The world is a twenty four hour market, and as one exchange sets the tone so another will pick this up and follow, with local news then overlaying the broader market sentiment. Big news items from the big four economies of the US, China, Japan and Europe will influence all markets, and when the cash markets are closed it is the futures markets which continue to reflect the ongoing sentiment.

The underlying futures markets which trade around the clock will signal whether the open of the cash market is likely to be higher or lower than the previous day's close. This often leads to gap up and gap down opens as trading in the cash index catches up. This is one reason why, as a binary trader of options, you need to watch both the cash and the futures. When I started trading I always had the cash and futures charts running side by side. The futures market will always move first as the big operators position themselves ahead of moves by the market makers in the cash, which are revealed by applying volume price analysis. This is why this method is a key tool and will give you an immense advantage.

The benchmark indices are as follows:

- S&P 500
- NASDAQ 100
- DOW 30
- Nikkei 225
- DAX
- Euro Stoxx 50
- FTSE 100
- S&P ASX 200
- Hand Seng
- S&P TSX
- Shanghai Composite

The last of our four markets is the foreign exchange market which is the central axis around which the others rotate. This is where real money is exchanged from one currency to another. It is the quickest way to shift risk, from high to low and back again. Buying or selling large size in other asset classes has its problems. It can be slow, and for the big operators moving the price against an asset when buying or selling in volume, is always an issue. In the forex market, large volumes can be moved quickly and easily, and in addition, true intent can be hidden from view.

A seller wishing to sell US dollars and buy British pounds, may execute this through the GBP/USD. But they could also transact this via a third currency, buying euros in the EUR/USD and then selling against the UK pound. The result is the same, but the route is different.

Before moving to consider the characteristics of the various currencies, and the focus for any analysis, the first point to bear in mind is this. All markets now operate on a twenty four hour basis, and as with equities, where the focus may be global but also local, so the same applies to the world of currencies, both in terms of the price action on related pairs, but also in terms of volatility.

Currency Focus London

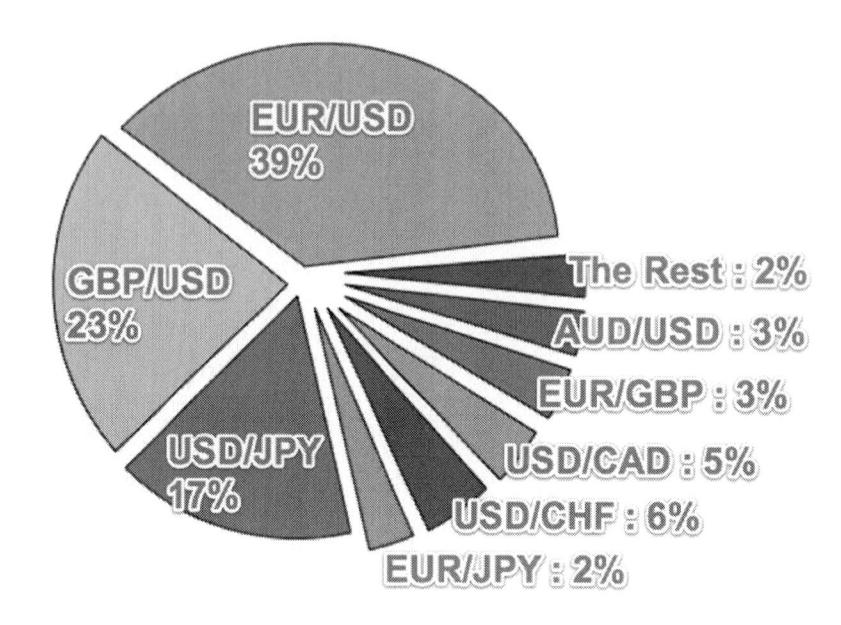

- EUR/USD 39%
- GBP/USD 23%
- USD/JPY 17%
- USD/CHF: 6%
- USD/CAD: 5%
- EUR/GBP: 3%
- AUD/USD: 3%
- The Rest: 2%
- EUR/JPY: 2%

Fig 10.12 - Currency focus during the London session

What is immediately clear from Fig 10.12, is which currencies are the primary focus during the European and London session with the euro and the British pound dominating, along with the US dollar. Now compare this with the trading session as it moves into Asia and the Far East in Fig 10.13.

Currency Focus Tokyo

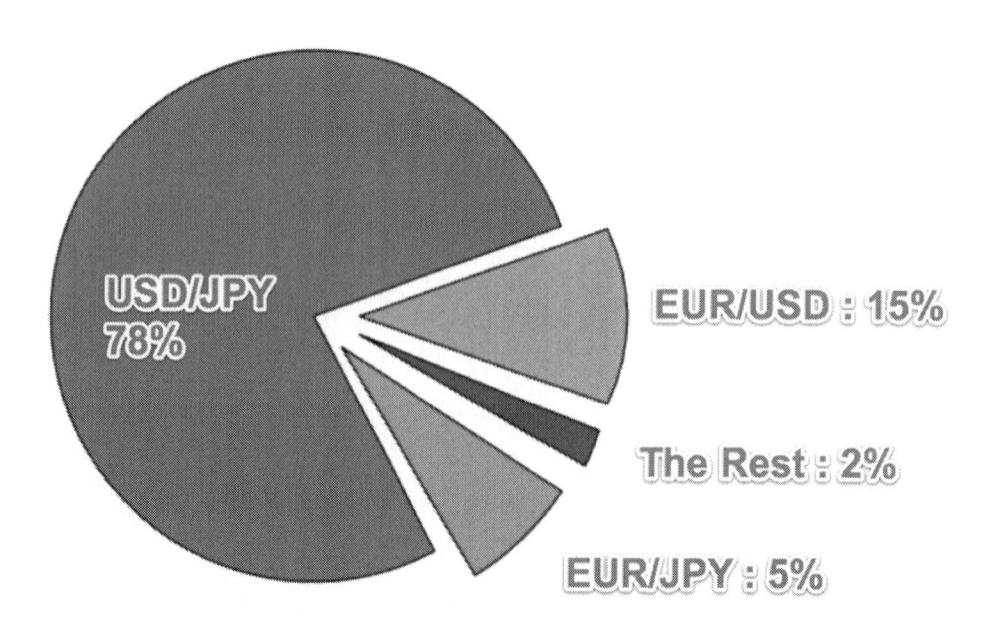

- USD/JPY 78%
- EUR/USD: 15%
- EUR/JPY: 5%
- The Rest: 2%

Fig 10.13 - Currency focus during the Tokyo session

The shift in focus is dramatic with the USD/JPY now dominating market activity.

The starting point for any analysis in the forex market is always the same, namely the US dollar. Paradoxically the same is true for all the other markets. It is the currency of first reserve, and the primary funding currency for liquidity. To take any position in any market without analyzing the US dollar is foolhardy. It underpins the world's largest economy, and is the currency every major central bank will hold as the greatest percentage of their foreign exchange reserves. The US dollar also underpins the largest debt market, and is the currency for pricing commodities.

The key index to follow here is the US dollar index. It is one of the most important charts to follow as it reveals strength and weakness in the US dollar. If the US dollar is rising then other major currencies are likely to be falling and vice versa. As with all the other charts mentioned here, this too is freely available, and the index charts the US dollar against a basket of currencies which are weighted. The most well known is the DXY or USDX. The components in the index are as follows:

- Euro - 57.6%
- Japanese yen - 13.6%
- UK pound - 11.9%
- Canadian dollar - 9.1%
- Swedish krona - 4.2%
- Swiss franc - 3.6%

In my opinion, the euro carries a disproportionate weighting, and moreover the Australian dollar is not represented. The 'Europe' weightings are extremely heavy with the euro, the pound and the krona at over 70 %, which I do not believe truly represents the picture for currencies today. Whilst this is a perfectly valid index, and one many traders follow, there are alternatives. The one I would suggest is a collaborative venture between Dow Jones and FXCM who have created a simplified US dollar index, based on an equally weighted basked of four currencies as follows:

- Single currency euro - 25%
- Japanese yen - 25%
- British pound - 25%
- Australian dollar - 25%

I feel this gives us a more balanced index, reflecting an equal weighting for the principle currencies. Equally of interest is an index for the Japanese yen. Dow Jones and FXCM have developed this index on the simple equally weighted principle, this time against the following currencies:

- US dollar - 25%
- Single currency euro - 25%
- Australian dollar - 25%
- New Zealand dollar - 25%

Both of these indices are useful and if you are a client of FXCM you may already have these on your trading platform. If not, the DXY is perfectly acceptable and also very easy to find. Whichever you choose, having a view of the US dollar is paramount as it underpins everything. It is the starting point for any analysis, and whether you are trading longer term binaries, or intraday the US dollar index is the 'go to' chart before you begin any deeper analysis. You can find details on both these indices here:

http://www.djindexes.com/fxcm/

To round off, here are some of the relationships and the characteristics of individual currencies and currency pairs, which will help to broaden your view and assist you in making better decisions trading these as binary options. This is only a brief overview of the subject as I have written two other books which explore this, and many other aspects of the forex market, in much greater detail. You can find both of these on Amazon here:

http://www.amazon.com/Forex-Beginners-Anna-Coulling-ebook/dp/B00GBHQXZC/ref

http://www.amazon.com/Three-Dimensional-Approach-Forex-Trading-ebook/dp/B00CX2QCVO/ref

If we start with the two most important currencies, these are the US dollar and the Japanese yen. Both currencies, in their own way, are considered as safe haven and reflect risk which is one reason why the USD/JPY can be a tricky currency pair to trade.

The US dollar is a safe haven currency in its own right, whilst the Japanese yen is associated with 'risk on' and 'risk off' through the carry trade. The carry trade is a trading strategy which takes advantage of differential interest rates. Money is borrowed at a low interest rate to fund an asset at a higher rate. In terms of a currency pair, the yen is sold and the higher yielding currency is bought. This leads to huge inflows and outflows for the yen. In a risk on environment, the yen is sold whilst in a risk off phase, the yen is bought. The yen is closely linked to the Japanese stock market. When the Nikkei 225 index is rising, the yen is likely to be selling off against the US dollar and the yen cross currency pairs. Equally, when the index is falling, yen buyers will be in the market as equities are sold in favor of a move back into the home currency. So viewing the yen when trading indices is paramount.

Next comes the euro. This is a political currency, beloved of the ECB and Eurozone elite and managed accordingly. Like many other currencies at present, the price action is driven by central bank policy and political rhetoric. Since the financial turmoil of 2007, free floating exchange rates have become a thing of the past, with most currencies now managed one way or another by their respective central banks.

The commodity currencies come next with the Australian dollar, the New Zealand dollar and the Canadian dollar, and here we have the linkages between commodities and currencies. For the Australian dollar (AUD) it's the country's trading relationship with China which is the key. As a major exporter of base commodities, any Chinese economic data has a direct impact on the Aussie dollar, with any bad news suggesting a fall in demand for commodities such as iron ore and coal, and good news suggesting a rise. This in turn is reflected in the Australian currency particularly in the AUD/USD and cross currency pairs.

For Canada it's oil that dominates the commodity export market, and with the third largest reserves in the world, after Saudi Arabia and Venezuela, it is not hard to see why. It's no surprise therefore the linkage between oil prices and the Canadian dollar is relatively close, and one pair to watch in particular is the CAD/JPY. The relationship here is a direct one, and as oil prices rise then the CAD/JPY is likely to rise too, and vice versa.

The reason this relationship exists is based on the characteristics of the two economies. Japan has virtually no natural resources, and as a major exporter of finished products, has to import virtually every base commodity, of which oil is one. Canada is a net exporter of oil, with the US and Japan two of its largest customers. This export/import relationship for oil is then reflected in the CAD/JPY pair as a positive correlation. However, correlations can and do break down.

The third commodity currency is the New Zealand dollar, and whilst the country is rich in natural base commodities, it is soft commodities which are the principle export, with milk, milk powder, butter and cheese the main constituents. For New Zealand commodities, once again it is China which has the greatest impact with changes in the Whole Milk Powder index reflecting prices and demand. In recent months there has been a fall in demand from China for milk and milk related products, and this has been reflected in the currency.

In addition to the relationship to commodity prices, the New Zealand dollar is also driven by interest rate differentials, with relatively high interest rates in New Zealand attracting the speculative carry trade, resulting in consequent strength in the New Zealand dollar.

The last currency in this brief introduction could also be considered a commodity currency of sorts, and it is the Swiss franc. This is another currency that has seen huge inflows over the last few years as investors have sought out safe havens. Moreover, the Swiss franc is underpinned by huge gold reserves, (the fifth largest in the world) so much so the currency is heavily influenced by the price of gold.

These are just some of the many relationships that exist between the four capital markets. There are many others, and all I have tried to do here is to introduce you to some of the concepts and ideas which you may not have considered for yourself. Some of these relationships do fall in and out of correlation, as nothing is ever guaranteed in trading, whether intraday or longer term. But in having a deeper understanding of the role each market plays, their characteristics and their relationship will, I hope make your analysis deeper and more rounded.

The best place to find all the information on the four capital markets is at investing.com http://www.investing.com

It is one of the best online resources available and here you will find live prices for both spot and futures, as well as live cash market quotes and prices for the indices along with bond prices and bond yields. All the information is free.

So far, we have yet to look at a chart, and simply considered some of the relationships which shape money flow and the consequent price action. Before we do, there is a further aspect which deserves deeper consideration, and it is the impact of fundamental news. Far too many traders are simply ambushed by unexpected, or even expected news. There are, of course, news events which none of us can plan for - geopolitical events, natural disasters, speeches from politicians and bank governors, and many others. But fortunately, most news events and economic releases are planned well in advance and published on an economic calendar.

The question then becomes one of interpretation and use.

For options traders, whether binary or vanilla, I hope I have convinced you that volatility in all its forms is a crucial and vital concept to understand. It is neither good nor bad, and can be high and low. The key is to match volatility to the appropriate option and appropriate strategy.

Fundamental news is one of the primary triggers for intra day volatility, and there are several decisions to make when considering any intra day position in relation to the option being considered.

The first question is whether you are seeking volatility or seeking to avoid volatility. In the first case, you may be seeking volatility for one of two reasons:

- To take a new position that requires volatility
- To leverage volatility in order to shift the probabilities

If, on the other hand, you are seeking to avoid volatility, this may be for the following reasons:

- To take a new position that does not require volatility
- To continue holding an existing position with favorable probabilities.

The decisions you make and take with regard to the news will also be influenced by time. If you have a strong position ahead of the news, do you hold or close and take any profits off the table, (assuming you can). If you have no position ahead of the news, but are thinking of opening a position requiring low volatility, it may be best to wait.

The degree of any intraday price volatility will depend on the news item itself and its importance, and once again http://www.investing.com has an excellent calendar, as does http://www.forexfactory.com. Both sites rank the releases. Forex Factory with a red flag and Investing.com with three bulls. Of the two, Investing.com offers a slightly more comprehensive calendar.

Judging the market's reaction to any release is always difficult, not just in terms of direction, but also range. The last thing you want on an existing position built on a trend is for the market to reverse, even temporarily, against the longer term trend. Alternatively, any reaction may increase the momentum in the trend, provided it is in the same direction. The question is whether there are any tips and techniques which can help us as traders when assessing the news. Either from the perspective of an existing position, or from the standpoint of a new position in the market. And here is where Forex Factory may be able to help.

Fundamental news is cyclical, and by that I mean the weight the market gives an item of economic data changes according to the economic and business cycle. At present, for reasons we all know, most major economies are deep in recession, with interest rates at historic lows and likely to remain so for some time to come. What was once a key release, is now almost a 'non event', since the prospect of any dramatic change in interest rates in the short term is unlikely. Of far more interest is the associated statement from a central bank chairman, who may deliver some clues or hints as to the future. The markets do not expect any change, so any reaction is consequently muted. For any economy to move out of recession, jobs, job creation, employment and unemployment are far more important as leading indicators of economic growth. Inflation too becomes increasingly important as central banks attempt to drive demand into the economy.

You can think of fundamental news as a leader-board on a golf course. Names are changing places all the time, moving up and down the board - it is the same with the priorities of economic data, and their position on the leader-board will reflect the current economic landscape.

Bond purchases have recently been included on the monthly calendar, something that was of little interest a few years ago. These releases never appeared, but now they are a regular feature, with the European bond auctions taking centre stage. As the markets settle and the threat of defaults wanes, these will fall out of the limelight once again. This is just one example of the cyclical nature of fundamental news.

Do not assume local news only affects local markets. It does not. At present, the market data that influences world markets the most is from China. China is one of the few, if not the only economy to be growing. The second largest economy in the world is now so influential in this context, any slowdown here has a dramatic impact. If China were to slow and even move into recession, the effects would be catastrophic. China and other economies in Asia are doing well and as long as this continues, the major economies of the USA, Europe and Japan can continue to languish and remain waterlogged in recession.

Nowhere is this more graphically illustrated than in the release of equivalent data from China and the USA. Under normal circumstances you would expect a GDP release from the world's biggest economy to carry more weight than one from the second largest. In fact the reverse is true. China is such a pivotal market for everything from base commodities to US bonds, if China sneezes the rest of the world catches a cold.

Next it is always important to consider the release in the context of its trend, and not simply against the forecast or the previous. Many traders are surprised and wrong footed when markets rise on bad news and fall on good. How can this happen? The answer is news is relative, and has to be seen in the context of its trend. This is where Forex Factory steps in to lend a hand.

On the right hand side of each release is a small icon which, when clicked, opens a chart of the previous releases. This helps to frame the release in the context of the data trend. If it is line with the general trend, market reaction will be muted. If it is not, then expect a volatile reaction. Markets rarely if ever change direction on one release. It is the longer term trend that is important.

If you are trading a binary in the commodities market, you will need to hunt out the important releases. The principle one released weekly on a Wednesday is the oil inventories report. This reports whether oil stocks have increased or decreased at the Cushing oil hub, and even though this is a US release, the impact is generally more pronounced in the Canadian dollar, and of course in the price of oil.

For other markets, particularly the soft commodities, you will need to check the USDA (United States Department of Agriculture) http://www.usda.gov for regular news and releases, covering these markets. This report also includes weather updates and forecasts, another key element for soft commodities.

For gold, you need to keep a close eye on inflation data which can help to move gold higher, and the US dollar on the dollar index. Shock news events may trigger a flight to safety, and there is little that can be done in advance of these events. Also be aware there are buying seasons for the precious metal, particularly in India from late September through to January. India is one of the largest buyers of gold for jewelry, and as the wedding season gets underway, gold prices will often lift as a result driven by demand in the region.

If you are trading binaries in the energy sector, global events will have a huge impact, as indeed will the seasons. Even for oil, there is a season, most notably the 'driving season' in the summer in the US, when demand for oil should rise, whereas in the winter it is demand for natural gas which takes priority. For oil and gas, tensions in Russia or the Middle East will also have a huge effect, and any hint of conflict is likely to send prices soaring.

Having considered the relational and the fundamental aspects in preparing to trade, now I want to consider the third element, namely the price chart itself for the underlying market. This is where volume price analysis becomes an invaluable method in helping you validate moves in all timeframes, and even more so in the binary world where we are dealing, not only with assessing price action, direction and range, but also time.

In trading we only have two leading indicators, they are volume and price. Volume validates price and price validates volume. They are both free, and provided the market you are trading has volume displayed, whether as a proxy for volume, futures volume or true volume, it works equally well. Once you have learnt the basics of volume price analysis, I truly believe this approach will help you achieve greater consistency in your trading results.

I also truly believe it is essential for trading binary options. Volume provides the insight into price action. It reveals when markets are in congestion, or preparing to breakout. It reveals the strength of trends, the reversals in trends, and the minor pauses and pullbacks. In short, it gives you that inside view of the market, at the leading edge. Learn to interpret price action using volume, and you will move the probabilities of binary trading heavily in your favor.

Volume price analysis is a methodology. It underpins everything. You may decide it is for you, alternatively you may not, but whatever methodology you adopt, it has to provide the foundation for your trading, whether binary options, vanilla options, or any other instrument or market.

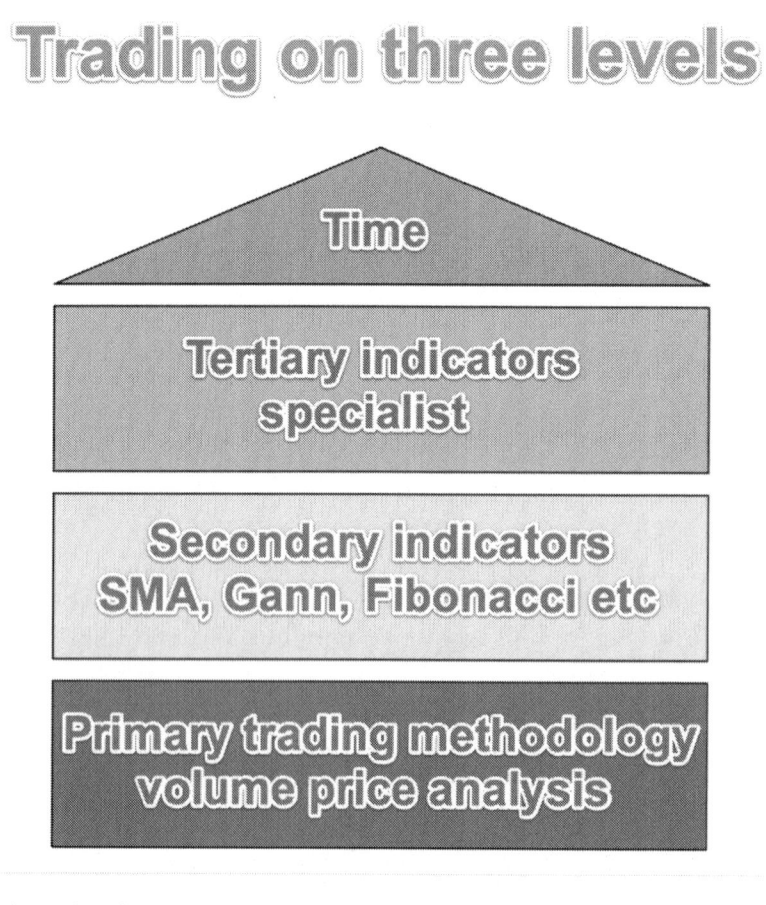

Fig 10.14 - Trading on three levels

Fig 10.14 lays out the basic principles. The foundation is the trading methodology which in my case is volume price analysis. To this you apply your secondary indicators. These are generally freely available with most charting packages. Next we have our tertiary level where we apply specialist indicators and tools to complement our trading method. The roof of the house is completed with the over arching element of time, which binds the whole approach together using multiple timeframes.

Fig 10.15 expands the first two levels in more detail.

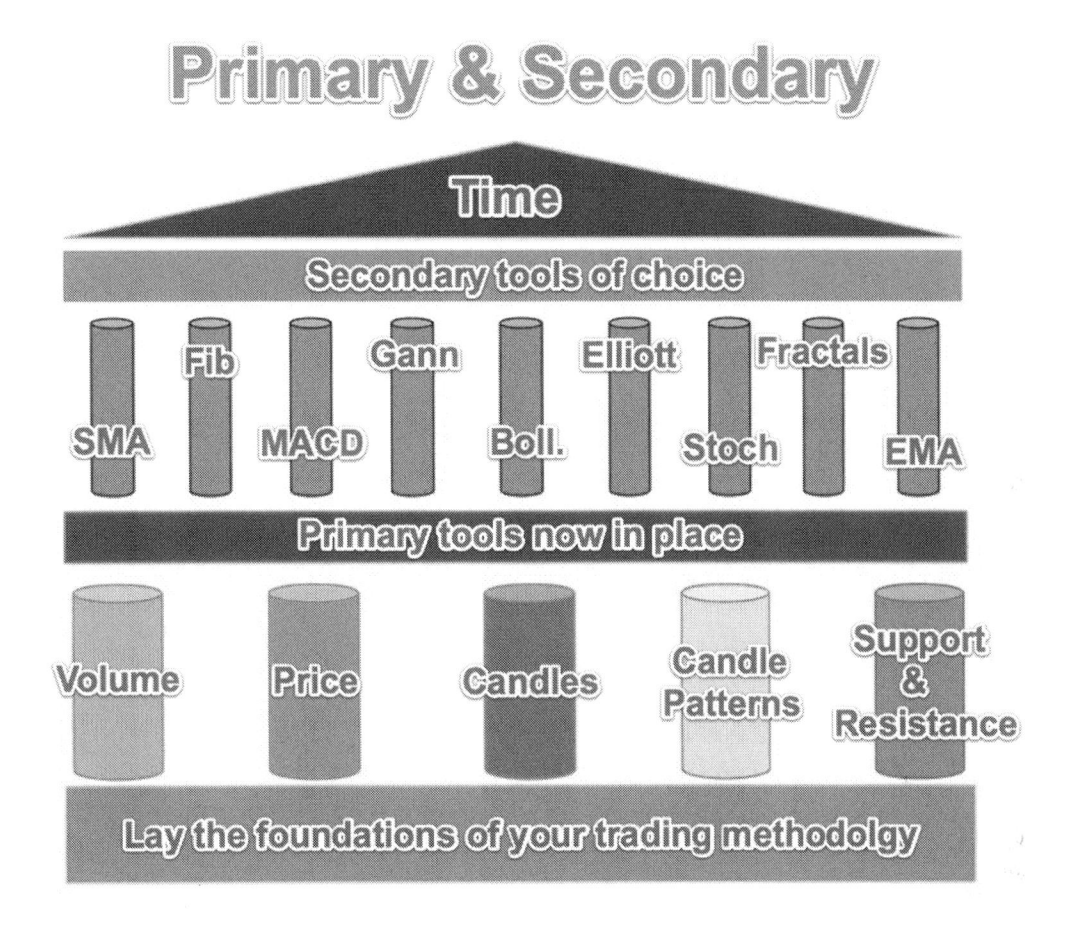

Fig 10.15 - The primary and secondary approach

Volume price analysis lays the foundations, using volume, price, candles, candle patterns and support and resistance. To this we apply our secondary indicators such as simple moving averages, MACD, Bollinger bands and Stochastics, but herein lies a problem. Many of these secondary indicators work well in one type of market but not in others. Moving averages are a classic example. They work perfectly when a market is trending with the price action bouncing off the average as the market moves higher or lower. However, they fail miserably when a market is in congestion crossing back and forth as the market moves in a tight range.

Bollinger bands are another example, and one we looked at in great detail earlier in the book. They are superb as volatility indicators, but not so great for price action. And if you are in any doubt, let me just highlight the point with an example from Investing.com. This is for the USD/CAD on an hourly timeframe and is shown in Fig 10.16.

A Mixed Picture

Symbol	Value	Action
RSI(14)	48.415	Neutral
STOCH(9,6)	80.287	Overbought
STOCHRSI(14)	72.723	Buy
MACD(12,26)	-0.000	Sell
ADX(14)	19.706	Neutral
Williams %R	-30.108	Buy
CCI(14)	2.8274	Neutral
ATR(14)	0.0022	High Volatility
Highs/Lows(14)	0.0000	Neutral
Ultimate Oscillator	51.001	Buy
ROC	-0.128	Sell
Bull/Bear Power(13)	0.0012	Buy

Buy: 4 Sell: 2 Neutral: 5
Summary: BUY

Fig 10.16 - USD/CAD directional analysis on the hourly chart

A mixed picture to say the least. Some of the indicators are saying this is a neutral market, a few are suggesting a sell, whilst others are suggesting a buy. What's the solution?

This is where volume price analysis steps in, and for those of you who have read my other books, you will know I love using analogies to describe markets and market behavior. The best analogy I can use here is the sea and sailing. Why does one team win the America's cup and another fail? Why does Ben Ainslie win more gold medals in sailing than anyone else? All things being equal, it's an understanding of the wind and associated sea state, which allows the helmsman or woman to trim the sails and the boat, to take maximum advantage of the conditions.

Understanding and interpreting wind direction and sea state are the building blocks of their success. They do it better than their competitors. It's the same with the market. To succeed, you have to understand the sea state of the market. Are we in the doldrums? If so, we set our sails accordingly. Or are we sailing along nicely in a force 4 or 5 ? Are we heading into choppy waters, or a full blown storm, in which case we reduce the sails and batten down the hatches. It is exactly the same in trading.

If you can understand and interpret the sea state of the market, you can then select the most appropriate indicators which will match the conditions, and perhaps more importantly the conditions for which the indicators were developed. You would not sail with a spinnaker in a force 10 gale. At best the boat would capsize and at worst sink. Instead the sails are reduced to the minimum, while you ride out the storm. Equally, you would not take this approach in the Doldrums. Here you want maximum sail area to catch whatever breeze is available. It's about matching the set up of the boat to the conditions, and the same applies in trading.

For those of you who have sailed a boat, you will know that attached to the sails are small little 'laces' which lie alongside the sail. These are called 'telltales' and do precisely that. When they are lying flat and horizontal to the sail, the boat is perfectly trimmed, but when they are flapping around, the boat is sailing off the wind. The 'telltales' are like our trading indicators, helping to guide us to maximize our profits and reduce risk, but only once we understand the prevailing sea state of the market. You cannot sail just using telltales, and you cannot trade just using indicators. In both cases you have to understand the sea state or market conditions first, and move to your indicators second.

Volume price analysis does just this. It describes the sea state for you as the price action unfolds, at the live edge of the market. If you can understand when the market is moving into a congestion phase, a volatile phase or a measured trend, you can apply the correct indicator to those market conditions. You are then matching indicators to market conditions. Here are some charts with some examples.

Forecasting The Sea State

Markets can only move in six different ways. These are the six different sea states you will encounter on any chart, and they are as follows:

- Trend
- Trend with momentum
- Trend with volatility
- Trend with momentum and volatility
- Congestion without volatility
- Congestion with volatility

The following example is from the $GBP/JPY pair on a 30 minute chart from the NinjaTrader platform. The small up and down triangles are a simple pivot indicator which is based on a three candle pattern. When the centre candle of the three has a higher high and a higher low, a pivot high is created. When the centre candle has a lower high and a lower low, a pivot low is created. This simple indicator helps to define the various sea states as they develop at the live edge of the market.

Fig 10.17 - $GBP/JPY 30 minute chart NinjaTrader - *phase 1*

Here we are considering the price action in isolation without volume. Volume will validate the price action, but understanding the sea state simply from the price action, is the first step.

As the price action unfolds from the left of the chart, the first point of reference would have been the pivot low, suggesting a possible pause. At this point, we would not have known what was to follow, but simply waiting for any sign the market was indeed entering a phase of consolidation. In other words, a possible floor of support had been signaled and now we have to wait for a pivot high to establish the potential resistance region. This duly arrived, setting the initial potential levels for floor and ceiling, but again we cannot be sure we are in a congestion phase just yet, and must wait until the price action and further pivots confirm this for us.

A further pivot high then appears, confirming the congestion phase, and with the price action also testing the floor of support, we are now confident the market is pausing and waiting for a potential breakout. We have no idea whether this will be to the upside or the downside. All we can be sure of is a breakout will arrive, and it is just a question of being patient. The market appears to rally, but reverses back to post a further pivot low, before the breakout finally arrives on wide spread up candles, surging higher before narrowing as it reaches the top of the move.

At the top of the move a pivot high is posted, followed by an extremely volatile shooting star candle, signaling possible weakness. Two further pivot highs follow, with the price action below building a platform of support, but on this occasion with no pivot lows to confirm. Nevertheless, the price action to the downside is defining this region for us, and with the pivot highs sliding lower, this suggests weakness as the market continues to move into a tight congestion phase.

This phase of congestion finally comes to an end with a move lower this time, before a pivot low then signals a further possible pause point, which is duly confirmed with a subsequent pivot high.

Once again this defines the potential floor and ceiling of a further congestion phase. Three pivot highs confirm this view, with this extended phase failing to breach either the floor or the ceiling. The next phase of price action then unfolds in Fig 10.18.

Fig 10.18 - GBP/JPY 30 minute chart NinjaTrader - ***phase 2***

Towards the end of the congestion phase arriving from the left of the chart in Fig 10.18, the price spreads were tightening, until finally the market broke out, to the downside, before moving into a further minor period of congestion. Here a single pivot high defined the upper region of price resistance, with the floor defined by the price action itself, before the market broke lower once again, punctuated with a short pause, before continuing lower in a classic price waterfall.

Markets always fall faster than they rise, because the market makers and big operators are in a hurry to accumulate stock or contracts.

The price waterfall then comes to an end, and we enter a further classic phase of price congestion as shown on the right hand side of the chart in Fig 10.18. Again we see the market pause, rally slightly and mark the upper level of potential resistance with a pivot high. The floor of support is duly defined with a pivot low, before the price action continues to move sideways, with a further pivot high as we move to the extreme right of the chart. Now let's add in the volume component which adds depth, definition and confirmation to our analysis.

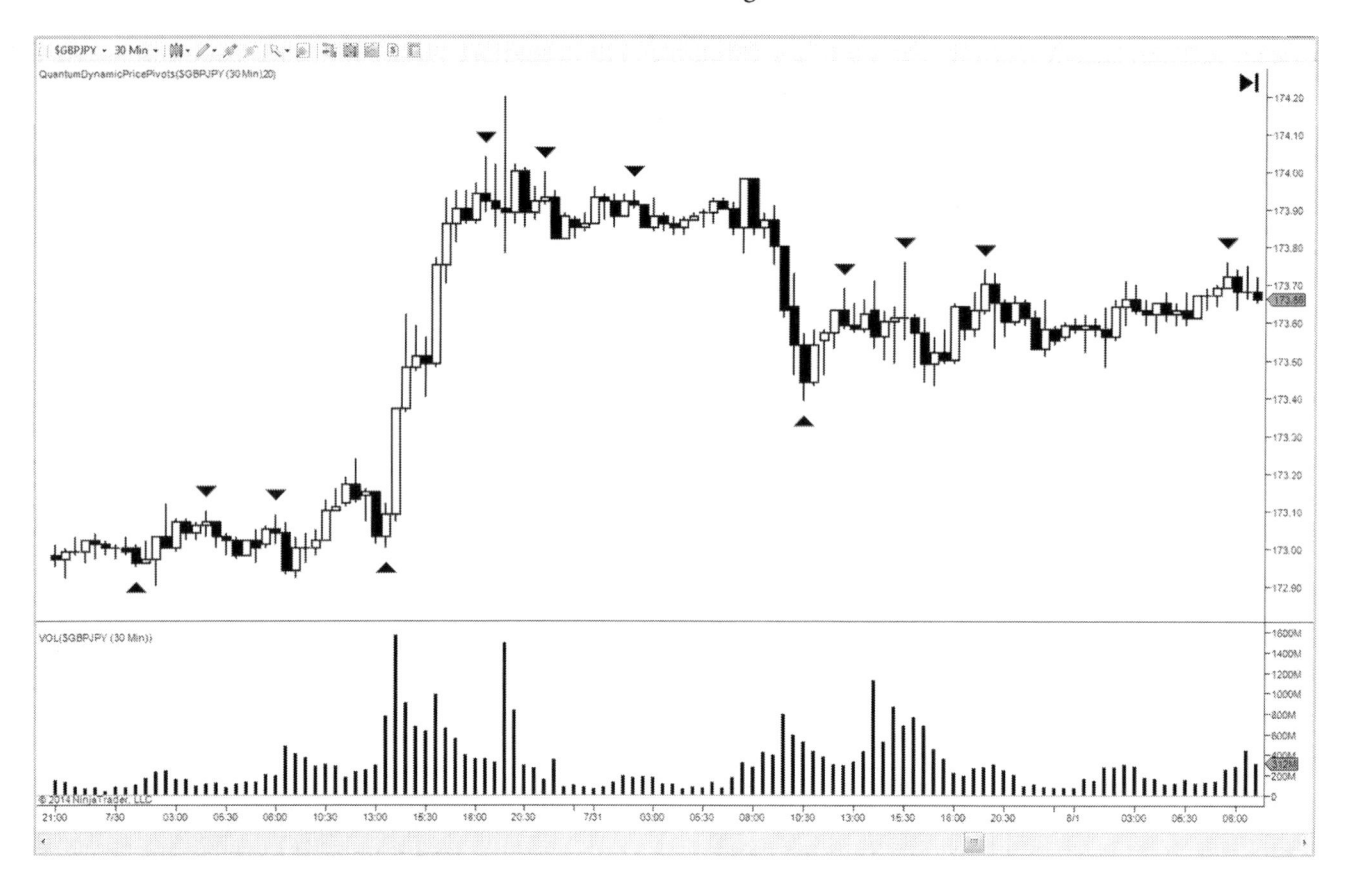

Fig 10.19 - *Phase 1* price action with volume

Starting from the left of the chart in Fig 10.19 we now have the complete picture, with price validating volume, volume validating price, and all the volume price anomalies clearly visible.

During the initial congestion phase on the left of the chart, the volumes are low, and as we would expect from the price action, confirming this as a period of sideways consolidation. The only increase in volume is towards the end of this phase with the attempt to rally accompanied by falling volume, sending a clear signal this minor rally is weak. This is something the price action alone would not have revealed. Without volume you might have been tempted into the breakout early. With volume, it's safe to wait. The breakout arrives with a wide spread up candle clearing the price congestion and closing well above it. The price is accompanied with ultra high volume, validating the price action, and more importantly confirming the big operators are moving into this market and buying.

Now it is safe to join in as the market moves higher still, before coming to a pause point as the volumes steadily decline towards the end of the move. This is a classic part of volume price analysis. In other words, not simply considering the candle in isolation and the associated volume, but also the candle clusters. A rising market on falling volume is not going to travel far before it reaches an exhaustion point. It may continue with the trend in due course, or it may not. In this case the market paused and then reversed, but pause it did. The pause may be long or short, but volume will confirm the direction of the next move.

In this example, not only was volume signaling exhaustion, so too was the price action, and as we reach the top of the move two consecutive shooting star candles arrive on average volume. Before the third, a massive shooting star with ultra high volume, confirms this weakness dramatically. I suspect this may have been on a news release, and probably a major one given the volatile price action over the subsequent candles. The price action then subsides, as does the volume, moving into calm waters with low volumes and narrow spreads.

The market breaks to the downside, and as it does the move is validated with rising volume. This is a further classic signal of volume validating a move, before moving into the start of an extended congestion phase. We can see the rally is weak, as the volume is falling on the initial move higher, and this weakness is further validated with the high volume bar and narrow spread candle. This congestion phase then continues on average to low or very low volume, as the GBP/JPY waits for the next breakout to be signaled.

In Fig 10 .20 we now move to phase 2 of the price action with volume applied.

Fig 10.20 - *Phase 2* price action with volume

Once again the breakout is validated on ultra high volume, this time with the pair moving lower and down to the next phase of price congestion as the volume fades away. Just as a rising market and falling volume are signs of a forthcoming pause, so is a falling market with falling volume, which is precisely what we have here. The market then moves into the price congestion phase to the right of the chart, with volume fading away fast reflecting the calm waters of the narrow spread price action.

Now let's revisit the price action in this pair one last time, but this time adding in our Bollinger bands. The Bollinger bands are here for one reason and one reason only, to highlight volatility.

Fig 10.21 - **Phase 1** price action with volume and Bollinger bands

Starting from the left hand side of the chart, the bands are very narrow as they define the calm waters of very low volume and narrow spread price action. Gradually the bands begin to widen as volume increases, along with the price spreads. On the breakout, the bands widen dramatically as the market moves higher, and they are also followed by further volatility at the top of the move, before narrowing again as the market calms. Volume dies away and the price action settles.

The bearish breakout appears, the bands widen as volume increases with the wide spread down candles. At the bottom of this move, volatility remains for a period, before ultimately draining away as the volumes decline and price spreads narrow towards the right hand side of the chart.

Fig 10.22 - Phase 2 price action with volume and Bollinger bands

This narrowing of the bands continues for some time, until in Fig 10.22 we arrive at the final phase of price action with the market moving lower in the price waterfall, coupled with a widening of the Bollinger bands. The market then calms to the right of the chart as volume ebbs away, and the price action moves into a very tight range with the bands narrowing once again in the classic squeeze pattern.

In this single chart spread over several days, we have seen examples of five of our six ways the market moves. The only one missing is the trend with volatility.

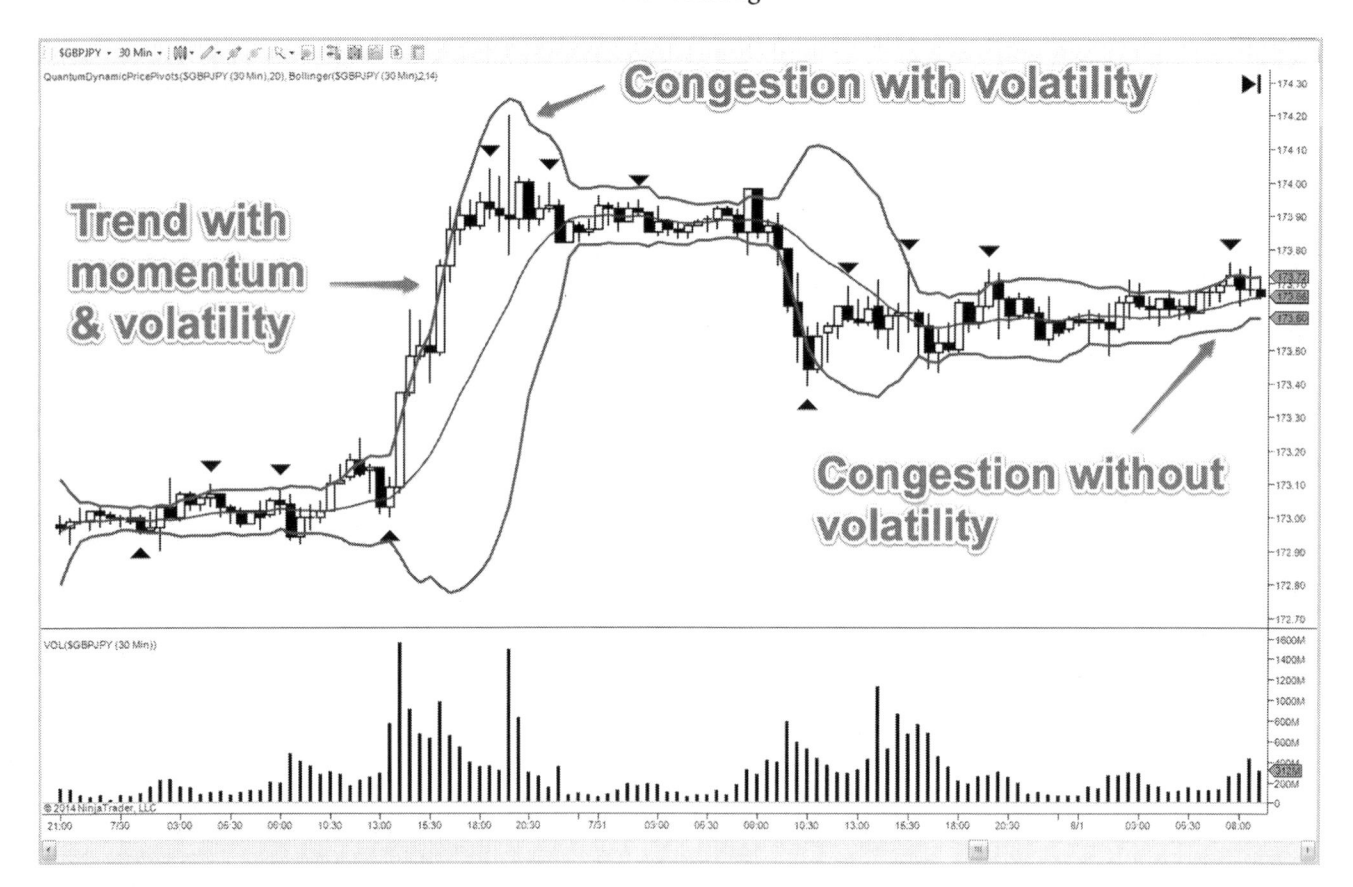

Fig 10.23 - Example of ways the market moves

In Fig 10.23 we can see three of the ways described on the 30 minute chart for the GBP/JPY. As the market climbs from the breakout the move is fast with wide spread candles signifying momentum, with spiky price action both at the mid point and to the top of the trend signaling volatility. This is not a smooth measured trend. Here the market is moving fast and in a volatile way.

Moving to the top of this phase, the price action moves into congestion, and here we have a short period of congestion with volatility. The market is whipsawing here, and if we were watching this on a faster timeframe, perhaps a five minute chart, the price action would be swinging wildly and describing this perfectly. We can see the congestion phase without volatility on the right hand side of the chart. The sea state is calm, the wind light, and our yacht is gently sailing along in benign conditions.

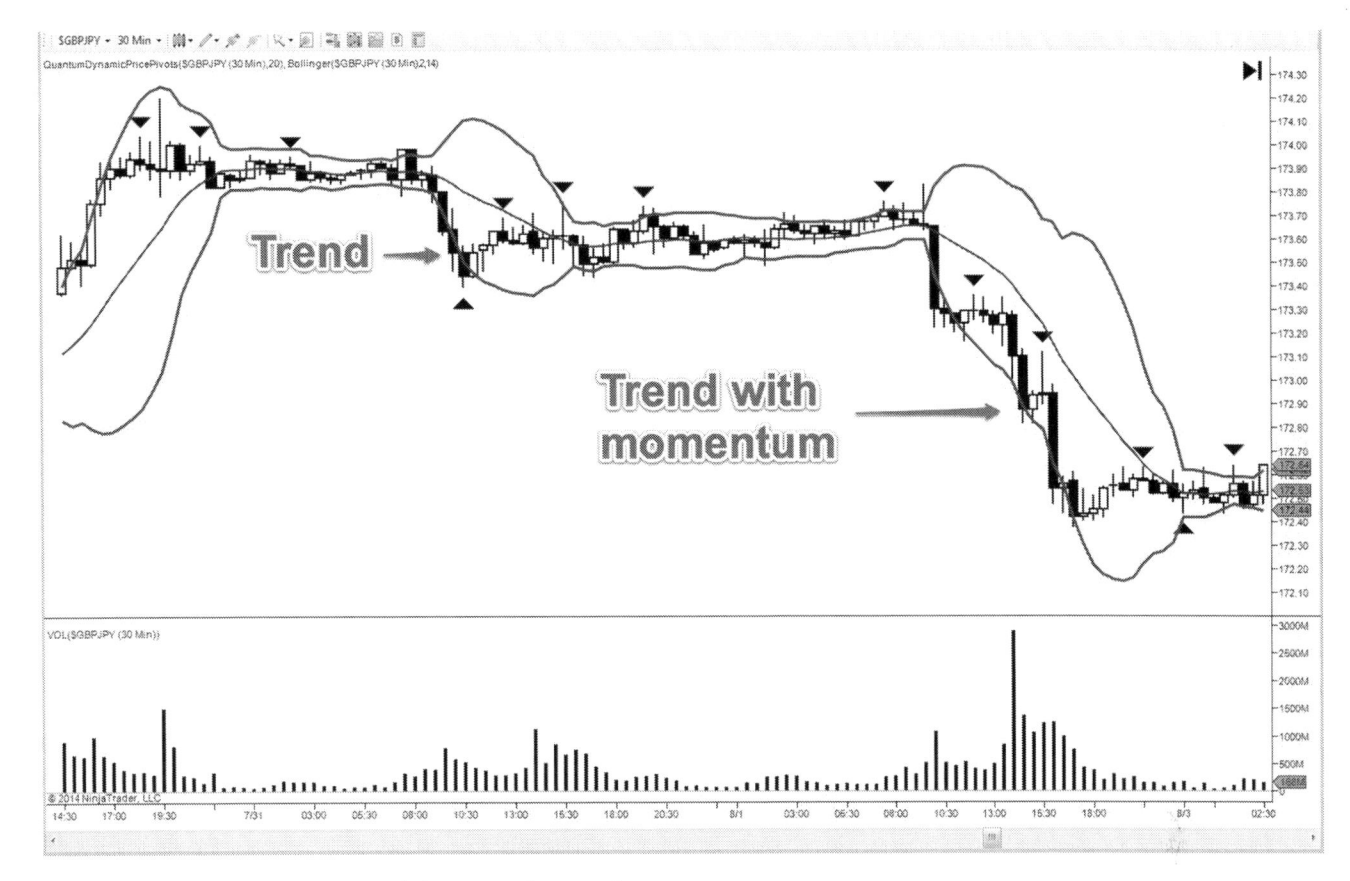

Fig 10.24 - Further examples of the way the market moves

In Fig 10.24 we have two further examples. The small trend run lower is a measured fall, with no great momentum nor volatility. These are often trends or moves you will see in a rising market where the move higher is steady, climbing in small increments of relatively narrow spread price action.

As the market falls and the trend develops lower, this is a trend with momentum. The price spreads are widening in a measured way and gathering momentum as they go, before moving into the final phase of price action which is congestion without volatility on the right hand side of the chart.

I hope this example which I have described at length, has convinced you this approach to the market works. It is what I believe in and it is what I teach and use in my own trading. What I have described using the 30 minute chart for the GBP/JPY is as follows:

- First, how to interpret market behavior based on price action alone
- Second, to then apply volume to create the alliance which is volume price analysis
- Third, to apply a secondary indicator to help with our analysis. In this case we used Bollinger bands to gain a better understanding of volatility
- Fourth, to use a simple indicator, the pivots indicator to help us in our analysis

This is the process I believe will help you succeed as a trader, whether in binary options and in other instruments. As an options trader, the above is even more fundamental, since so much depends on your understanding and interpretation of market conditions. The sea state of the market. If you are looking for calm and benign conditions, you have to learn how to identify them and recognize the factors which will confirm these conditions.

Equally, if you are looking for volatility, again knowing where and what to look for is crucial. This is not to say conditions do not change suddenly - they do - but at least using volume and price coupled with a volatility indicator you will have a more profound understanding of the likely market conditions in the short term, and whether any sudden change is a full scale storm or simply a minor squall and one which is likely to pass soon.

Seeing the volatility directly on our charts is just one way. The volatility indices and other simple volatility tools will also provide that additional context and background. The information is all there, and even if you do not have a live feed for some of the more esoteric indices, I hope in the volatility chapter you will find one or two to help you, whatever market you are trading.

Whether you are trading a ladder, a tunnel, a one touch, a no touch, pairs, bull spreads, calls and puts, off exchange or on exchange - this is your starting point. The price chart is the focal point with the relational and the fundamental then providing the three dimensional view. The volatility tools, indicators and indices then complete the picture. This is your trading house which you can now furnish with whatever other indicators, whether secondary and free, or tertiary and paid, to help you in your analysis.

Now we come to time, which is the critical element when trading options. This is the roof of our trading house. Not only are we being asked questions about range, volatility or trend, we are also being asked to specify the timescale of every proposition.

Using Multiple Timeframes

It is often said there is nothing new in trading, and this is certainly true using a multiple timeframe approach. It is one which has been used by traders for decades. The same could also be said of volume price analysis, which is simply an extension of tape reading. What is perhaps different is that binary option traders rarely consider using multiple timeframes. In my opinion a huge mistake. And extending the concept further, I would suggest not only should this technique be applied to the charts, but also to any associated trading indicators.

Furthermore, the same approach can also be applied to a type of chart rarely used by intraday traders, namely a tick chart. This is yet another powerful way to visualize momentum and activity, as it is created and displayed directly on the chart as the candles develop. Tick charts are devoid of time, providing an additional and powerful way to trade.

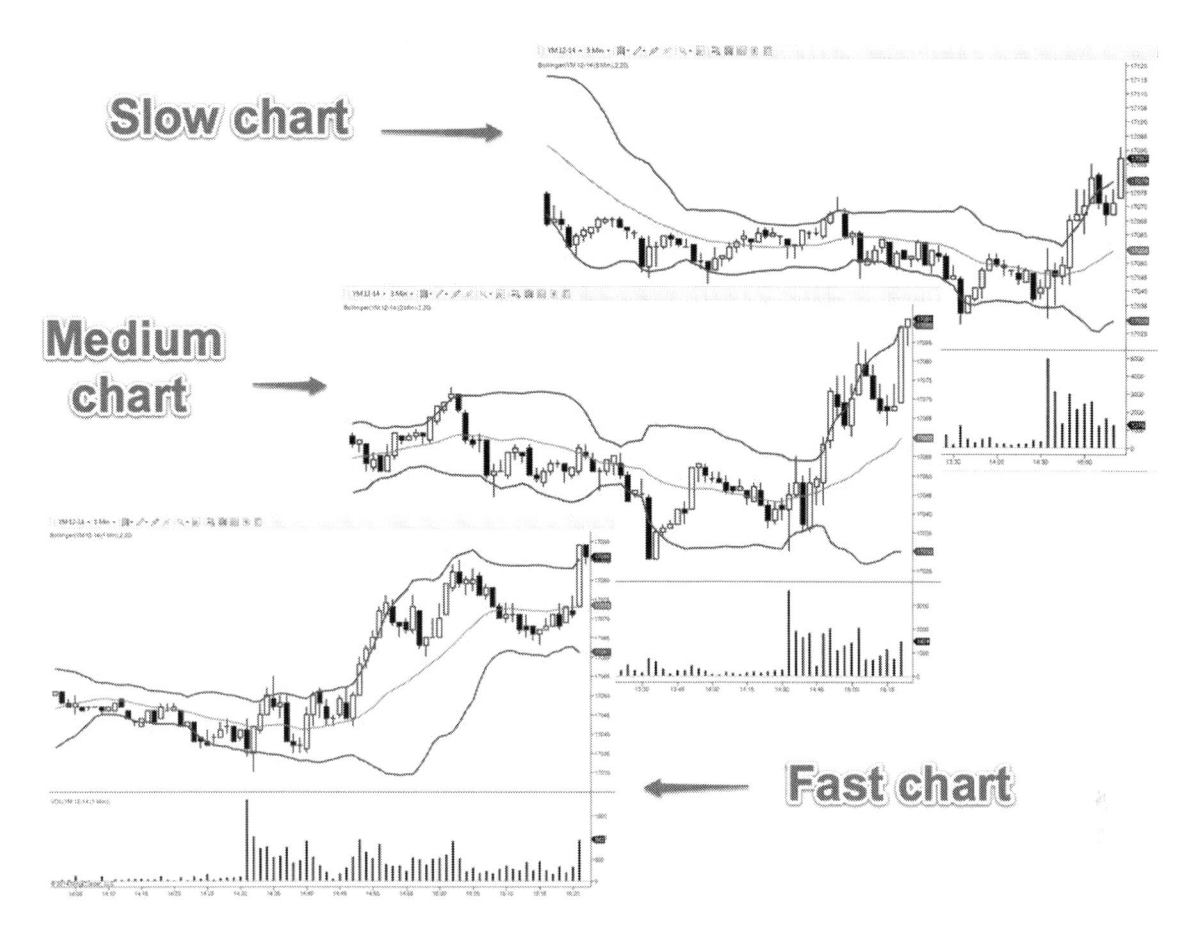

Fig 10.25 - Trading using multiple timeframes

The concept of trading using multiple timeframes is very straightforward yet powerful, and you can think of it in two ways. The first is in terms of the price action, and the second is in the application.

The analogy I use here is to describe price action in terms of throwing a pebble in a pond. Once the pebble lands the ripples move out and away from the landing point eventually reaching the side of the pond. This is the broad principle of price action when using a multiple timeframe approach. The fast chart reacts first, the price action ripples through to the medium timeframe chart before it finally arrives on the slow timeframe chart. Any significant changes in price direction moves through the three charts, rather like our three dimensional approach to analysis.

In this trading set up it is the medium speed chart which is the focus. It acts as the filter, slowing down the faster price action below, whilst giving a heads up on the slower timeframe above, which is the dominant timeframe. If the dominant trend is bullish, then trading with the trend carries a lower risk, all things being equal. The same is true for a bearish trend. Whilst there is nothing wrong with trading pullbacks and minor reversals, inherently they carry more risk. For binaries, we are also looking for congestion phases along with trends, and if your slow chart is in a congestion phase with no volatility, any positions taken from your medium speed chart would reflect this view.

Using three charts not only helps to reduce the noise of the faster timeframe, but will also give a more considered view of the slower time chart. This principle also works in reverse. When you have a position in the market based on your middle chart, and are perhaps worried the market may be reversing, a check on the faster time frame will help to clarify the price action in more detail. Using three timeframes to view the price action is simply a way of zooming in and out to enlarge and then reduce the focus. Using this approach will also help with candle patterns. It's difficult, if not impossible to layer candles one on top of another. A simple two bar reversal creating a hammer candle is straightforward, but several candles creating the same is more difficult to spot. With multiple timeframes each candle and its importance is defined, along with the related volume profiles and any associated indicators on the charts.

In terms of applying this method you can think of this in another way, as driving a car on a three lane highway. You are in the centre lane with your wing mirrors on either side providing constant updates and information. One is telling you what is happening in the fast lane, the other is telling you what is happening in the slow lane. As the driver in the middle lane, you have the complete picture of traffic flow.

The same applies to your trading. You now have the complete picture allowing you to assess risk in the context of the faster and slower timeframes. As you trade you move from fast, to medium up to slow and back to medium and down to fast. Up and down constantly checking, scanning, analyzing and assessing risk and sentiment as the money flows drive price action back and forth.

This principle can also be applied to associated charts and indicators. If you are trading the currency binaries, a currency strength indicator will help you enormously, and here again you can use the same approach. If a currency is rising across all three timeframes, this is a strong signal the trend has momentum. Equally, if a currency is overbought in a faster timeframe, and appears to be reaching overbought in a slower one, then again this is signaling a possible low risk position. Alternatively, the currencies may all be bunched in the centre of the indicator and if so the markets are in congestion.

In fact, I would suggest a currency strength indicator is essential, giving you an insight into every currency in every timeframe from a minute to a month. In Fig 10.26 we are using a multi timeframe approach on the currency strength indicator.

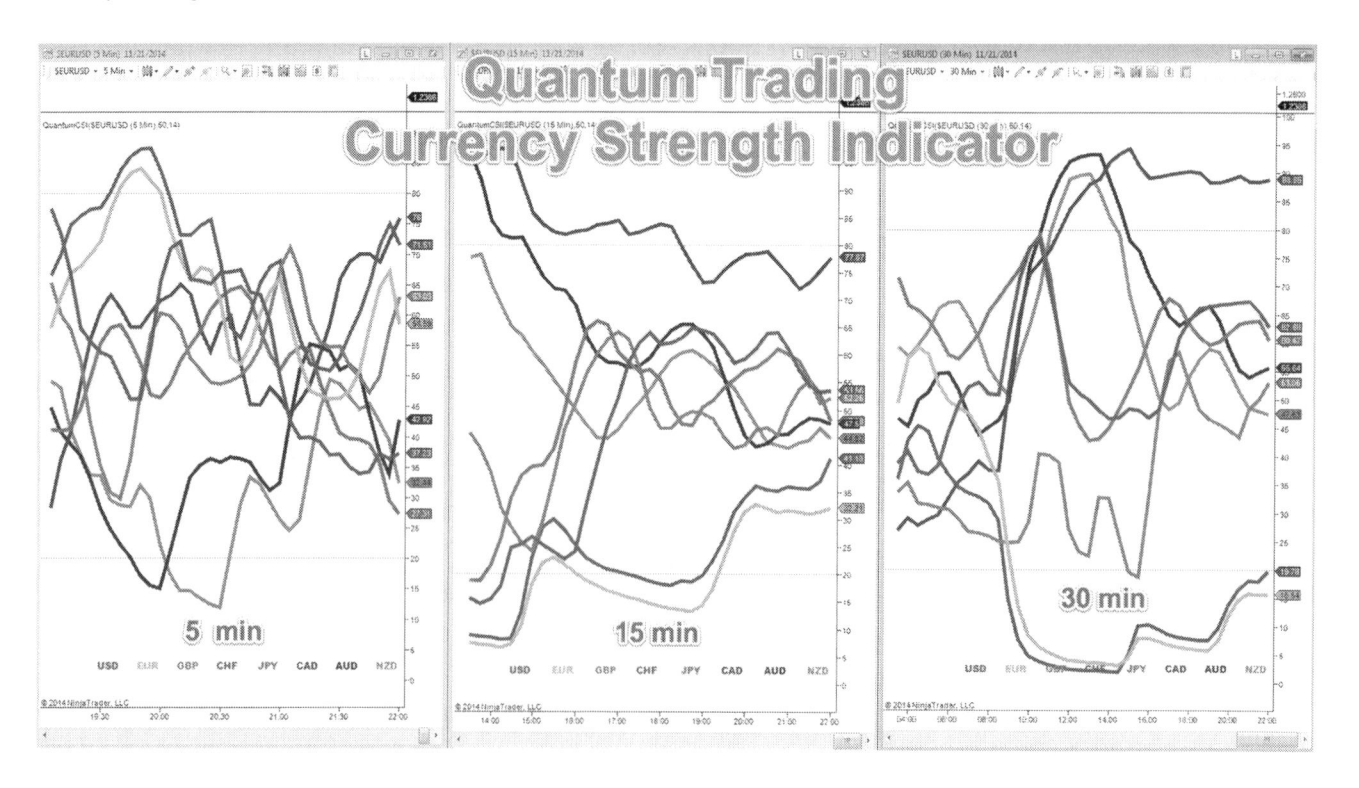

Fig 10.26 - Currency strength indicator available from www.quantumtrading.com

Tick Charts

Tick charts are a perfect way to trade binary options on an intraday basis. As I mentioned earlier, the primary advantage of a tick chart is that it is independent of time. A tick chart reveals surges of momentum coupled with volatility which are simply not visible on a time chart. Tick speeds vary throughout the session. As the market opens tick activity surges with the candles formed in seconds. The market then settles as tick activity falls away and candles are formed at a much slower pace, until perhaps a news item injects both momentum and volatility back into the price action once more. Using a combination of time and tick charts is a perfect way to apply this approach to trading binaries. A tick chart will provide precise and early entries and faster exits.

A further variant of multiple timeframes is to use multiple charts from related markets. For example if you are trading index futures make sure you have the cash equivalent also displayed along with the VIX. The VIX is a powerful chart for trading binary indices. Having the VIX in multiple timeframes will help reinforce your trading decision and give you the confidence to manage your trade.

These are the building blocks of trading binaries. The relational, technical and fundamental provide the perspective and landscape for sentiment and risk. The volatility indices provide the deeper and all important perspective on volatility. The charts in multiple timeframes and other indicators complete the approach.

In the next chapter we are going to consider some strategies appropriate for the sea state of the market.

Chapter Eleven

Binary Options Strategies

I never hesitate to tell a man that I am bullish or bearish. But I do not tell people to buy or sell any particular stock. In a bear market all stocks go down and in a bull market they go up.

Jesse Livermore (1877 - 1940)

Let me start this chapter with a further paradox of the binary instrument, and one which will also explain why I spent so much time in the previous chapter explaining the preparation phase for trading binaries. And the paradox is this. Simple they may be, but it is time which sets all options apart.

In trading conventional instruments we can afford to wait. Time neither influences nor dictates whether a position is ultimately profitable or not. For binaries, time is the ultimate arbiter of success. Fail to plan, or interpret the sea state accurately, and time will quite literally shipwreck your positions. This is the reason all trading strategies ultimately fail when applied with no regard to the market conditions. Typically a strategy will work for a while and then fail. The reason it fails is the market conditions have changed, and the strategy no longer works in those conditions.

This is why understanding and interpreting the market's sea state is critical to your success, and why binary options require market analysis of the highest calibre. Forecast the sea state accurately, and you will succeed with these instruments. Fail to plan or take the time required, and you will ultimately fail. Time, like the devil, always collects, and the devil is in the detail. Focus on the detail and the options will look after themselves.

Mapping Strategies To Markets

When choosing and applying a binary option strategy, whether off exchange or on exchange, there are four distinct approaches you can take. The one you ultimately select will be dictated by your experience, knowledge of the markets, and the time you have available. And perhaps more than any other, binary options are instruments that lend themselves to a 'set and forget' approach. Even more so on the Nadex platform where all orders are executed using a limit order, allowing entry and exits to be accurately planned in advance.

When considering a strategy to adopt (trading binary options or any other instruments), there are four approaches you can take, and these are as follows:

- Multiple markets and multiple strategies
- Single market and multiple strategies
- Multiple markets and single strategy
- Single market and single strategy

Multiple Markets & Multiple Strategies

Using this mapping strategy, you are happy to consider applying any strategy to any market. Your trading is indiscriminate and you are happy to select an appropriate strategy and apply this to the sea state in any market. You could consider this as the 'Jack of all trades, and master of none' approach, where you are simply looking for trading opportunities in all markets, in all timeframes and for all strategies.

Single Market & Multiple Strategies

This is a more targeted approach. Here you are focusing on one market, but prepared to apply a range of strategies which suit the sea state of the market. However, you are focused on one market which you understand well, and are simply identifying a market condition and then applying the appropriate strategy.

Multiple Markets & Single Strategy

This is the reverse of the above approach. Here you have focused and become an expert in one binary option strategy, which you then apply to any market. In this case you understand the strategy intimately, and are then hunting for opportunities to apply it, in whichever market has the appropriate sea state conditions.

Single Market & Single Strategy

This is the laser guided approach. Here you are mapping a single strategy to a single market. This requires patience. In this case you are a specialist both on the market and the strategy. All other trading strategies are ignored, and you only take a position in the market when this single strategy is relevant. The focus is on one market only, which you understand intimately and a strategy which you apply with precision.

These are the choices available to you as a binary options trader. Whichever you choose will depend on many factors, but choosing one and then honing this over time will help to shape your success using these instruments. I cannot stress this too strongly, and of the above, I would suggest you consider the more focused approaches of a single market or single strategy as your starting point.

And let me reinforce this aspect with a personal anecdote. One of my good friends, who is a proprietary trader, trades binary options on his personal account. He only trades one strategy which is then applied across all markets, and over the longer term timeframes of days, weeks and even months. This suits his trading style and personal life.

You can think of this in much the same way as a sniper. Here you are using a single shot from a high powered rifle for a high probability kill. The guiding principles are patience and planning, and it is just a question of waiting until the target is in the crosshair of your sights. Then fire. The strategy my fellow trader employs is the one touch/no touch option.

If you recall, this is one of the products which does indeed offer a significantly higher return in the off exchange world. The problem is, traders are attracted by the returns, and trade using a scatter gun approach. If you are prepared to wait, select your target with care, and only execute it when you have conducted a full and complete analysis of the underlying market, then and only then are you likely to take advantage of the high returns on offer. As with everything in the binary world - these are perfectly valid instruments when used correctly and with care. Used incorrectly, and with little thought, such returns will remain elusive. But with preparation, planning and patience, such returns become attainable. This is the approach my trading friend adopts, with great success. I would urge you to explore this approach for yourself.

Off exchange binary products are straightforward and appealing. They offer a fixed risk proposition, and one which you can take many times a day.

Let's consider a couple of examples trading a trend and a channel, before moving on to look at some more sophisticated strategies for on exchange binary spreads and options.

In these examples I have used futures charts, but please be aware off exchange binary options brokers may or may not provide charts. In addition, and unless you ask specifically, you will have little or no idea where their data feed is originating. If you are using futures charts for your analysis, as here, then there may be a big divergence in the price, depending on the time to rollover and the contract, when the futures and spot prices converge.

If you are trading currencies the spot prices are readily available and free through platforms such as MT4 and elsewhere. For spot prices on other markets such as gold, you can find these at http://www.netdania.com as well as http://www.freestockcharts.com and of the two I would suggest the latter, as it also covers many of the other markets we have featured in this book. In addition it's easy to apply the trading tools and indicators to the charts, such as Bollinger bands.

In the first example we are looking at a possible position on the AUD/USD. The charts below are for the 4hr, daily and weekly timeframes and following the breakout on the daily chart, the pair has been bearish for the past few days. We are in trend momentum here, and the general picture is one of a continuation of the current move, perhaps with some increased momentum in due course. The options we could consider here might be a one touch to the downside, a no touch to the upside, or a simple target price. We could also consider a ladder option if available.

These are the steps we would follow:

- Check the USD index across multiple timeframes looking for bullish breakouts, or any recent move through strong areas of resistance. Ideally, we want to see the dollar rising steadily with technical downside protection in the event of any reversal. This can be confirmed on instruments such as the ETF UUP dollar bullish fund
- Check the CRB index for commodities and the trend
- Check the gold charts across multiple timeframes
- Consider the fundamental news across the period under consideration. Any major announcements in Australia or China which could reverse sentiment. Make sure there are no major local news releases particularly from the Royal Bank of Australia and also be aware of US news
- Check the volatility charts on OANDA or Investing.com for signs of confirming price action and trend
- Check the GVZ volatility index on the CBOE
- Finally move to the three timeframes for the charts themselves

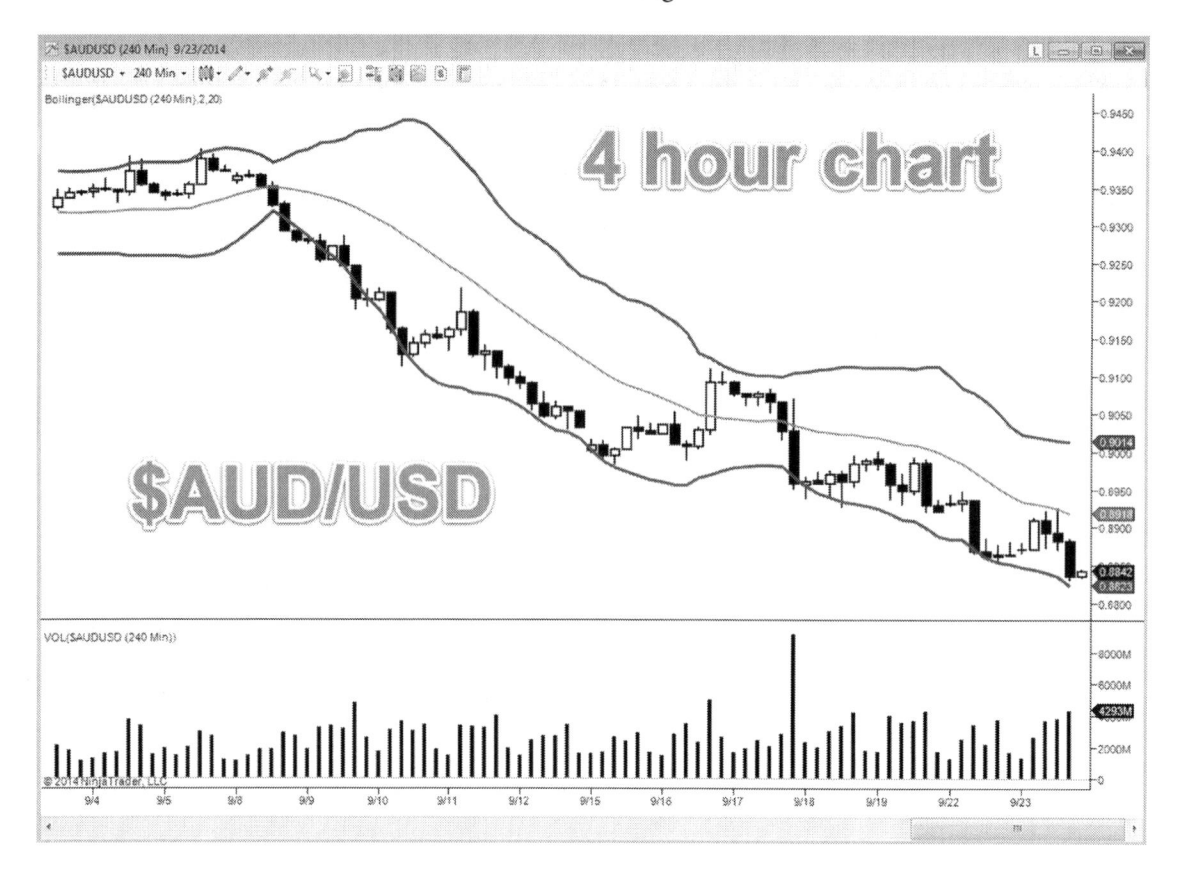

Fig 11.10 - AUD/USD four hour chart NinjaTrader platform

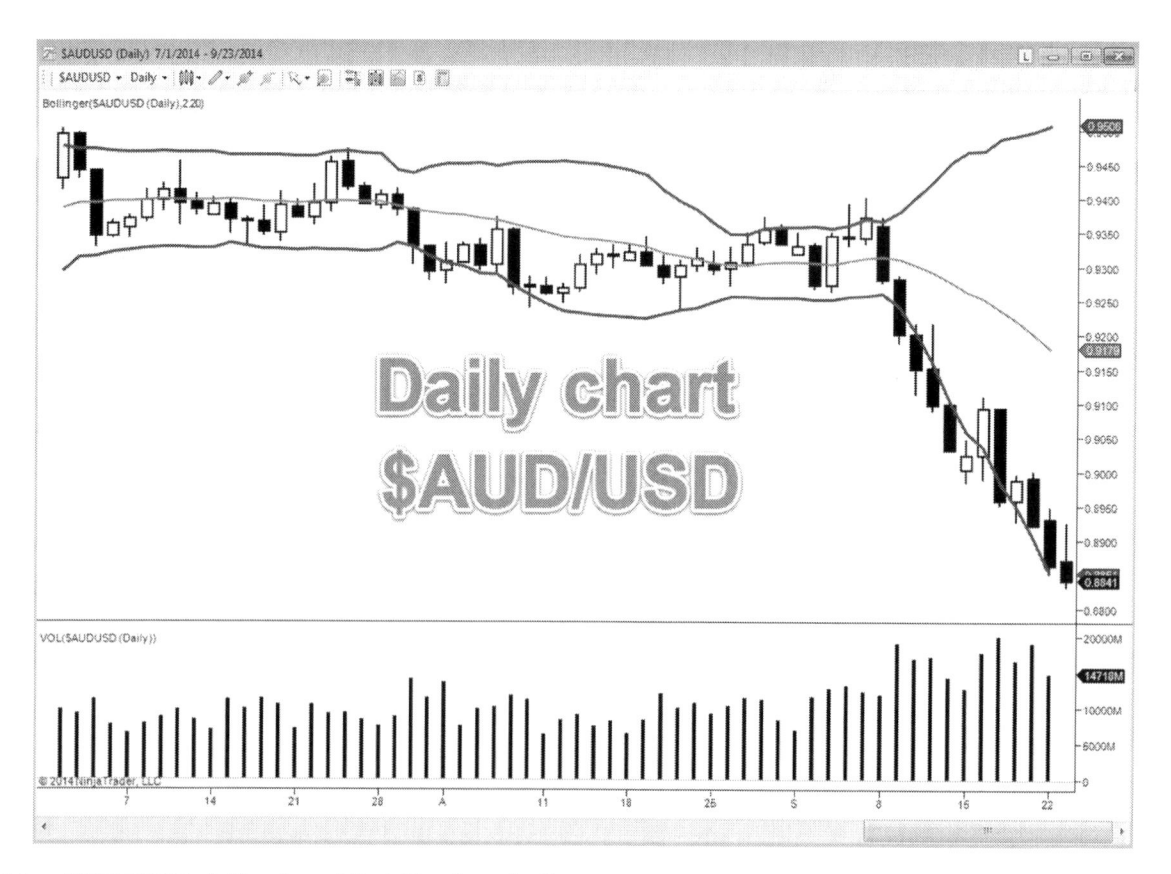

Fig 11.11 - AUD/USD daily chart NinjaTrader platform

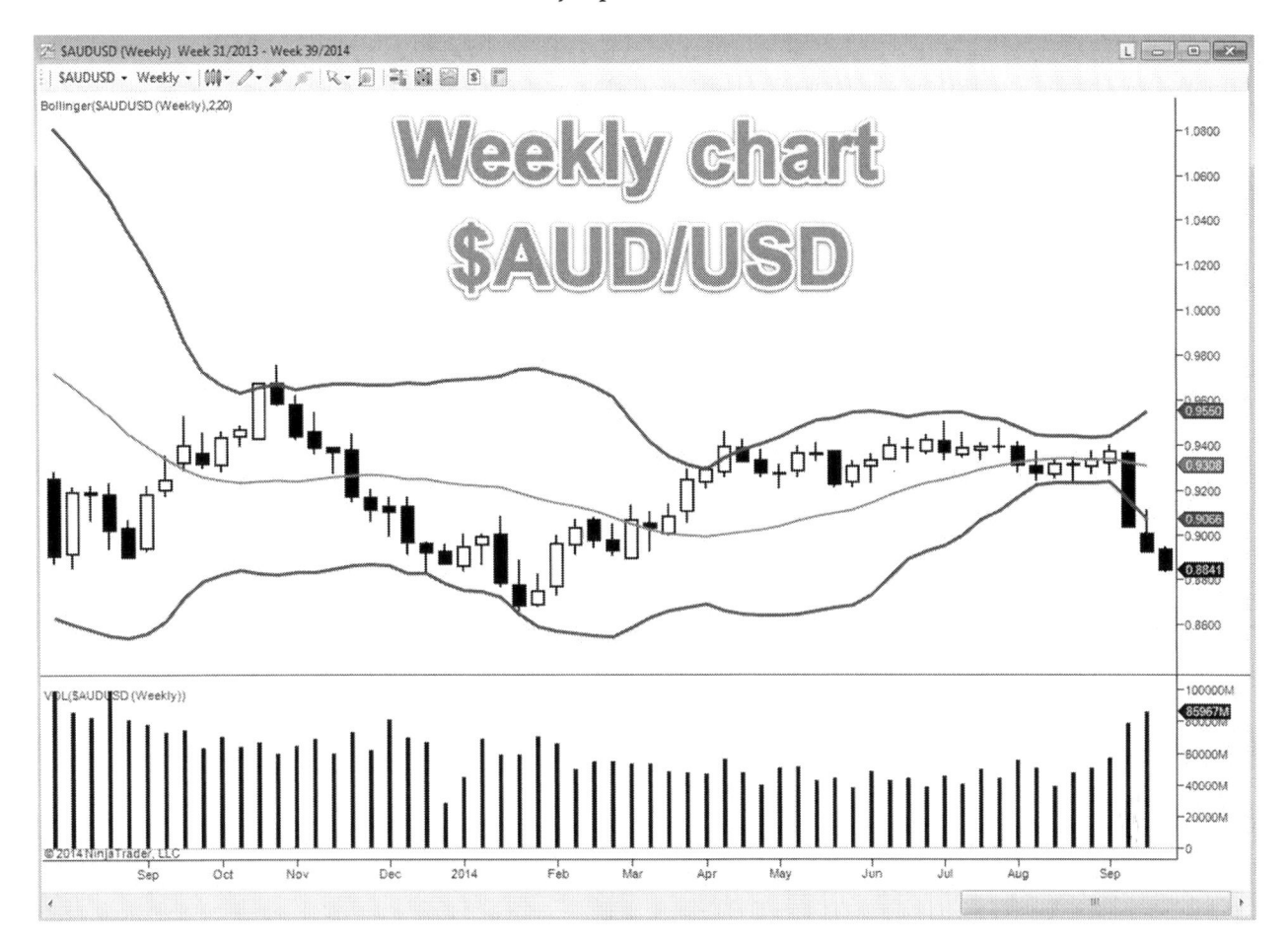

Fig 11.12 - AUD/USD weekly chart NinjaTrader platform

For the Aussie dollar it's been a steep fall, ever since the breakout from the congestion phase in the 0.9400 to 0.9200 region, most clearly evident on the daily chart. Since then, the pair has moved lower on rising volumes with increasing momentum suggesting a deeper move to come. The most recent candle on this chart has a deep upper wick signaling further weakness. There is no sign at present of any stopping volume on this timeframe, or of a buying climax.

The weekly chart confirms this picture, with the AUD/USD falling on rising volume, and breaking out from the recent narrow phase of price congestion as confirmed by the Bollinger bands. The only technical issue of concern here is the potential support waiting from earlier in the year in the 0.8700 region. If this is breached we should expect to see the pair continue lower in the short to medium term.

Given this analysis the decision now is whether we opt for a touch/no touch or perhaps an option with a specific strike price. There are advantages and disadvantages to both. With the one touch/no touch option you are relinquishing some flexibility in the instrument for substantially increased returns. However, provided you are considering a longer term timeframe then time is on your side, and given the current market analysis, I would suggest the no touch option would be the best choice here, since the market has already fallen dramatically, and likely to pause and move into congestion at some point. The other alternative would be a target based option with a strike price.

Moving to silver where we could consider a range binary such as a tunnel. Here we are looking for low volatility, with no prospect of a trend in the near future. In this case it is the December contract for the metal, and is based on the 15 minute, 30 minute and 60 minute timeframes, so an intraday opportunity. Once again the steps would be much the same as in the first example:

- Check the USD index for congestion in multiple timeframes. This can be confirmed on other instruments such as the ETF UUP bullish fund
- Check the CRB index for commodities and the trend
- Gold and silver correlate closely - check the gold charts across the same timeframes for any contradictory signals
- Consider the fundamental news across the period under consideration.
- Check the VXSLV volatility index at the CBOE both intraday and daily
- Check the GVZ volatility index at the CBOE both intraday and daily
- Finally move to the three timeframes for the charts themselves

Fig 11.13 - Silver futures 15 minute chart

Fig 11.14 - Silver futures 30 minute chart

Fig 11.15 - Silver futures 60 minute chart

If we start with the 60 minute chart, the picture here is of a market in congestion, and where it has been for the last two days. The Bollinger bands have narrowed, and despite the modest move during the day have remained tight with the price action narrowing. The volumes too are confirming this lack of volatility present in this timeframe. Both the 15 minute and the 30 minute charts confirm this picture, and the associated volumes are in agreement. The question, as always, is whether this lack of volatility is likely to continue for the duration of the option, which is where the tools, analysis and indicators in our checklist will help to complete the picture, and from which it is possible to assess the risk on the position.

From our analysis, we have concluded that the lack of volatility is likely to continue for the duration of the option and the choices here would be for a tunnel from one of the leading off exchange brokers, or alternatively the construction of a range trade which is one of the strategies we are going to look at in the next section.

Before moving foreward to the on exchange products and strategies, let me make one final point concerning Binary.com. You may recall I used a horse racing analogy to explain how with this broker you are in complete control of your own race, for most binary products. It is you who decides when your option starts, and it is one of the unique features offered on this platform. As you will see when you select an option from the platform, the drop down menu allows you to select between duration or end time.

Giving you these choices puts you in control, and when combined with the approaches outlined above helps to shift the probabilities in your favor.

I cannot stress this too strongly or make the case more forcefully. This is a game changer. If you can apply VPA successfully, along with all the other techniques, you can choose when to trade, and as a result move the probabilities in your favor immeasurably.

On Exchange Strategies

In this section I want to consider more advanced examples for on exchange binary options products, and two in particular. First a strategy using one of the CBOE options, and then move to the Nadex exchange to look at an example using a binary option as a hedge in the spot market.

If we begin with the CBOE and a low volatility strategy using the BSZ binary option for the S&P 500 index. These are currently monthly, and what we are going to construct is a position which creates a range by buying and selling a call option simultaneously, but with different strike prices. This is the simplest, and the cleanest way to create an option strategy where the range is defined. In many ways it is similar to a condor strategy, except with the condor the boundaries of the range are not quite so clearly defined. With binary options they are, owing to the unique characteristic of the binary option profile.

If we start with the underlying index, namely the S&P 500. It is the 26th September and the index is trading at 1982.85. We check the options chain, and find we have the following strike prices available:

- Strike price of 1950 - in the money binary call option is 0.73
- Strike price 2000 - out of the money binary call option is 0.38

Each binary option will either settle at $100 or $0, and for simplicity let's use a factor of ten. In this case we are buying ten in the money call options, and selling ten out of the money call options. This is how the figures work out:

- 10 x 0.73 x 100 = Cost of buying the options $730
- 10 x 0.38 x 100 = Income from selling the options $380

The net cost of creating the position, in other words the maximum risk on the position is:

- $730 - $380 = $350 maximum loss

We now have three possible outcomes which are as follows:

- The index settles below 1950
- The index settles between 1950 and 2000
- The index settles above 2000

If we take each of these in turn as follows:

- ***If the index settles below 1950***
- The long binary option loses $730
- The short binary option wins $380
- The net P/L on the position is $380 - $730 = ($350)

- ***If the index settles between 1950 and 2000***
- The long binary option wins $270
- The short binary option wins $380
- The net P/L on the position is $270 + $380 = $650

- ***If the index settles above 2000***
- The long binary option wins $270
- The short binary option loses $620
- The net P/L on the position is $270 - $620 = ($350)

If we consider this in terms of the risk profile for the binary strategy it would look like this:

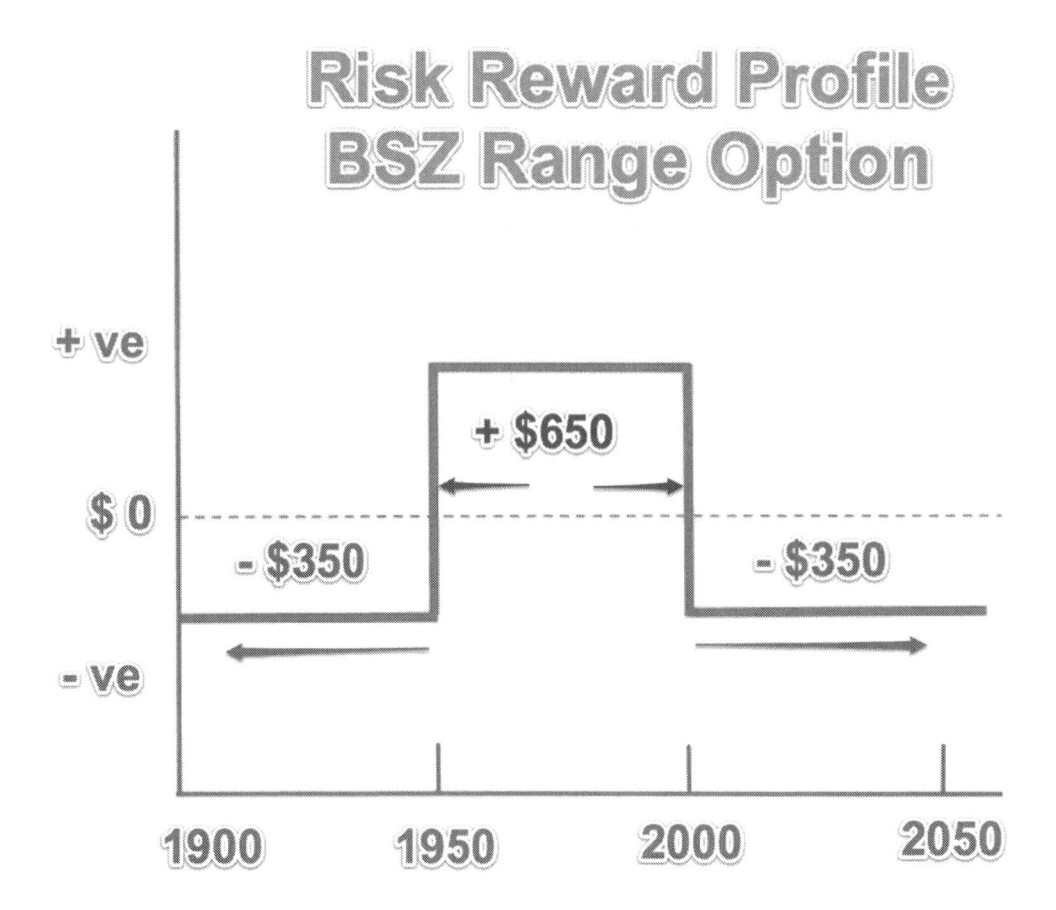

Fig 11.16 - BSZ options range strategy risk and reward profile

As we can see, provided the index closes between the two strike prices the profit is $650, but anywhere outside of the range specified the option closes at a loss of - $350. As with all binary options, it is the all or nothing proposition which defines the precise limits of the risk and reward profile.

Whilst I have used an on exchange binary option to explain this strategy, it is one which can be applied equally well to Nadex binary options and to off exchange options too. The risk and reward profile is the same, and all we are doing in creating the range is applying our knowledge of the underlying market to define this 'range of expectation' for the construction of the position. It is a stress free way to trade, and in addition is entirely flexible allowing risk and return to be balanced and matched to the underlying sea state conditions precisely. Employing this strategy on the Nadex platform you will be spoiled for choice.

This strategy can be extended further by considering cross instrument hedging, either in the same market such as forex on other pairs, or in related markets where correlation plays a part. Their use is only limited by your imagination. And remember with the Nadex platform you also have the additional flexibility of closing out early to take profits off the table, something which may not be available off exchange.

Staying with Nadex here I want to explore the Nadex bull spread option product, once again, but here we are going to combine the binary option with the underlying spot market to create a simple hedging strategy.

Before constructing the hedge, I would like to clarify the terminology. What Nadex refer to as the 'bull spread', is perhaps a little misleading, and I believe Nadex will be renaming this product the 'Nadex spread' in the near future.

Perhaps the easiest way to think of these instruments is as a box on the chart with a defined floor and ceiling. The spread is the difference between these two levels, and it is important to appreciate from the start, this instrument is not the same as the binary option in terms of the expiry. It still has a fixed risk and fixed reward profile as we saw earlier, but settles at the underlying market, and not at 0 or 100.

This is a hybrid instrument, which draws together elements of the binary world and elements of the vanilla options world. In this case the instrument settles to the underlying spot market and not to the traditional zero or one hundred of other on exchange binary instruments.

The options can be both bought and sold, and are quoted across the complete range of markets for indices, commodities and currencies.

The floor and ceiling (the strike prices if you like) are defined by the exchange and not by you as the trader. This is a key difference, because in the vanilla world, you create the two strike prices and the two legs. Nadex have made this very simple by creating the instrument for you, thereby negating the need to construct the two legs of the position yourself.

This is an example based on a 2 hour expiry for the EUR/USD. The bull spread option will be quoted in the following way:

- The spread - in this case 1.3100 to 1.3200
- The expiry date and time - in this case 2 hours

Nadex Bull Spread EUR/USD 2 hour

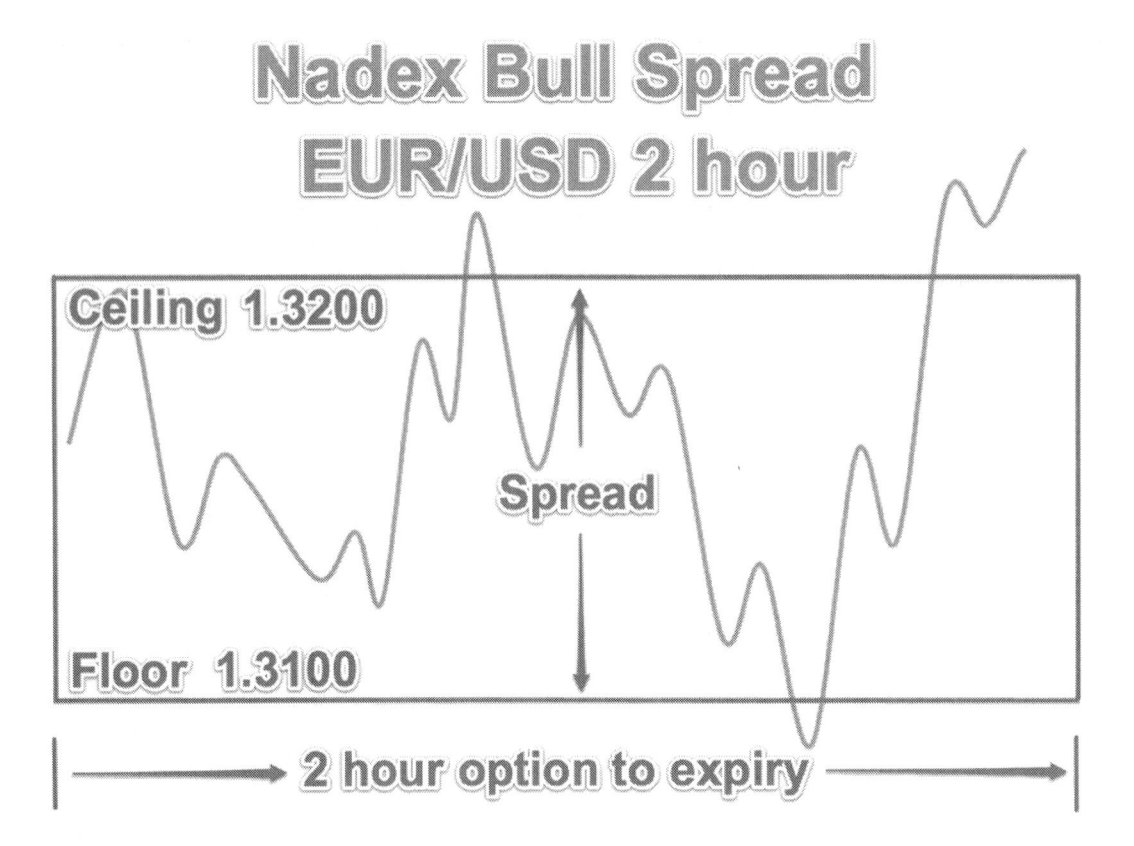

Ceiling 1.3200

Spread

Floor 1.3100

2 hour option to expiry

Fig 11.17 - EUR/USD 2 hour bull spread option

Here the spread is 100 pips from the floor of 1.3100 to the ceiling of 1.3200 with a 2 hour expiry period. The box confirms the start and the finish, with the floor and the ceiling defining the top and bottom of the box.

If you were to sell this spread at say 1.3190, the risk and reward profiles would be as follows:

- Maximum risk = 1.3200 - 1.3190 x $1 = $10
- Maximum profit = 1.3190 - 1.3100 x $1 = $90
- Even if the market moves below 1.3100 before or after expiry the maximum profit is capped
- Even if the market moves above 1.3200 before or after expiry the maximum loss is capped
- The option can be closed at any time before expiry or left to expire

If you were to buy this spread at say 1.3110, the risk and reward profiles would be as follows:

- Maximum risk = 1.3110 - 1.3100 x $1 = $10
- Maximum profit = 1.3200 - 1.3110 x $1 = $90
- Even if the market moves above 1.3200 before or after expiry the maximum profit is capped
- Even if the market moves below 1.3100 before or after expiry the maximum loss is capped
- The option can be closed at any time before expiry or left to expire

Now let's look at applying the above example to a spot forex position.

Suppose the EUR/USD is trading in the spot market at 1.3200 and we are bullish, and trading a full lot contract. In other words each pip in the spot market is + or - $10, so we buy at 1.3200. We are going to add the binary bull spread with a floor at 1.3100 and the ceiling at 1.3200, and sell at 1.3185.

At this point we have two positions in the market. A long in the spot market, and protection to the short side with the binary spread option. As we now have the protection of the spread to the floor of 1.3100, we can also place our stop loss in the spot market at the same level. It is a huge distance from the market price at 100 pips. If we were trading a simple directional spot position over this timeframe, any stop loss might only be in the range 20 to 30 pips. A 100 pip stop loss might only be considered if we were trading a much longer term strategy, of perhaps days or weeks.

With the addition of the binary spread, not only have we moved the stop loss dramatically, but the risk on the position has also been reduced equally dramatically, as it is covered with the spread of the option. In effect, what we have done here is to buy ourselves some protection which is costing us $15, or the difference between 1.3200 and 1.3185.

There are several different concepts at work here, and of course several different outcomes which we will explore in detail. But let's start with a schematic of the trading position we have created. This is shown in Fig 11.18, and please bear in mind this is just one strategy - there are many different ways to use the bull spread in combination with the underlying spot market. This approach works equally well where you could be trading a futures contract on a commodity such as gold, or an index future. I just happen to have used a currency pair, but it can be applied to any other market in exactly the same way.

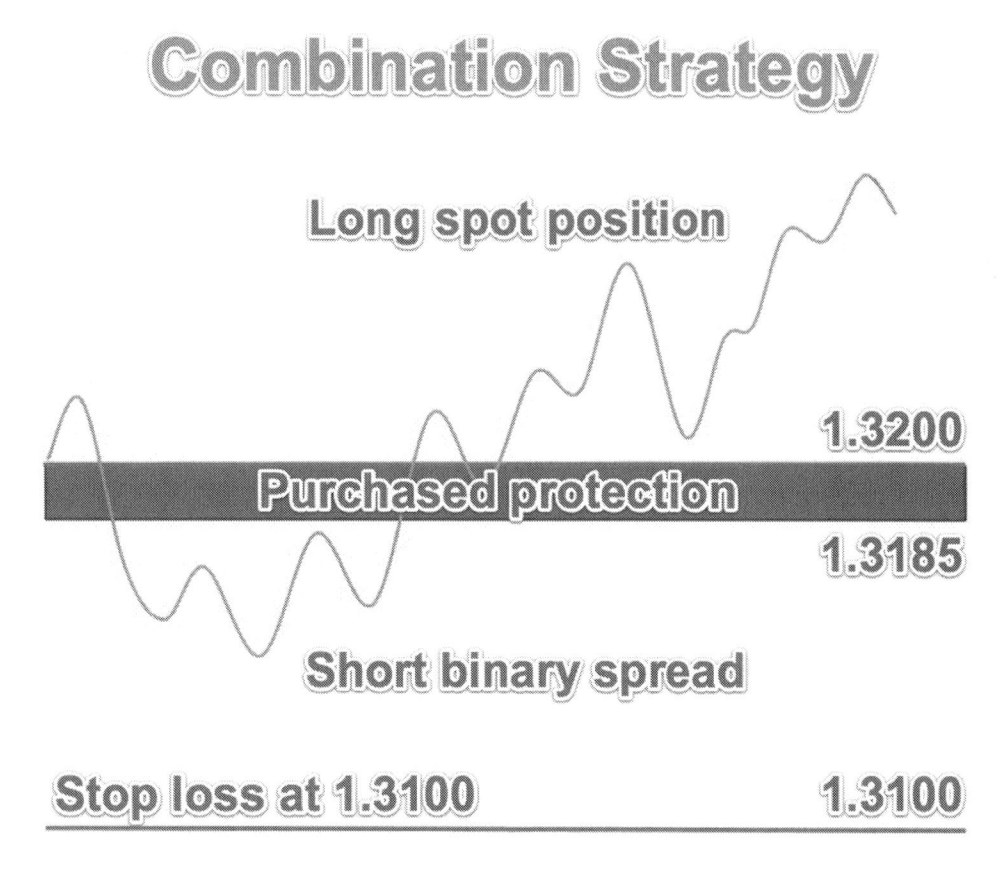

Fig 11.18 - Combination strategy using spot and Nadex binary bull spread

If we begin by considering the two components in isolation. First we have a spot position, where we have entered the market at 1.3200 with a stop loss of 100 pips below at 1.3100. For such a large risk, we would expect to be looking at a substantial move in our favor, perhaps over days or weeks. Here however, we are considering an intraday position, and one where we would normally place any stop loss perhaps 20 or 30 pips below, and in line with an expected move in this timeframe.

Moving to the binary bull spread. Here we have sold the option at 1.3185, 15 pips below the ceiling. This is the 'protection' we have purchased. You can think of this as a premium on the position - it's the cost of the insurance if you like. In marrying the two approaches, our purchased protection becomes our maximum risk. It is the cost of the position, and in addition has allowed us to increase the depth of our stop loss giving the position room to breathe. In a way, we have bought ourselves time. Time to allow the position to move into profit, remembering that we can always close out either or both whenever we like. In addition, in overlaying these two approaches we have also opened up the risk reward profile, having moved from the fixed risk and fixed reward of the bull spread, to fixed risk and unlimited reward with the addition of the spot position.

And there is a further, perhaps more subtle reason for adopting such a strategy, and it concerns the stop loss. If you were trading this as a simple intraday trade to the long side, any stop loss would probably be placed to within 20 or 30 pips of the entry price. By introducing the bull spread our stop loss has moved much deeper, but with no equivalent increase in risk. We are now in a situation where the market can move against us in a meaningful way, but the position remains intact. We have bought ourselves time for the position to breathe, and potentially move into profit which would probably not be achieved with a conventional stop loss. A conventional stop loss set close to the entry is always at risk. It is a subtle point, but one that is often lost when considering this strategy.

Furthermore, if the position moves in our favor to expiry, further spreads can be added against the position with an associated move in the stop loss, allowing us to manage the position further.

It is important to ensure the binary spread is matched to the spot position. If you are trading a full lot at $10 per pip, in the above example you would need to sell 10 contracts to equate to $10 per pip in the option.

And here are the possible outcomes, using a full lot in the spot market:

The spot market moves to 1.3250 at expiry:

- Profit in the spot market = 50 x $10 = $500
- Loss in the bull spread option = 15 x $10 = ($150)
- Total profit = $500 - $150 = $350

The spot market moves to 1.3140 at expiry:

- Loss in the spot market = 60 x $10 = ($600)
- Profit in the bull spread option = 45 x $10 = $450
- Total loss = $450 - $600 = ($150)

The spot market moves to 1.3210 at expiry:

- Profit in the spot market = 10 x $10 = $100
- Loss in the bull spread option = 15 x $10 = ($150)
- Total loss = $100 - $150 = ($50)

The market could collapse and trigger the stop loss at the floor of 1.3100, but even so the maximum loss would once again be the 'insurance premium' you have paid to protect your position, as in this case the binary spread would be in profit at $850 against a loss in the spot market of $1000.

Considering the first outcome, you may be thinking you have had to forego $150 of potential profit, making only $350 against a possible $500. Whilst this is certainly true, this opens up the debate surrounding trading emotion, and the stress you would feel trading a position which was moving heavily against you. Which of the following scenarios would you rather have?

- The prospect of $1000 loss in your account
- The prospect of $150 loss in your account
- The prospect of a reduced profit
- The prospect of a very small loss

If you are a seasoned trader with years of experience, you may be equipped to deal with this pressure. However, if this were your second or perhaps even a third losing trade, the pressure is not so easy to handle. Insurance always comes at a price, but in using this strategy, you have not only bought yourself time, but also a certain amount of peace of mind.

What this strategy does is to define the risk on the trade. If you are keen to trade other markets such as commodities, or perhaps have come from the futures market, and familiar with the margin requirements for oil or gold on the full size contracts, you will already know the amount of margin that is required, simply to manage your risk and position. Using this strategy will give you the tools to trade more comfortably, and with a clearly defined level of risk. Nadex offer this very simple option across all the markets and they are available throughout the trading session. As one expires others become available. There is always plenty of choice, whatever the market you are trading, and there is a wide range of timeframes to choose from. Nadex also offer a demo account, so it is easy to practice this strategy and others for yourself.

I would urge you to investigate all the Nadex binary products in more detail. If nothing else, this one strategy will help you manage your emotions and risk more easily so you can enjoy your trading to the full.

Chapter Twelve

Are Binary Options For Me?

If you want to have a better performance than the crowd, you must do things differently from the crowd

Sir John Templeton (1912 - 2008)

Perhaps this is the question that prompted you to buy this book, and I hope I have managed to answer it for you. Throughout this book, I have tried to provide a balanced and objective view of the binary options world as it is at present. As the tagline of the book suggests, there are the good, the bad and the downright dangerous, which I think neatly sums up the world of binaries.

As with anything new, there will always be those out to make a quick return, and to take advantage of the unwary or ill-informed. And my objective in writing this book has been to try and inform and educate.

There are many good things in the world of binary options, but there are also many not so good things. At present this market is at an embryonic stage. Legislation will come, and come quickly as the regulators seek to protect the public. Whilst this is a good thing, it is only part of the solution, since this simply drives the less scrupulous into unregulated jurisdictions.

However, as binary option traders become more educated and competition grows, this market will mature in much the same way as is happening in the world of spot forex. In many ways it is very sad the good always get tarnished by the bad. Companies such as Binary.com, Nadex, IG Index, and of course the exchanges, stand head and shoulders above the rest. With these companies you will find integrity, security, opportunity and creativity in equal measure. The products offered have validity and authenticity.

At present, the question that is perhaps vexing the authorities more than any other, and is also the focus of many conversations in the chat rooms and forums is simply this. Are binary options betting or trading? And here let me give you my thoughts.

Perhaps the starting point is the CBOE. The CBOE is akin to the CME, CBOT, the NYSE and other major exchanges, and the mere fact that binary options are listed, places this instrument fairly and squarely in the trading world. It is impossible to argue otherwise. The same is true of Nadex. Here again, we have an exchange, albeit one where you can become a member with a 'seat' on the exchange for just $100. Not something you could ever buy on the CBOE or CME. Both offer binary options, and as with any other exchange traded instrument, it is the financial chart and market analysis which underpins the buying or selling decision.

The debate then becomes one centered on off exchange offerings. Are these instrument betting or trading? And this is not an easy question to answer.

Betting

If we start with the casino, this is a fixed odds proposition, but with no underlying market. There is no analysis we can undertake, other than to study the mathematics and probability of chance.

Next comes sports betting, and perhaps horse racing is a good example. Whilst a horse race does not have an underlying market, what it does have is a level for analysis, and that of course is the horse itself. Here we now have something to study, namely the form of the horse, which is reflected in the odds being quoted. And one could argue that if we are prepared to study the form of the horse in depth, and compare this with the going, the conditions, the length of the race and the course itself, all things being equal we are basing our decision on sound analysis. And perhaps it is not so far fetched to suggest horse racing may be a 'better bet', if we are prepared to put in the work and study the form. But then so do the bookmakers, which is how the odds are derived.

Next comes spread betting which introduced the word betting into the trading lexicon. This instrument covers every market from financial to sports, having been introduced originally for trading gold. CFDs are a further example in this category.

My own thoughts are as follows, and follow two very distinct paths.

First, if the proposition I am considering has some underlying scope for analysis, it moves up the scale from outright betting to speculation, and ultimately into investing and trading.

Second, it is perhaps time which is the defining factor. Consider two examples from the same market with the only difference being time:

- The EUR/USD being higher than 1.2820 in 60 seconds
- The EUR/USD being higher than 1.2820 in 4 hours

The proposition is the same. The market is the same, and the underlying analysis would be the same. The only difference is time. Why then is the first considered to be betting, and the second to be trading? And ultimately it does all boil down to time.

Time is a wasting asset, and one we have to have on our side. The time to be right. Outside of the world of options, we can afford to be patient, provided we have sufficiently deep pockets and wide stop loss orders. In the world of options, we are constantly considering time. For a binary option, time can be both a friend and an enemy. In binary options we need time on our side. Time for the outcome to occur, and 60 seconds is simply insufficient in this respect. The greater the time element, then the more an instrument moves towards the speculative and trading environment, and away from betting. You may find this simplistic, but it is just my view.

Finally, everything starts with the chart, and from there it's a question of risk analysis, part of which includes the time element. If you can get time working for you, rather than against you, you push the odds and probabilities heavily in your favor. For me, on exchange binary options offer the greatest opportunity and flexibility.

Those offered by Nadex may not be available to you as a non US customer, although I believe this is changing, and you will need to check with Nadex for the current situation. IG Index offer many of the same options. The CBOE options, whilst limited, will be widely available and may also encourage you to explore the world of vanilla options, more fully. And don't forget the NYSE which has a broader range of binary options available.

There is one thing however, I can guarantee. This market will change, and it will change very fast over the next few years, as competition forces out many of the less scrupulous, and new players will enter this market. Products too will change fast, and indeed as this book goes to print, Binary.com have announced their new pairs trading products, whilst Nadex have launched a binary option for Bitcoin.

I hope in reading this book, it has given you the confidence at least explore these instruments in more detail for yourself, with eyes wide open. There are many traps for the unwary, but there are also some solid gold nuggets if you know where to look.

As always, I would like to thank you for purchasing this book, and if you do have questions I would be delighted to hear from you.

You can contact me on my personal email at anna@annacoulling.com and you will receive a reply. This is one of several books I have published with those below:

These include *A Three Dimensional Approach To Forex Trading* which explains how to forecast forex market behavior using the combined power of relational, technical and fundamental analysis.

Another is *Forex For Beginners*, along with *A Complete Guide To Volume Price Analysis*. You can find details on all of these on my personal site at http://www.annacoulling.com

Further books are planned, including one about forex options, a book about vanilla options, as well as one on stock trading and investing. Once again, thank you so much for buying this book, and may I wish you every success in your own trading.

Warmest regards,

Anna

PS - please do follow my market analysis on my personal site and check for the latest book, or join me on Twitter or Facebook. In addition I also run regular seminars, webinars and trading rooms where I explain the concepts and methodologies in more detail. I look forward to seeing you there.

http://www.annacoulling.com

http://www.twitter.com/annacoull

http://facebook.com/learnforextrading

Acknowledgments & Trading Resources

Appreciation is a wonderful thing. It makes what is excellent in others belong to us as well.

Voltaire (1694 - 1778)

Acknowledgements

Before I thank all the people and companies who have kindly agreed to be included in this book, there is one person to whom I owe the greatest debt of gratitude, and that is my husband and trading partner David. Trading for us has been a joint adventure, and one we began almost twenty years ago. Some of you reading this will know David from our weekly trading rooms which we host together. This book has been a joint collaboration and one which would not have been possible without his help.

And what is perhaps ironic, given the subject and debate between betting and trading, is that David spent his teenage years ensconced in his local bookmaker's office. In those days it was a dark, dingy and slightly seedy establishment, full of cigarette smoke, discarded betting slips, and old copies of the Racing Post. The 'bookies', as it was affectionately known was populated by grizzled old gamblers, ever hopeful of the next big win. The perfect apprenticeship for a budding student of the turf. This was a fact I only discovered in the course of writing this book, and hence the number of horse racing analogies used throughout. I am extremely grateful to him for checking all the maths of odds and probabilities, and coming full circle, we are now looking to become part owners in our own racehorse soon. And this perhaps sums things up neatly. Racing is for fun and enjoyment. Trading is a business about making money.

I would like to extend my personal thanks to the following companies for kindly allowing me to publish images from their sites and platforms.

http://www.binary.com

Binary.com were awarded the coveted 'Best Fixed Odds Firm' title in 2012, and whose platform is featured in several images. In the last few months, they have added several innovative products to their platform, and in my opinion are the gold standard for fixed odds instruments. More recently the company has added pairs trading to its range of instruments.

http://www.nadex.com

Nadex is the innovative binary options exchange whose instruments and images are used extensively throughout the book. Their binary options and binary spreads are unique, offering traders of all risk appetite an innovative and creative approach to trading the financial markets. Binary options are now available for Bitcoin.

http://www.ninjatrader.com

Many of the chart examples in this book are from my NinjaTrader trading platform. The NinjaTrader platform with the Kinetick data feed is one of the most powerful combinations in the market, and is available on a free, end of day basis. I am a NinjaTrader parter and showcase the platform in my day trading room.

http://www.oanda.com

My thanks to OANDA for allowing me to publish details of their volatility indicator for currencies and associated markets. OANDA are a leading broker for spot forex offering a range of platforms and services for currency traders.

http://www.fxstreet.com

Thank you to my friends at FXStreet for allowing me to use an image from their site. As the host of the FXStreet London MeetUp, I enjoy working closely with them, as one of the largest and most respected forex portals.

Trading Resources

My Other Books

Here are the links to my other books which are available on Amazon, in both Kindle and paperback versions.

http://www.amazon.com/Three-Dimensional-Approach-Forex-Trading-ebook/dp/B00CX2QCVO/ref

http://www.amazon.com/Forex-For-Beginners-Anna-Coulling-ebook/dp/B00GBHQXZC/ref

http://www.amazon.com/Complete-Guide-Volume-Price-Analysis-ebook/dp/B00DGA8LZC/ref

Free Resources

http://www.investing.com

One of the best sites available for all markets. Here you will find live prices for all the instruments mentioned in the book

http://www.forexfactory.com

The best site for the latest financial news with an excellent economic calendar

http://www.freestockcharts.com

Another excellent site for live charts for a variety of markets including ETF's and indices. Volume is also reported on the charts

http://www.annacoulling.com

My own site for regular market analysis across all the markets including commodities and stocks. You can also contact me there (or leave comments on posts which are much appreciated) or email me personally on anna@annacoulling.com

http://www.cboe.com

Here you will find all the latest volatility indices as discussed in the book, along with details of the binary options from the exchange

http://www.cmegroup.com

Another of the principle futures exchanges where you will find a wealth of information for all major markets

https://www.nyse.com/products/options-byrds

Here you will find further information on the binary options referred to as Byrds and available from the New York Stock Exchange

http://www.netdania.com

Another excellent resource site for live data, including the US dollar index

Specialist Trading Software

http://www.quantumtrading.com

A range of trading tools and indicators for various platforms including MT4, NinjaTrader and Tradable, with other platforms to follow soon.

Printed in Great Britain
by Amazon